HOW TO SAY IT

Helpful Hints on English

BY

CHARLES N. LURIE

G. P. PUTNAM'S SONS

NEW YORK   LONDON

The Knickerbocker Press

1926

The
Knickerbocker
Press
New York

Made in the United States of America

PREFACE

It has been the intention of the compiler of this book to bring together, in as small a compass as possible, the most common errors that are committed by the users of the English language. Its purpose is, of course, the teaching of the avoidance of such errors. With that end in view, the errors are stated and the corrections are given. The examples—the "horrible examples," in many instances—have been culled from a wide range of newspapers, magazines and books. The present is the first publication in book form of the material contained herein, the articles having been printed in newspapers in many of the states of the United States, and in other parts of the English-speaking world.

The claim is not made that every possible error in the use of English is to be found in these pages. Some readers will look in vain for their "pet" errors. Long experience in writing, and in editing the writings of others, has taught the compiler that the possibilities of error-making in the use of the English language are almost infinite. But it is believed that the book contains most of the common errors of which the "man in the street"—for whom the book is intended, primarily —is guilty. Often he sins without knowledge; and it is to point the finger of conviction at him that the book is issued.

This book is not a grammar, and it cannot take the place of a grammar. Perhaps it is best to look upon it as a supplement to a formal grammar, although it should be written that most, if not all, of the errors pointed out herein are corrected in the various grammars. The study of grammar is to many a student—young or old—a dreary process, with the learning of rules by rote, and with the noting of exceptions that try the ingenuity of the instructor and the patience of the pupil. Some say that English is a grammarless tongue; others assert that we have too much grammar. Perhaps, therefore, the pointing out of errors, with the substitution therefor of correct words and forms, is the best method of inculcating good English. In the end, however, it will be found that the man or woman who knows the commonly accepted rules, and applies them to speech and writing, will be the one to use the language with the closest approximation to correctness.

In compiling the articles, reference was made to many grammars, dictionaries and books that follow the ways of words—ways that are often devious—in English speech. A list of those cited in the text will be found elsewhere. Grateful acknowledgment is made to the authors and the compilers of these books.

The largest division of the book, and the first, is the one that is called "Words and Phrases Commonly Misused." In the other divisions, "Adjectives and Adverbs," "Articles," and the rest, are included examples and rules which might have been put with the others in the first section. However, the compiler has thought it best to divide the book into sections. A full index has been provided, so that reference to any of the divisions should be easy.

C. N. L.

CONTENTS

(See also Index in the back of the Volume)

BOOKS CITED

American Language, Mencken
Americanisms, Bartlett
Art of Writing English, Meiklejohn
Better Say, Fernald
Composition Grammar, Bain
Dictionaries:
    Webster's International
    Standard
    Century
    New English Dictionary
English Grammar, Carpenter
English Grammar, Longman
English Grammar, Maetzner
English Synonyms, Graham
English Synonyms, Antonyms and Prepositions, Fernald
Expressive English, Fernald
Good English, Gould
Grammar of English Grammars, Brown
Handbook for Newspaper Workers, Hyde
Handbook of Composition, Woolley
History of the English Language, Lounsbury
Institutes of English Grammar, Brown
Lessons in English, Lockwood
Manual of Good English, MacCracken and Sandison
Our English, Hill
Principles of Rhetoric and Their Application, Hill
Queen's English, Alford
Rhetoric and English Composition, Carpenter
Slips of Speech, Bechtel
Standard of Usage in English, Lounsbury
Standards of English, Mahoney
Structure of English Prose, McElroy
Study and Practice of Writing English, Lomer and
    Ashmun
Use of Language, Lomer and Ashmun
Verbalist, Ayres
Words and Their Uses, White
Words and Their Ways in English Speech, Greenough
    and Kittredge
Working Grammar of the English Language, Fernald
Written English, Woolley

WORDS AND PHRASES COMMONLY MISUSED

A, An and The (See also The)

Errors in the use of the little words "a," "an" and "the," known in grammar as articles, are quite common, as will be seen from the following examples:

"Shakespeare was a greater writer than an actor." The word "an" is not required; say, "Shakespeare was a greater writer than actor." This error is especially common in connection with such words as "kind" and "sort." We hear frequently, "What kind of a man is he?", which should be, in correct English, "What kind of man is he?" Say "This is the sort of tree that grows in tropical countries," not, "This is the sort of a tree," etc.

"The official called the provost is the head of the university," should be "The official called provost," etc.

"An eagle is the emblem of the United States," should be "The eagle is the emblem of the United States."

A Day, A Year, etc., see *Per Day.*
A Pair, etc., see *The Pair.*

A or An

Everyone who has studied English grammar knows the rule which says that "a" is to be used before words beginning with a consonant, and "an" before words beginning with a vowel,

I

but should such words as "eulogy" and "eucalyptus" be preceded by "an" or "a"?

"English usage," says one writer, "is to employ 'an' before a vowel sound, but in cases such as those of 'eulogy' and 'eucalyptus' the sound is not vowel, but of 'y,' therefore we must employ before such sounds the article 'a,' not 'an.'"

Say, therefore, "He pronounced a eulogy over his friend's body"; "There was a eucalyptus tree before the house of my friend in Australia."

Ability and Capacity

These two words are often used incorrectly—so frequently, in fact, that many persons think they are synonyms; that is, words with the same meaning. But they are not. "Ability" implies the power of doing; "capacity," the faculty of receiving. Do not say, "He has the capacity for doing great things." Say, instead, "He has the ability to do great things."

"'Capacity' is the power of receiving and retaining knowledge with facility," says Graham in his book on English synonyms; "'ability' is the power of applying knowledge to practical purposes. Both these faculties are requisite to form a great character; capacity to conceive and ability to execute designs. Capacity is shown in quickness of apprehension. Ability supposes something else; something by which the mental power is exercised in executing, or performing, what has been perceived by the capacity."

About

"Have you finished that piece of work?"

"No, but it is about done."

This use of the word "about" is condemned by some writers, who say that we should say, instead, "almost." But there is good authority for "about," including the Standard Dictionary, which gives one of the meanings of "about" as "nearly; approximately; almost; used of numbers, quality, degree, etc.; as, 'about completed,' 'about right.'"

Acquaintance, see *Friend*.
Acquainted, see *Know*.
Act, see *Bill*.

Admission or Admittance

The question is asked sometimes, Is it correct to say, "No admission to this building," or "No admittance to this building"?

So far as the dictionary definitions of the two words "admission" and "admittance" are involved, it may be said that there is no difference. Both are correct, and you may post either sign on your building without fear of its being held ungrammatical.

There is this, however, to be said: Some authorities hold that it is preferable to say, "No admittance to this building," rather than "No admission," because the word "admittance" has but one meaning, "the act of admitting, or the state or fact of being admitted; entrance or the right or permission to enter." On the other hand, the word "admission" has additional meanings, as "a concession, or acknowledgment, or confession," as in the phrase, "An admission of guilt."

Admit, see *Confess*.

To Advise

The verb "advise" is often used incorrectly, as in the following sentence:

"We beg to advise you that your shipment of the tenth was received today."

This should read, "We beg to advise you of the fact that your shipment of the tenth was received today." According to the dictionary and other authorities, "advise," when used in this sense,

3

must be followed by "of." The dictionary defines "advise" as follows: "To give information or notice of; to apprise; inform; with 'of'; as, 'We were advised of the risk.'"

The common use of "advise," in the sense of "to give advice or counsel to," is well known. There is another sense of the word that is not so common, meaning "to take counsel or consult." It is then followed by "with," as, "I will advise with my friends concerning the matter."

Aeroplane or Airplane

The vote of modern authorities is for "airplane," as being simpler and more easily pronounced than "aeroplane." In fact, the correct pronunciation of the latter term is very difficult, if not impossible, for most persons, and in the mouths of the careless or unthinking it easily becomes "areoplane," which is, of course, grossly incorrect. Therefore, the newer word, "airplane," has come into being to fill a need, and is being recognized more and more, by the makers of dictionaries and others.

Affable

The word "affable" is used sometimes as though it meant "polite," "courteous," but such use is incorrect.

We hear, for example, such sentences as the following: "The salesman was very affable to me, and seemed to be pleased to show me the goods, although I did not buy any." Say, instead, "The salesman was very polite, or very attentive, or very courteous."

"Affable" and "affability" are used properly only when speaking of the bearing of a superior to one who is socially or otherwise an inferior. For examples: A king may be affable to a petitioner,

4

a conqueror to a captive. "Affable," therefore, implies condescension.

Affect, see *Effect*.

Aggravated and Provoked

"I was so aggravated that I almost became ill," said a woman to whom something vexatious had happened. She was guilty of an error of speech which is quite common, and which is condemned by all authorities on English. The word "aggravate" is derived from a Latin word meaning "to increase in weight," and in English usage it should be employed only to mean "to increase in gravity or severity, to become worse." Therefore, it is correct to say that a disease or a misfortune may be aggravated, but not the person who has the disease or is subject to the misfortune.

"Aggravated" does not mean and should never be used in the sense of "angry," "vexed," "exasperated," "irritated," etc. In the sentence with which this article begins, any of these four words, or a word of similar meaning, should be substituted for "aggravated."

Ago, see *Since*.

Agreeably Disappointed

This phrase, "agreeably disappointed," is used, as is the phrase "to enjoy poor health," by careless persons. To be disappointed means to have one's hopes blasted, one's plans balked, one's expectations defeated, etc. How, therefore, can one be agreeably disappointed? Since "agreeably" means in an agreeable manner—that is, in a manner to cause pleasure—it is not possible to be agreeably disappointed. We may be agreeably astonished or surprised, but not agreeably disappointed.

Airplane, see *Aeroplane*.

Ain't

The word "ain't" is surely to be included among the "utility" words, for it is used in many places, and it is used incorrectly. The dictionary calls it "colloquial and illiterate." We hear "I ain't," "we ain't," "he ain't," etc., instead of "I am not" (or "I'm not"), "we are not" (or "we're not" or "we aren't"), "he is not" (or "he isn't"), etc. "Ain't" is a contraction of "am not" or "are not," and it may be contended that it should be used instead of those words. It is condemned, however, and it should never be considered a contraction of "is not." Instead of saying "Ain't I?" say "Am I not?"

All

It happens sometimes that in the use of the word "all" the speaker or writer fails to make his meaning clear. Indeed, often the sentence in which the word is used conveys a meaning that is the exact opposite of the one intended.

For example, suppose we say, "All will not go." Does that mean that the entire body to which reference is made will not go, or that some of them will go and some will not? In the first case we should say, "None of them will go," which makes the meaning entirely clear, and in the second case we should say, "Some of them will go and some will not go."

All or All of

According to some of the best authorities on the use of English, we should not use the expression "all of," as in the sentences, "I saw all of them," "all of the boys were there," etc.

Omit the word "of"; say, in the sentences quoted, "I saw them all"; "All the boys were there."

6

Dr. Fernald, in "Better Say," writes:

"'He drank all of it.' Better say, 'He drank it all.' 'All of' is a popular idiom to emphasize the totality of that which is referred to; as, 'How many of those men did you see?' 'I saw all of them,' 'How much of this shall I take?' 'All (that is, the whole) of it.' But the best literary usage omits the 'of' as needless, preferring 'I saw them all,' 'Take it all,' etc."

All, You, see *You All.*

Allow

Do not use the word "allow" when you mean "assert," "say," "express an opinion." For example, consider the following sentence: "He allowed that he would go to the ball game this afternoon." Say, rather, "He said that he would go," or, if you wish to use a longer word, "He asserted that he would go."

"I allow that she's the prettiest girl that ever visited this town." Say, instead, "I regard her as (or consider her) the prettiest girl that ever visited this town."

In some parts of the United States, especially in some of the Southern states, the word "allow" is used to express an intention, as in the sentence, "I allow to visit my mother next Sunday." This use of the verb "allow," which properly should be employed only as another word for "let," "permit," "tolerate," etc., is also condemned by authorities on English.

Allude and Refer

The word "allude" is frequently used in the sense of "refer" or "mention," even by some writers and speakers who are ordinarily careful, but such use is incorrect. "Allude" means to re-

7

fer to lightly and indirectly, as in the sentence, "The speaker described the riots in the city, and alluded to his belief in the guilt of the city officials." Observe that the speaker did not refer directly to his belief; he merely mentioned it in passing. "It is not correct to say that the speaker alluded at great length to the tariff," says the Standard Dictionary.

You cannot "allude" to whatever you mention directly, or speak of, or describe. You may "refer" to these things, and even refer to them at great length, if you wish, but you cannot "allude" to them. Further illustration of the proper use of "allude" may be gained from the following example, in which the noun "allusion"—from the verb "allude"—is employed: "He made a passing allusion to the difficulties of the Government in dealing with the question."

Almost, see *Most.*

Alone and Only

The word "alone" is often used improperly instead of "only." A thing or person that is alone is unaccompanied; one that is only is one of which there is no other. If we say, for example, "Virtue alone makes us happy," we mean that virtue unaided or unaccompanied is sufficient to make us happy. But if we say, "Virtue only makes us happy," we mean that nothing else can do it, that virtue and that only (not alone) can do it.

"This means of communication is employed by man alone," says one author. He should have written, "This means of communication is employed by man only"; that is, it is not shared by the animals, but is the exclusive possession of man.

"For myself," says Professor Brander Matthews, in discussing questions of usage, "I strive always to put 'only' in the place where it will do most good. It is ever my aim to avail myself of the phrase which will convey my meaning into the reader's mind without the least friction."

Aloud, see *Out Loud*.
Alternative, see *No Other Alternative*.

Amateur and Novice

These two words are often confused, especially by writers on sporting topics. The meanings of the two words are quite distinct. An amateur is one who follows a line of activity—in sport, science, art, etc.—as a diversion, or perhaps as his occupation, but does not do so professionally, or for gain. A novice, on the other hand, is a beginner, one who is new or inexperienced in any art or business. He may be either an amateur or a professional follower of the art or business. Thus, a professional actor who is new and unskilled in his art is a novice, but not an amateur.

Among (see also Between)

It is not correct to use the word "among" as it is used in the following sentence, taken from a letter to a newspaper:

"There is no doubt that among the medical profession many commercial doctors are for their own good trying to undermine the practice of this new method of treatment."

This should be changed to read:

"There is no doubt that among the members of the medical profession many commercial doctors," etc. Or, "There is no doubt that there are many commercial doctors, in the medical profession, who are trying," etc.

Another example of the same error, as noted in a newspaper article:

"As the coach said the other day, there is no jealousy among his team." This should read,

9

"There is no jealousy among the members of his team."

Anarchism and Anarchy

There is a difference between "anarchism" and "anarchy." The latter is what the advocates of anarchism seek to bring about. According to the dictionary, "anarchism" is the "principles, practices or characteristic spirit of anarchists; the theory that all forms of government are wrong and unnecessary." "Anarchy" means "absence or utter disregard of government; an unregulated and chaotic condition of society; social and political confusion and disorder."

An anarchist is one who believes and teaches that the condition of mankind would be improved if all forms of government were abolished.

Ancient and Old

Do not use the word "ancient" when you mean "old." For example, a suit of clothes or a dress cannot be "ancient," unless it was made a long time ago, in historic time. The suit of clothes which you bought a few years ago is "old," but it is not "ancient." A careful speaker will be sure to discriminate between the two words.

Angry, see *Mad*.

Answer and Reply

Many writers on correctness in the use of English have given their views on the difference or differences between the words "answer" and "reply." Alfred Ayres, in "The Verbalist," says: "These two words should not be used indiscriminately. An 'answer' is given to a question; a 'reply,' to an assertion. When we are addressed, we answer; when we are accused, we reply. We 'answer' letters, and 'reply' to arguments, statements or accusations they may contain. Crabb is in error in saying that 'replies are used in personal discourse only.' Replies, as well as answers, are written. We very poorly write, 'I have now, I believe, answered all your questions and replied to all your arguments.' A rejoinder is made to a reply. 'Who goes there?' he cried; and, receiving no answer, he fired. 'The advocate replied to the charge made against his client!' "

"A reply is an unfolding, and requires more thought and intelligence than an answer," says the Standard Dictionary.

Any, see *Each Other*.

The Use of "Any"

"I know the family well, and the youngest son is brighter than any of them." This sentence is incorrect, and should be changed to, "I know the family well, and the youngest son is brighter than any other one of them," or, "brighter than any of the rest of the family."

When the sentence first quoted is analyzed— that is, taken apart and examined critically—it seems to say that the youngest son is brighter than himself; for, of course, he is one, or any one, of the family. Such a statement is absurd, and to express clearly the meaning of the writer or speaker it is necessary to insert some word or words (such as "other" or "the rest of") to show the comparison between the member of the family under discussion and the rest of the family.

If you say, "The blacksmith is stronger than any man," you imply that the blacksmith is not a man. Say, therefore, "The blacksmith is stronger than any other man."

Apart and Aside

In a report of a court proceeding, it was said,

"The lawyer took the witness apart to confer with him."

Now, strictly speaking, this is not incorrect English, since "apart" means "separately, away from others, to one side," etc. But it has another meaning, "in pieces or to pieces," and therefore its use as in the sentence quoted is open to criticism. It is better to say, and thereby avoid such criticism, "The lawyer took the witness aside to confer with him."

When a word has two or more meanings, and its application in a given case is in doubt, it is better to substitute another word, if one can be found that expresses exactly the meaning of the speaker or writer. Fortunately for us, the English language has a larger number of words than any other, and a person who is accustomed to thinking about his vocabulary should seldom be at a loss for a word.

Aren't I?

For the expression, "Aren't I?" meaning "Am I not?" there is no authority. Although it seems to be creeping into use, in plays and novels, it is certain that many years will elapse before the critics recognize it; if, indeed, they ever admit it into the ranks of permissible expressions.

Apparent, see *Evident*.

Argue and Augur

In an article describing an important international conference the following expression was noted: "The course of action taken by the delegates does not argue well for the success of the conference."

This should have been: "The course of action taken by the delegates does not augur well for the success of the conference." The word "argue," which is in common use, means to give reasons for or against; to debate about; to discuss, etc. To "augur" means to foretell; to prophesy concerning; to foretoken; to give signs of, etc.: as in the sentence, from "Ivanhoe," by Sir Walter Scott: "Have you never found your mind darkened like a sunny landscape by the sudden cloud, which augurs a coming tempest?"

The error noted has its origin, as in the case of "resource" and "recourse," "exorcised" and "exercised," etc., in the similarity, in spelling and pronunciation, of words.

Artist

What is an "artist?" Many persons, when they use the word, mean by it a man or woman who paints portraits, landscapes, battle scenes, and so forth, on canvas, wood, ivory or some other material. But an artist—that is, one who excels in any of the fine arts,—may be a sculptor, a musician, a goldsmith, an engraver. Therefore, to apply the term "artist" to a painter only is not only an incorrect use of language, but is an injustice to those who create worthy things in other lines of endeavor. Consequently, if you wish to describe a painter do not call him simply an artist; call him a painter, or, if you desire, call him a landscape painter, portrait painter, or the like.

However, it is well to note that some painters have asked that the use of the word "artist" be restricted to themselves, on the ground that "painter" describes also a man who applies paint to a house, a fence, a barn, etc. "The excuse is weak as water," says Richard Grant White; "if they are liable to such confusion, or fear it, so much the worse for them."

As and So (see also Like)

Grammarians generally make a distinction in meaning between the two sets of words, "as . . . as" and "so . . . so."

13

For example, it is held to be proper to say, "This suit is as good as the one I bought last year," but not, "This suit is not as good as the one I bought last year." In the second case, use the word "so" instead of the first "as." Say, therefore, "This suit is not so good," etc. The rule reads, "'So' is generally used after a negative." One authority gives as an example of both uses the following:

"He is as well grounded in grammar as his brother, but he is not so quick in arithmetic."

Some authorities make another distinction. One of them says: "When you say, 'William is not as tall as Henry,' you do not imply that either William or Henry is tall; you merely compare their heights. But when you say, 'William is not so tall as Henry,' you imply that Henry is uncommonly tall."

As Regards That

According to some authorities, the phrase "as regards that" is incorrect, and we should say "in regard to that" or "with regard to that." But there is good authority, on the other hand, for the use of "as regards that." For example, Webster's International Dictionary says:

"Regard, verb; to have relation to, as bearing upon; to respect; to relate to; to concern; to touch; as, 'an argument does not regard the question; I agree with you as regards this.'"

In this case, as in so many others, the language seems to have gone on in its own way to manufacture a phrase to meet its needs or desires, without regard to the opinions of grammarians.

Aside, see *Apart*.

Aside From

An amusing instance of the ease with which words may be made to convey a meaning that is not in the mind of the writer or speaker was found in the following:

"Miss Robinson will enter the speaking contest and will read her selection. Aside from this, a very interesting program will be given."

What the writer meant to say, was: "Miss Robinson will enter the speaking contest and will read her selection. In addition to this, there will be other features of an interesting program." If the writer had expressed himself properly, he would have saved himself from criticism and Miss Robinson from embarrassment. He seemed to say that her part of the program would not be interesting.

The case affords a good example of the value of exactness in the choice of words. Sometimes a wrong choice will make you say exactly the opposite of what you mean.

Assassinate and Murder

May we say that a person was assassinated, when the victim is not prominent?

There is nothing in the authorities to support the belief that the word "assassinate" may not be applied to persons who are not prominent, as well as to those who are. The definition, as given in one of the latest dictionaries, reads:

"Assassinate, to kill by surprise or secret assault; to murder by treacherous violence."

The word has an interesting history. It is derived from "assassin," and that in turn comes from the Arabic "hashshash," meaning one who has drunk of "hashish," a narcotic or intoxicating drug used in the Orient.

Assist At

According to some authorities, it is incorrect to use "assist at" in the sense of "to be present." Professor Carpenter cites, "Many guests assisted at the ceremony," and asserts that it is an incorrect expression, taken from the French, for "were present at." Another authority who calls it incorrect to use "assist at" in this sense, is Professor Hill, but the latter declares that the authority for the expression is increasing. As he wrote this fifty years ago, it is safe to say that we may now use to "assist at" in the sense of "to be present," and give good authority for it. The Standard Dictionary supports it, and says that it was used by Macaulay, who was a careful writer.

Astonished and Surprised

There are critics who tell us that we should make a distinction between the words "surprise" and "astonish," and they are fond of quoting the old story of the boy who was caught stealing jam. "I am surprised, Johnny," said his mother. But the boy was as fond of using correct English as he was of jam. "No, mother," he said, "You are mistaken; it is I who am surprised. You are astonished."

But the dictionary and other good authorities do not agree with the boy. Standard books on good usage in English, such as "The Verbalist," by Alfred Ayres, and "Principles of Rhetoric," by Professor Hill, do not mention any distinction between "surprise" and "astonish." According to the Standard Dictionary, "astonish" means "to produce a strongly confusing or disturbing emotion in the mind of; affect with wonder and surprise; amaze; confound"; while "surprise" means "to strike with astonishment by some unexpected act or event; affect with surprise."

It will be seen that the difference in meaning between the two words—if, indeed, there is any difference—is very slight.

At, see *Where Am I At?*

At a Distance Away

The following extract is taken from "The Book of a Naturalist," by the late W. H. Hudson, who wrote excellent English, as a rule:

"It was in Savernake Forest that, on emerging from a beech wood, I noticed at a distance of seventy to eighty yards away a number of rabbits."

The sentence contains two errors. In the first place, it is not correct to say, "at a distance of seventy to eighty yards away." He should have written either "at a distance of seventy to eighty yards," omitting the word "away," which is not needed, or "I noticed, seventy or eighty yards away," omitting the words "at a distance of."

In the second place, the use of "a number of" is not in accordance with the usage of the best writers. It is too indefinite. How many are "a number of?"

At Length and At Last

Between the meaning of the phrase "at length" and that of the phrase "at last" there is a distinction that is often ignored by writers and speakers. Of course, in this case, as in so many others, failure to make the distinction is not a capital offense; but those who desire to speak and write correctly should endeavor to train themselves in the making of fine distinctions.

Both "at length" and "at last" are used in reference to something that occurs after long waiting; but the former is used to denote an action or a state that continues, or is yet to come, while the latter indicates something that has happened. Thus, we say, "I have long desired to visit the national capital, and at length I am going there next month"; and "I have long desired to visit the national capital and at last I find myself in Washington."

17

Audience and Spectators

"Audience" means an assemblage of persons gathered to hear something; the word is derived from the Latin verb, "audire," which means "to hear." "Spectators" are those who have come together to see something; the word comes from the Latin "spectare," which means to see, to observe.

It is correct, therefore, to speak of the audience at a concert, and of the spectators at a horse race. An incorrect use of the word "audience" is found in the following sentence; "The audience held its breath while the aviator spun round in the air."

Aught, Ought and Naught

These three words are confused sometimes by careless writers. The word "aught" is a noun, and means "anything." For example, "If there is aught in your life to make you ashamed, seek to correct it." The word "ought" is a verb, and means "to be under obligation to do or to perform"; as, "Resolve to perform what you ought; perform without fail what you resolve," says Franklin in his autobiography. The word "naught" is a noun, and means "nothing"; it means also a cipher, or zero, the figure 0. "No noble human thought, however buried in the dust of ages, can ever come to naught," says the poet Saxe.

In business offices, the word "aught" is often used incorrectly to indicate "naught," in speaking of figures. Thus, we hear a person reading a line or column of figures and saying, "The figures are one, five, aught, six, three." The correct term to use in this case is "naught."

Augur, see *Argue*.

Authoress, etc.

Especially in recent years, good usage has tended away from the use of "ess" in such words as "authoress," "poetess," "editress," etc., to express a female author, poet, editor, etc. Edward S. Gould, in "Good English," says: " 'Poet' means simply a person who writes poetry, and 'author,' in the sense under consideration, a person who writes poetry or prose—not a man who writes, but a person who writes. Nothing in either word indicates sex; and everybody knows that the functions of both poet and author are common to both sexes. Hence, 'authoress' and 'poetess' are superfluous. If the 'ess' is to be permitted, there is no reason for excluding it from any noun that indicates a person; and the next editions of our dictionaries may be made complete by the addition of writress, officeress, manageress, superintendentess, secretaryess, treasureress, walkeress, talkeress, and so on to the end of the vocabulary."

Therefore, do not say, "She is a well known authoress or poetess," but say, "She is a well known author or poet." However, "actress" is the recognized and required form for the feminine of "actor," and there are other examples of the proper use of "ess."

Autumn, see *Fall*.
Avocation, see *Vocation*.

Awful, Awfully (see also Terribly)

Few words that go to make up the long list of abused terms in the common use of English are employed so frequently, and so erroneously, as "awful" and "awfully." Everything is "awful," as in the following example: "Do you like that cake?" one asks of a schoolboy. "Yes," he replies, "it's awful nice." And not alone schoolboys and schoolgirls, but grown men and women, fall into this error. Of course, the word to be substituted for "awful" or "awfully" is "very."

The adjective "awful" and the adverb "awfully"

are derived from the word "awe," which means "fear or dread, mingled with reverence and veneration." The words "awful" and "awfully" have their proper place in the language, but it is not that of a substitute for "very."

Avenge and Revenge

There is a difference between the meanings of the two words, "avenge" and "revenge," although the distinction between them is frequently forgotten. The New English Dictionary says that this distinction, though not absolutely observed, largely prevails.

The Standard Dictionary says, "'Avenge' and 'revenge,' once close synonyms, are now far apart in meaning. To 'avenge' is to visit some offense with punishment, in order to vindicate the righteous, or to uphold and illustrate the right by the suffering or destruction of the wicked. 'And seeing one of them suffer wrong, he avenged him that was oppressed, and smote the Egyptian.' Acts vii. 24. To 'revenge' is to inflict harm or suffering upon another through personal anger and resentment at something done to ourselves. 'Avenge' is unselfish; 'revenge' is selfish. 'Revenge,' according to present usage, could not be said of God!"

The Average Man

It is questioned whether we may say, correctly, "the average man." Should it not be the "ordinary" man?

In reply it may be said that while some grammarians object to the use of the word "average" in this sense, there is excellent support for it, among others the authorities on grammar who helped to compile the Standard Dictionary.

The "Manual of Good English," by MacCracken and Sandison, tells us that the word "average" has been overworked, and says that,

20

strictly speaking, the word relates to an arithmetical mean, medial size, etc. We should not say, this book cautions us, "The average audience was unruly," but "the ordinary audience was unruly."

But one of the meanings of "average" is, according to the Standard Dictionary, "Of a moderate or medium character; possessing general or typical characteristics; ordinary."

Back, to be, see *Be Back.*

A Bad Cold

"I am suffering from a bad cold," your friend tells you when you inquire concerning his health. If he tells you that he has "a good cold," you will be astonished, no doubt.

"Inasmuch as colds are never good, why say a 'bad' cold? We may talk about 'slight' colds and 'severe' colds, but not about 'bad' colds," says one authority.

Bad Friends

The expression "bad friends" is sometimes heard, as in the following sentence:

"We used to be very intimate, but we are bad friends now."

There seems to be no authority, dictionary or other, for the use of this expression. It sounds like a Germanism, and involves what the logicians call a "contradiction in terms"; that is, a contradiction involved in the very nature of a statement.

To express the meaning desired, say:

"We used to be very intimate, but we are not friendly now," or, "we are no longer friends."

Badly

The word "badly" is misused frequently. A case that is amusing is found in the sentence,

"The chair is broken, and needs to be mended badly." To mend it badly would not improve its condition. Therefore you should say, "The chair is broken, and needs mending very much." Do not say, "I shall miss you badly when you are gone"; say, instead, "I shall miss you very much when you are gone."

Back Of for Behind

"Where's your pencil, Willie?" asked the teacher.

"I dropped it back of my desk," was the answer.

In England, this use of "back of" instead of "behind" is considered incorrect by many authorities; in America it is in common use, and no reason for condemning it, or finding fault with it, is found in the works of several writers on the subject of good English.

Balance and Remainder

A distinction should be made between "balance" and "remainder."

A "balance" is the amount that must be added to or subtracted from one side of an account to make the two sides agree; the word should not be employed to indicate the amount or the number left after a part is taken away. When it is necessary to express the latter meaning say "remainder" or "rest." For example, do not say, "I ate half of the apple this morning, and expect to eat the balance this afternoon." Use "remainder" or "rest."

Bathos, see *Pathos*

Be Back

"Are you going out of town?"

"Yes, but I'll be back in a few days."

This phrase, "to be back," is in common use, but

it is not approved by grammarians or other authorities, save, perhaps, those who hold that usage makes any expression correct. It is better to say, in the sentence quoted above, "I shall come back (or I shall return) in a few days."

"Be back" is a common, though unwarranted colloquialism," says one authority; "'I'll come back' is legitimate, 'back' denoting direction toward the starting point; but 'be back' has no such significance. The following is taken from Shakespeare's "Midsummer Night's Dream":

"Fetch me this herb; and be thou here again,
Ere the leviathan can swim a league."

Beautiful, see *Handsome*.

Beautifulest

"I saw the beautifulest dress displayed in the window; the color was one of the delicatest blues I ever saw."

The speaker, in her enthusiasm over the gown, forgot to weigh her words. "Beautifulest" and "delicatest" certainly violate the precept which tells us that the ear is sometimes a good guide to the proper use of English. How much better the sentence sounds when worded thus:

"I saw the most beautiful dress displayed in the window; the color was one of the most delicate blues I ever saw!"

"Of two forms of expression otherwise in equally good use, the one which is more agreeable to the ear should be chosen," says Professor A. S. Hill in "The Principles of Rhetoric and Their Application." He says also: "The principle of euphony (good sound) has, perhaps, a greater influence upon the language than some grammarians admit. Not infrequently, it overrides other principles."

Because, see *Reason, Because*.

Before Me or Before I

Should one say, "He was there before me," or "He was there before I"?

According to the Standard Dictionary, "before" may be an adverb, a preposition or a conjunction. If it is considered as a preposition meaning, "prior to, in time; anterior," as in "lilies come before the roses," we should say, "He was there before me."

But if we consider it as a conjunction, meaning "previous to the time when," we should say, "He was there before I," the words "was there" being understood after "I," and the complete sentence being, "He was there before I was there."

Beg to State

"In reply to your letter of yesterday, I beg to state."

Many letters begin thus. The expression "beg to state" is incorrect, however. When used in this way—that is, in asking permission to do something—the verb "beg" should govern a noun, such as "leave" or "permission." Therefore, the expression quoted should read, "In reply to your letter of yesterday, I beg leave to state."

The foregoing remarks apply mainly to written communications. In common speech we often hear the expression. "I beg to differ with you." That is incorrect. One should say, "I beg leave to differ with you," or, simply, "I differ with you."

Begin, see *Commence; see Initiate.*
Beginner, new, see *New Beginner.*
Behalf, see *In Behalf of.*
Behind, see *Back of.*

Began or Begun

It is common to hear someone say, "I begun to do that work yesterday"; "the battle begun between the two armies," etc. This use of "begun" to express the past tense (sometimes called the preterit) of "begin" is not incorrect, according to some authorities on the uses of words, but there is a fairly general agreement that the better word to use is "began." If you wish to safeguard yourself against possible criticism, say "I began to do that work yesterday"; "the battle began between the two armies," etc.

It is incorrect, also, to say, "I have began" to express the perfect tense of "begin." Say, "I have begun," never "I have began."

Being Built

Shall we say, "the house is being built," or "the house is building"?

In "Rhetoric and English Composition," Professor George R. Carpenter writes concerning "being built":

"A long warfare has been waged over this and similar expressions, but they are perfectly correct. In 'The Verbalist,' by Alfred Ayres, there is a very long discussion of this subject—whether we should say 'The house is being built' or 'The house is building'—with quotations from a large number of authorities. But Ayres declares that in his opinion the student of English who has honestly weighed the arguments on both sides of the question must be of the opinion that our language is the richer for having both forms of expression.

"Certainly most writers of English of the present day would write 'The house is being built,' without any thought that the expression could be called into question."

Beside and Besides (see also Except)

If you say, "There were two men there beside me," you mean that the two men were at your side. But if you say, "There were two men there

25

besides me," your meaning is that there were two men there in addition to yourself. It should be noted, however, that these two words, "beside" and "besides," were formerly used interchangeably, and that only in comparatively recent years have the best writers made a distinction between them.

The word "besides" is sometimes used incorrectly for "except," as in the sentence, "No trees will grow here besides the pine."

The Better of Me or The Best of Me

"I argued with him, but he got the best of me in the argument," said a man. He should not have said, "got the best of me," but should have said, "got the better of me." It should be remarked, however, that the expression, "got the best of me" is recognized by the dictionaries, although most authorities hold that the use of "better" is preferable, since it stands analysis by grammatical tests, while "best" does not.

Better Than

"How far is it to the nearest town?" asked a traveler in one of the Southern states. The reply was, "Well, I reckon it's a little better than four miles."

This use of the word "better" instead of "more" is not wholly condemned by grammarians, but is held generally that it is "colloquial," which means that it belongs to that large class of expressions which are in common use but are not looked upon as good or literary English. Therefore, anyone who desires to speak or write the best English should avoid them; in the case cited, one should say: "I think it is a little more than four miles."

It should be borne in mind, however, that many colloquial expressions are really vigorous, "homely"

English, and not to be condemned. To learn just where to draw the line requires long and careful study.

Between

"I applied to my physician for advice recently on the subject of smoking," says a friend, "and he told me 'Limit yourself to one cigar between each meal.' I know what he meant, but I am puzzled by his English. Was it correct?"

"Limit yourself to one cigar between meals," or, "Limit yourself to one cigar between each meal and the following one," would have been the proper expression.

Between and Among

Generally speaking, "between" must be employed when reference is made to two objects, "among" when there is reference to more than two. However, it is correct sometimes to use "between" even in reference to many objects. Thus, "There are eighty trees in my orchard, and there is a space of ten feet between them," meaning that the space lies between one tree and the next one. In this case it would not be correct to use "among."

"Between" should never be used as in the following incorrect phrase from Dickens: "And with a gap of a whole night between every one." It should read, "And with a gap of a whole night between each one and the next."

Big

"You don't know Henry Smith? Why, he's the big man of our town!"

This use of "big" is not approved by authorities on English. It is called "colloquial," which means "in common use." One writer, in the Standard Dictionary, tells us that "big" is not the equivalent of "great" and is in many ways a word of less dignity. A "big" man may be very far from being a "great" man.

In the example criticised here, we should say: "He's the leading man of our town, or the chief man, or the great man." Any of these words conveys the idea, and it is not necessary to take "big" away from its proper employment, which is to show greatness of amount or size. For example, we may say of a writer whose writings abound in words of three or more syllables that he is too fond of big words.

Bill, Act and Law

The three words, "bill," "act" and "law," are often used incorrectly.

The proper term for any special measure while it is in process of enactment is "bill," not "law." After enactment and approval by the executive it is an "act," not a "bill." The term "law" is a generic term for all legislation of a general type; for example, a banking law, while an "act" is a special measure. The two are related as genus and species.

To Blame On

"Blame on" is a crude expression, in the opinion of "The Study and Practice of Writing English," by Lomer and Ashmun, while the Standard Dictionary and others condemn it less harshly, saying that it is colloquial, or in common, every-day use. The former book tells us not to say, "He blamed it on me," but to say, instead, "He put the blame on me," or, "He attached the blame to me." The latter book gives as correct usage, "The conductor was blamed for the accident."

Don't say, therefore, "Don't blame that on me"; better say, "Don't blame me for that."

Is it wrong to condemn such colloquialisms as "blame on"? That is a question which cannot be answered with absolute authority. Precise grammarians frown upon them; others, more lenient, hold that usage has given them a proper place in the English language.

Both, see *Either*.

Both Alike

When a person, writing or speaking of two persons or objects says, "They are both alike," you grasp his meaning, which is that the two are similar or resemble each other. But consider the sentence a moment. Is there not one word too many?

It is better to say, "They are alike," or, "The two are alike." Other sentences in which there is this error of redundancy, or the use of too many words to express an idea, are as follows:

"The two children both resembled each other" and "John and I both went to the picnic." In each case, omit the word "both" and note how the sentence is improved.

One critic, James C. Fernald, tells us that the use of "both alike" jars on an ear accustomed to good English because the use of "both" means or shows a union, while "alike" denotes separation for comparison. "We must think of the two things separately in order to see that they are alike; we must think of them together in order to refer to them as both."

Boughten

In some parts of the United States which hold fast to old-fashioned ways of speaking inherited from the mother country, the expression "boughten goods" is still heard. It means goods that are bought, as distinguished from those that are made at home. In one of her New England stories Mary E. Wilkins wrote: "She could not think

29

of such things as boughten trimming for her poor
little wedding outfit."

However, the proper form is not "boughten,"
but "bought," which is the imperfect and past
participle of the verb "buy." There is no reason
for adding the extra syllable "en" to the word.
The English language, in its growth and development toward uniformity, has grown away from
such old-fashioned forms of speech as "boughten,"
and it is well to avoid them if one wishes to use
one's mother tongue without the admixture of
provincial or outworn expressions.

Brave and Courageous

The question is asked sometimes, "What is the
difference in meaning between 'brave' and 'courageous'?"

The following answer is made in "Synonyms,
Antonyms and Prepositions," by Dr. James C. Fernald: "'Courageous' is more than 'brave,' adding
a moral element; the 'courageous' man steadily encounters perils to which he may be keenly sensitive, at the call of duty; the 'gallant' are 'brave'
in a dashing, showy and splendid way; the 'val-
iant' not only dare great dangers, but achieve great
results; the 'heroic' are nobly 'daring' and 'daunt-
less,' truly 'chivalrous,' sublimely 'courageous.'"

Probably the reader will be able to decide from
this explanation of the shades of meanings of these
words which will meet his needs; but in this case,
as in so many others, improvement of speech or
writing, or of both, depends upon long and careful
study of the meanings of words. The English
language contains many examples of the making
of such nice distinctions.

Bring, see *Carry*.

Broadcasted

Whenever an invention or sport or game, or

anything else that affects a large number of persons, comes into vogue, and requires new terms, the English language finds or invents such terms. This is true of the radio, as it has been true of so many other matters in the past.

Among other terms, the wireless has introduced "broadcast," in its newer sense. Many persons, however, are saying and writing "broadcasted," which is incorrect.

"Broadcast" is derived from the simpler verb "cast." The past form of "cast" is not "casted," but "cast." Therefore, the past or participial form of "broadcast" is not "broadcasted," but "broadcast."

Builded or Built

A form "builded" is in good standing, although "built" is also correct and is in more common use. The expression, "He builded better than he knew" is from the poem, "The Problem," by Ralph Waldo Emerson. Poets use the word "builded" more frequently than writers of prose, or than speakers, but poets use also the word "built," as in Tennyson's "Palace of Art," "I built my soul a lordly pleasure house wherein at ease for aye to dwell."

A Bunch and a Crowd

"I wouldn't be seen with that bunch; I belong to a much nicer crowd."

There are two errors in the foregoing sentences, the use of "bunch" and "crowd," in the sense of an assemblage or company of persons gathered together or associating for social or business purposes, etc. Although both of these words have been used in this sense for many years, they are not recognized as good English, and the books call them slang. Therefore they should be avoided.

The girl should have said, "I wouldn't (or would

not) associate with that set. I belong to a much nicer set."

Bunk

"Bunk," meaning humbug, false or misleading statements, etc., is not good English, although it is in common use. It seems to fill a want, and in time it may be admitted to the ranks of acceptable words, but the best that the dictionaries can yet do for it is to call it "colloquial" or "slang."

It is an abbreviation of "bunkum," and that word, in turn, comes from "buncombe." The latter word is the name of a county in North Carolina, which was represented in Congress, long ago, by Felix Walker, an old mountaineer. He spoke, and persisted in speaking, when the rest of the House of Representatives wanted him to stop, so that they could take a vote. But Walker refused to sit down. He insisted that his constituents wanted him to speak, and shouted: "You can all go if you like; I am speaking for Buncombe."

To Burgle

"Burgle," like "enthuse," makes every grammarian "see red" when he hears it used in speech or beholds it on paper. There is no authority for its use, and it should not have a place in the vocabulary of any person who desires to speak and write correctly. "The man was caught trying to burgle the house," says a newspaper report. Say, instead, "The man was caught trying to commit burglary." You may say, with less fear of criticism, "The man was caught trying to burglarize the house," although objection is made also to the verb "burglarize," which is a "newspaper word," according to A. S. Hill in "Our English."

Lounsbury, in "The Standard of Usage in English," calls "burgle" one of "certain terms which are technically called back-formations. Many of these are particularly objectionable, and sometimes, it must be added, with sufficient reason. The idea which serves as the basis for their creation is the desire of expressing in a single word what would otherwise require a phrase of more or less length.

Busted and Bust

There is a real and very great difficulty to be met when a writer sets out to condemn the use of the words "busted" and "bust." That difficulty lies in the fact that the words seem to have driven out of the American language the older form "burst," which all grammarians hold to be correct. It seems, almost, that only those who wish to call attention to the fact that they speak correctly will say nowadays, "One of my automobile tires burst," instead of using the everyday language of "the man in the street" and saying, "One of my automobile tires bust" or "busted." As no one wishes to appear affected in his speech, it seems almost certain that the older, correct form, "burst," will in time disappear from the American language, if not from the English. "Bust" has taken its place, by favor of the American people, and what are grammarians that they should oppose the will of the people?

"'Bust,' in truth, has come into a dignity that even grammarians will soon hesitate to question," says Mencken, in "The American Language." And he goes on to ask, "Who, in America would dare to speak of 'bursting' a broncho, or of a 'trust-burster'?"

But That and But What

"There is no doubt but that he is the greatest living statesman." We often hear this expression and similar expressions. It is not correct, for it uses too many words to express an idea. Besides, it is grammatically awkward. Say, instead,

"There is no doubt that he is the greatest living statesman," omitting the word "but." Here is another example: "I do not know but that I shall go there tomorrow." This is very much better in the simpler form, "I think I shall go there tomorrow."

There is equal objection to the use of "but what." Take, for example, the sentence, "I shall never believe but what I should have done better by investing the money." This is a poor construction that can be corrected best by recasting the sentence. Say, "I shall never cease to believe that I should have done better by investing the money."

Calculate

"I calculate to go to the ball game to-morrow."

This use of the verb "calculate," in the sense of "intend, purpose, expect," is incorrect, and is condemned by all authorities. Some writers go so far as to call it vulgar. At best it is a provincialism, and therefore to be avoided by all who wish to speak and write correctly.

There is a use of "calculated" in the sense of "likely" or "apt," that is criticised, as in the sentence, "His course of action is calculated to harm him in the eyes of the people." Those who object to this use of "calculated" say that the verb means only "to ascertain by computation, to reckon, to estimate." But good authority can be found for such use of "calculated" and those who object to it may lay themselves open to the criticism that they carry their objections too far. In this, as in many other points connected with English grammar, opinions differ.

Capacity, see *Ability*.

Can and May (see also Could)

The two auxiliary verbs "can" and "may" are

frequently confused. "Can" is used to express power or possibility; that is, it means to be able to do, or to have the power of doing something. "May" expresses permission or probability; that is, it indicates the permission or the right to do something. Thus, the pupil may ask of the teacher, "Can I speak to my seatmate?" and the teacher may reply, "Yes, you can speak to him" (meaning that the questioner has the power or the ability to do so), "but you may not do so" (meaning that the teacher's permission is withheld). "Can you lend me a dollar?" the chronic borrower might ask, and the reply might be, "Yes, I can lend you one, but I will not."

Grammarians make a similar distinction in the use of "could" and "would," when the past tense or the subjunctive is employed.

Carry, Bring, Fetch

To "carry" means, simply, to bear or convey from one place to another; to "bring" means to convey something, from another place, by a person addressed, to the one who issues the command or request; to "fetch" means to leave the person speaking, go for something and return with it. The following sentences will make clear the distinctions in the uses of these three words: "John, carry that package to the station—I think you will be able to carry it on your shoulder—and bring back the package which is there for me"; and "John, as we are now in the garden, it will be necessary for you to fetch the rake from the barn."

The word "fetch" has, however, other definitions, such as are shown in the following examples: "Asiatic spices fetched a good price in the European market"; "the vessel fetched (reached) its harbor."

Casuality, Speciality

Careless or ignorant speakers frequently say "casuality" when they mean "casualty," and "speciality" when they mean "specialty." Now, the words "casuality" and "speciality" are found in English, but they are not to be used—or, rather, misused—to mean "specialty," something that is special or set apart, and "casualty," a fatal or serious accident or disaster, as in the phrase, "the casualties of war."

The insertion of the letter "i" in each case adds an unnecessary syllable to the word and thus betrays the error to the person who gives some thought to correct English.

Richard Grant White says of this and similar errors: "They ought to be, but I fear they are not, evidences of an utter want of education and of a low grade of intelligence." He means that persons who are not lacking in education and intelligence are sometimes guilty of such errors.

Caused By and Due To

These two expressions, "caused by" and "due to" are frequently used incorrectly. They should be employed only in connection with nouns to which they refer. The following give incorrect and correct uses of the two words:

Incorrect: "She did not return to the city, caused by her illness." Correct: "Her failure to return to the city was caused by her illness." Or, "Because of her illness, she did not return to the city."

Incorrect: "Due to an accident to his automobile, he did not arrive in the city on time." Correct: "His failure to arrive in the city on time was due to an accident to his automobile"; or, "Because of an accident to his automobile, he did not arrive in the city on time."

Character and Reputation

Your "character" is what you are, in your moral nature, your abilities, etc.; your "reputation" is what your friends, your neighbors, the world, think of you. Your reputation may be ruined by a false accusation, but your character cannot be injured by anyone but yourself.

Cheap and Low Priced

Do not use "cheap" when you mean "low priced."

While "cheap" may mean "inexpensive" or "low in price," as when we say, "He wore a cheap suit of clothes," at other times the word "cheap" may mean low priced only as a comparison. For example, a painting by Rembrandt or Murillo may be very cheap at $100,000, but it would hardly do to refer to it as a low-priced picture.

"The dictionaries define the adjective 'cheap' as meaning 'bearing a low price," says Alfred Ayres, in "The Verbalist"; "but nowadays good usage makes it mean that a thing may be had, or has been sold, at a bargain. Hence, in order to make sure of being understood, it is better to say 'low priced,' when one means 'low priced,' than to use the word 'cheap.' What is low priced, as everybody knows, is often dear, and what is high priced is often cheap. A diamond necklace might be cheap at ten thousand dollars, and a pinchbeck necklace dear at ten dollars."

To Chortle

The word "chortle" was coined by the late Professor Charles Lutwidge Dodgson, who used the name "Lewis Carroll" in writing his famous and delightful books, "Alice's Adventures in Wonderland" and "Through the Looking Glass."

In one of his verses he wrote, "Oh frabjous joy, callooh, callah, he chortled in his joy." The word struck the popular fancy, and it "stuck."

According to the latest edition of Webster's International Dictionary, it means: "Apparently, to sing or chant exultantly." But a short story writer recently said: "When the old man saw her enter the room, he seemed to chortle all over with glee."

Claim

"The detectives claimed that they saw the suspected man near the scene of the murder about half an hour before the shot was fired."

Such use of "claim," in the sense of "assert" was condemned generally by grammarians and others until recently, and some writers still hold that it should not be so used, but it has made a place for itself in common English. Until recently it was barred from the columns of a New York newspaper which has had for many years a list of prohibited words, but it is now admitted there as allowable.

However, if one wishes to be very careful in one's choice of words, it is best to use "claim" only when a real claim is involved, as in "I claim that land," and not when the word is merely equivalent to "assert," or "say," as in "I claim that it is going to rain."

College, Going to, see *Going to "the" College*.

Combine

There are authorities on English who denounce the use of the word "combine" as a noun, and one of them asserts that it was first employed about forty years ago by an ignorant New York alderman.

However, twenty years ago the word had already won recognition as "colloquial English"—that is, as a word in common use, if not accepted in literature—and it is now used frequently. It may, therefore, be accepted as part of the language. To

38

those who say that the word "combine" is not needed, that its meaning is expressed by "combination," the answer may be made that the two words differ greatly in meaning, and that "combine" conveys the suggestion of an illegal or underhand combination, or conspiracy, or unlawful "trust."

Commandeer

If any writer of English, in America or elsewhere, had used the verb "commandeer" before the Boer War, probably very few of his readers would have understood him. Now the word is in everyday use, in newspapers and elsewhere, and is generally understood. The naturalization of "commandeer" shows how hospitable the English language is to words of foreign origin—this one comes to us from the Dutch—and how easily the adopted children of the language take their places among the older members of the family.

In this case, we did not need a new word, as we already had an exact equivalent in "requisition." It is certain, however, that "commandeer" has come to stay, and perhaps in time it will drive out the older word "requisition."

Commence or Begin

The question is frequently asked, "Is there any difference in meaning between the words "commence" and "begin?"

These words have exactly the same meaning. "In significance there is no difference whatever between 'commence' and 'begin'; the former word is from the Latin, the latter is Saxon and is preferred before an infinitive," says the Standard Dictionary. That is, it is better, according to some authorities, to say, "I began to read the book," than "I commenced to read the book."

It should be said, however, that some writers hold that "begin" is the simpler word and, the e-fore, to be preferred. Alfred Ayres, in "The Verbalist," says of "begin" and "commence": "These words have the same meaning; careful speakers, however, generally prefer to use the former."

Company, Keeping, see *Keeping Company.*

Complete, Most, see *More Perfect.*

Compliment and Complement

Owing to the similarity in the spelling of these two words, and to their close resemblance in sound, they are sometimes confounded. But the meanings are entirely different. Of course, everyone knows what "compliment" means, since the paying of compliments is a fairly general practice. But not everyone knows the meaning of the word "complement." It means the complete amount or number necessary for a purpose, as, "The regiment has its complement of men"; or, something that completes or fills up what another number, quantity, supply, etc., lacks, as "The two curves of the crescent are complements of each other; without either, the other would be simply a curve."

Comprise and Compromise

Because of the similarity in appearance, these two words are sometimes confused. Although they look alike, there is no likeness in meaning.

"Comprise" means "to include, to contain, to encircle, to inclose," etc., as in the sentence. "A few words comprised his entire stock of French."

"Compromise" has various meanings, as "to adjust or settle by mutual agreement, to put in danger, to expose to suspicion or discredit, etc." We speak of a person being found in a "compromising" position.

It is this last definition of "compromise" that makes ludicrous an error in a recent "Book of Etiquette." The book gives as a sample invitation to the opera: "My Dear Miss Smith, I have been fortunate enough to obtain a box in the parquet, where those of us who will compromise the party will be comfortably seated." Of course, "comprise" is meant.

Confess and Admit

These two words, "confess" and "admit," are sometimes used incorrectly, or, at least, without proper regard for the differences in their meanings. We say, "I confess the power of his argument, but I cannot agree with him," when we should say, "I admit the power of his argument," etc. In other words, "confess" is misused in cases in which the idea of a confession (as of a fault) does not enter, and in which the proper word to use is "admit."

"The chief present use of the word 'confess,'" says the Standard Dictionary, "is in the sense of making known to others one's own wrongdoing; in this sense, 'confess' is stronger than 'acknowledge' or 'admit,' and more specific than 'own'; a person admits a mistake; acknowledges a fault; confesses sin or crime."

Consensus of Opinion

The question is sometimes asked, "Is the expression 'the consensus of opinion,' correct, or should the words 'of opinion' be omitted?"

This doubt is based on the fact that the word "consensus" means "a collective, unanimous opinion of a number of persons; a general agreement." A "consensus of opinion," therefore, seems to involve the use of too many words to express an idea; a repetition, or what the grammarians and rhetoricians call tautology.

But the expression, "consensus of opinion," has been used for many years, and has embedded itself in popular and literary usage. The Standard Dictionary, which has the definition of "consensus" quoted above, gives as an illustration a quotation from the "Westminster Review" which speaks of "the consensus of opinion."

Considerable

Do not say, "The weather has grown considerable warmer since this morning, as so many persons say. The proper form is, "The weather has grown considerably warmer since this morning." This construction is governed by the rule of grammar which tells us that an adjective, such as "warmer" is modified by an adverb ("considerably,") and not by another adjective ("considerable.")

Contagious, see *Infectious*.

Contemptible

"Do you know that fellow Jones?"

"Yes, and I have a very contemptible opinion of him."

The second speaker should have said, "I have a very low opinion of him," or, "In my opinion, he is beneath contempt." When he said, "I have a very comtemptible opinion of him," he declared that his, the speaker's, opinion was contemptible, or beneath contempt. An old story says a man once said to Dr. Parr, "Sir, I have a contemptible opinion of you." "That does not surprise me," returned the doctor; "all your opinions are contemptible."

Alfred Ayres, who tells the foregoing story in "The Verbalist," declares that what is worthless or weak is "contemptible," and that that word is used sometimes for "contemptuous." "Despicable" is a word that expresses a still more intense degree of contempt. A traitor is a "despicable" character, while a coward is only "contemptible."

Continual and Continuous

These two words "continual" and "continuous," are often confused; it seems to be, and probably is, very difficult for most persons to make the distinction between them. Perhaps that is due to the similarity in spelling and derivation of the two words.

However, the dictionaries and the other authorities on the use of words tell us that there is a great difference in the meanings of the words. Proper usage requires that we use the word "continual" when we speak of acts that are repeated at frequent intervals, as in "Continual dropping wears away a stone." "Continuous," on the other hand, is to be used when we wish to convey the idea of uninterrupted action, as "The continuous flow of the brook turned the water wheel."

"'Continuous' describes that which is absolutely without pause or break," says the Standard Dictionary; 'continual' that which often intermits, but as regularly begins again."

Continue On

"There was a loud explosion outside the hut, as though a shell had burst in front of the door. The general continued to read on, not disturbed by the cries of his men."

The word "on" in the foregoing sentence is not needed. The idea of the writer would have been expressed quite as well without it. Therefore, according to the rule against the use of superfluous words, it should be omitted. However, in the sentence, "We continued on our way," the usage is good, idiomatic English. The meaning in this case is, "We continued to travel on our way."

Could Instead of Can or Will

Probably everyone has had the experience of

43

hearing from a friend or acquaintance, "Could you lend me a dollar until tomorrow?"

It is incorrect to use "could" in this manner. If the speaker means, "Have you the ability to lend me a dollar until tomorrow?" he should say, "Can you lend me," etc. And if he wishes to say, "Are you willing to lend me a dollar?" he should say, "Will you lend me," etc. Of course, the hearer understands him perfectly when he uses the word "could," but perhaps he is more inclined to grant the request if it is expressed in better English.

Counsel and Council

Owing, probably, to the similarity in sound, "counsel" and "council" are sometimes confused, especially in writing. (Of course, in speaking the error is not noticeable, save by one whose ear is trained in the catching of fine distinctions in pronunciation.)

"Council" means a body of persons assembled for discussion of some matter of common interest or importance; it means also a body elected or appointed for the purpose of deliberating or giving advice, as, "the Governor's council."

"Counsel" means, as a verb, to advise, or interchange opinion; to consult; as a noun it means one who gives advice, and is generally used of a lawyer who is engaged to give advice or to present one's case in court. It is used also in the plural, so that when we hear of a client's counsel, we cannot tell without further information whether one man is meant, or more.

Couple

Do not use "couple" when you mean simply "two." And do not use it, as so many persons do, to mean "a few" or "several." "A couple" means "two," but two that are joined in some natural

44

connection, as a married couple. "He went to Chicago a couple of days ago," was heard recently. It was quite incorrect. Did the speaker mean that someone went to Chicago two days ago, or longer ago?

Courageous, see *Brave*.

Cracked Up

The verb "to crack up," meaning to praise highly, is one of the very numerous expressions which the authorities on English call "colloquial" —that is, it is in common use and is not considered incorrect, but it is also looked upon as not belonging to the best grammatical society.

The famous English preacher Spurgeon, who was fond of vigorous English, used the verb "crack up" in the sentence: "Those who crack themselves up are generally cracked."

Credible, Creditable, Credulous

"Credible" means capable or worthy of being credited or believed; it is applied to stories, relations, accounts, opinions, etc., and also to persons; as "He gave a credible account of his travels in Africa"; "Henry Adams is a credible historian of the events of the early Presidential administrations."

"Creditable" refers to something that is worthy of credit or esteem, as in, "Although Benedict Arnold was a traitor in later years, his actions in the early days of the Revolution were creditable to his patriotism."

"Credulous" means inclined to believe easily, or over-inclined; it is applied frequently to persons who are easily deceived in matters of belief; as "Although a man of considerable natural intelligence Louis XI was grossly credulous of tales of superstition, and easily led, therefore, by those who played upon this trait."

45

Credit

A newspaper article reported that Tomasso De Angelis, Italy's most notorious criminal, had just died, and went on to say:

"De Angelis was a member of the old Camorra, and had more crimes to his credit than any other criminal in the country. He had been in prison many times."

It is incorrect to say that he had "crimes to his credit." The word "credit," as a noun, means, according to the Standard Dictionary:

"Reputation derived from the confidence of others; title to trust or belief; character; repute."

The sentence should have read, "De Angelis was charged with more crimes," or "was blamed for more crimes."

Crime, Vice and Sin

These three words, "crime," "vice" and "sin," are sometimes confused or used incorrectly. Perhaps the best definition of the differences in meaning is the one in "The Verbalist," by Alfred Ayres:

"The confusion that exists in the use of these words is due largely to an imperfect understanding of their respective meanings. Crime is the violation of the law of a state; hence, as the laws of states differ, what is crime in one state may not be crime in another. Vice is a course of wrongdoing and is not modified by country, religion or condition. As for sin, it is very difficult to define what it is, as what is sinful in the eyes of one may not be sinful in the eyes of another; what is sinful in the eyes of a Jew may not be sinful in the eyes of a Christian; and what is sinful in the eyes of a Christian of one country may not be sinful in the eyes of one of another country."

46

Criticism

We should not use the verb "criticize" and the noun "criticism" without indicating whether we mean favorable or unfavorable criticism. Thus, one should not say, "I do not care to read So-and-so's latest book, because it was criticized in the newspapers," since the book may have been criticized very favorably. Criticism may be either favorable or unfavorable.

In common usage, however, to criticize a book, a painting, a theatrical performance, etc., has come to mean to pass unfavorable judgment upon it. Probably only students of the history of English will remember, in the course of time, that in a criticism one may mention favorable points as well as those that are unfavorable.

This is possibly due to the fact that the verb "criticize" has for a secondary meaning "to judge severely; detect and expose defects or failures in; censure" (Standard Dictionary), and the tendency in this case is toward the driving out of the primary meaning by the secondary definition.

Crowd, see *Bunch.*

Cunning

In America the word "cunning" has a use that is unknown, or at least rare, in England. Americans call a baby "cunning," meaning that it is quaintly pretty or interesting or attractive, and they apply the same term to small animals, dolls, etc. In "Words and Their Ways in English Speech," the authors, Professors Greenough and Kittredge, call "cunning" an "American nursery term applied to a bright or amusing little child."

The word "cunning" affords an interesting example of the manner in which the English language grows. It means, literally, "knowing," and had at first no bad sense. But in the course of centuries a person who was "cunning," or "knowing," became known as a crafty, sly or artful person, and today we speak, for example, of a "cunning thief" as one who possesses unusual skill. The distinction between "cunning" and "wise" became fixed in the language long ago. Bacon, who lived in the sixteenth and seventeenth centuries, wrote; "Certainly, there is a great difference between a cunning man and a wise man, not only in point of honesty but in point of ability."

Custom and Patronage (see also Habit)

Probably many readers have received letters or circulars in which they are told that "John Smith, having opened a tailoring establishment, solicits your patronage." What John Smith should solicit is not your "patronage," but your "custom."

Ayres says that the word "patronize" and its derivatives "would be much less used by the American tradesman than they are, if he were better acquainted with their meaning. Then he would solicit his neighbors' 'custom,' not their 'patronage." A man cannot have 'patrons' without incurring obligations; while a man may have customers innumerable, and, instead of placing himself under obligations to them, he may place them under obligation to him. Princes are the patrons of those tradesmen whom they allow to call themselves their purveyors; as 'John Smith, haberdasher to His Royal Highness the Prince of Wales.' Here the prince 'patronizes' John Smith."

Dangerous

"I heard that your friend was ill."

"Yes, he was pretty sick, but he was not dangerous."

To the student of English, or even to the person who is ordinarily careful in the choice and use of

48

words, this use of "dangerous" in the sense of "dangerously ill," or "in danger," is amusing. "Dangerous people," says one authority, "are usually most dangerous when they are most vigorous." Instead of saying "He is pretty sick, but not dangerous," say rather, "He is sick, but not in danger."

Data

One should say or write, "The data are," and not "The data is."

The word "data" is the plural form of the Latin word "datum," which means "a thing given," from the verb "dare," meaning "to give." A datum is, according to the Standard Dictionary, "Something assumed, known or conceded as the basis for an argument, or a ground for a conclusion, or as material for an investigation or statement; a premise, starting point or given fact; commonly used in the plural, as "We had not sufficient data to determine the question."

"Send me all the data in the case," wrote a lawyer.

Date

If you wish to be fastidious in your choice of words, you will not say, "I have a date with him," "I am going to make a date with him," etc. Although this use of the word "date" has found its way into the dictionaries, it is not yet recognized as perfect English, but is marked "colloquial," which means that it is in common use, but is not literary English. Use "appointment" instead.

Dearest, see *My Dearest Wife*.

Decline and Refuse

Careful search through many works on the correct use of English words and phrases fails to disclose any reason for doubting that the meanings of the words "decline" and "refuse" are identical.

" 'Decline' and 'refuse' agree in expressing the opposite of consent," says Webster's International Dictionary. 'Decline' is the more courteous term; 'refuse' is more positive, often implying decided, even ungracious rejection of what is offered; as, to decline an invitation; 'Meats by the law unclean, young Daniel could refuse,' Milton."

Words that have the same meaning are known as "synonyms"; words that have the same sound, but are spelled differently from each other, and differ in meaning, are called "homonyms." Thus, "large" and "big" are synonyms; "great" and "grate" are homonyms.

Some authorities hold that there are no perfect synonyms in English; "so-called synonyms almost always differ from each other in some shade of meaning," says one writer.

Demean

"Demean" does not signify, as so many persons seem to think, to conduct oneself in an unworthy manner, to misbehave, to disgrace oneself, to humble oneself, etc. In fact, one may demean oneself in a very worthy and dignified manner, so that the sentence, "He demeans himself in a gentlemanly manner" is quite correct. Of course, if "demean" had the meaning which so many persons ascribe to it, erroneously, it would be ridiculous to say, "He demeans himself in a gentlemanly manner." To demean means simply to behave or to conduct oneself, worthily or unworthily.

Depot and Station

The word "depot"—generally spelled in the French style, "depôt,"—should not be used in the sense of "station," meaning a stopping place for railroad or other trains. A depot is a place or warehouse for the storage of goods awaiting transfer or use, and the word comes from the same Latin word as does our word "deposit." Its introduction into the English language arose from a mistaken idea that the French used it to mean railway station; the French word for railway station is not "depôt," however, but "gare."

In recent years, the men who name the railroad stations of the United States have recognized the error—that is, the grammatical error—involved in calling a station a depôt, and they have avoided it in many cases. Thus, the great stopping place of the Pennsylvania Railroad in New York City is known as the Pennsylvania Station. The other large station in New York City is the end of two lines and is therefore known officially not as the Grand Central Station but as the Grand Central Terminal.

Deprecate and Depreciate

These words are so nearly alike in spelling that they may be confused, and it is well, therefore, to learn the difference between them.

"Deprecate" means "to beg or plead earnestly against; express disapproval or regret for, with hope for the opposite"; also, "to pray or desire deliverance from or the removal of, as a threatened evil" (Standard Dictionary). "Some senators have deprecated any attempt to pass tax legislation," said an editorial.

The meaning of "depreciate" is, according to the Standard Dictionary, "to lessen the worth of, lower the price or rate of; lower or attempt to lower the estimation of; to sink in estimation, or fall in price or worth," as in the sentence. "This is not a condemnation of logic, of course, nor a depreciation of its value." Another case: "He bought the stocks in July, and when he attempted

51

to sell them in August he found that their value had depreciated greatly."

Diagnosed

In a review of a play, the critic for a newspaper of one of our large cities wrote:

"Even the good old maiden aunt becomes suspect and is diagnosed for kleptomania."

Such use of the word "diagnosed" is incorrect. A person cannot be diagnosed: the thing that is diagnosed is a disease, a condition, etc. The critic should have written: "Even the good old maiden aunt becomes a suspect; a diagnosis of kleptomania is made." Possibly this will sound affected or stilted, but it is grammatically correct, and the same assertion cannot be made of the sentence that is criticized.

Differ With, Differ From

Between the proper use of the term "differ from" and the proper use of "differ with" there is a clear distinction, although it is forgotten frequently, even by some writers and speakers who are careful in the use of words.

For a person to differ "from" another, or for a thing to differ from another, he or it must be unlike, in appearance, in manner, or in some other characteristic, while to differ "with" a person means to disagree with him in opinion or belief. It follows, therefore, that while a thing may differ from another, it cannot differ with another, since only thinking beings can have a difference in belief or opinion. For example, "I differ from John in stature, and I differ with him in our views on the present national policy."

Different and Various

"Throughout his professional life he displayed the different characteristics of a man of talent—

industry, adaptability, open-mindedness, quick grasp of the principles of the law and ingenuity in applying them." So read an obituary notice.

The writer should have used the word "various" instead of the word "different." According to the Standard Dictionary, "different" means "not the same; non-identical; distinct; other"; while "various," according to the same authority, means "characteristically different from one another; diverse; manifold."

We say, "This house is different from that one," but, "Chief Justice Taft has held various public offices." We could not say, "This house is various from that one," or, "Chief Justice Taft has held different public offices," because the public offices that he has held have not been different from those that have been filled by other men.

Different From, Than, To

It is quite common to hear or read sentences containing the word "different" followed by an incorrect preposition. "Different" should always be followed by "from," and never by "than" or "to." One hears, "Yours is a very different case than his," whereas the proper form is "Yours is a very different case from his." One hears also, "I have heard your story, and John's is different to it"; correctly, "John's is different from it," or "differs from it." The Standard Dictionary says that the use of "different to" is an undesirable English colloquialism.

The word "different" denotes distinction or contrast (indicated by the use of "from"), while comparison is shown by "than"; thus, "My hat is different from yours, but your hat is better than mine."

Directly

The use of the word "directly" in the sense of

53

"immediately, at once, as soon as possible," is not approved. It is a faulty use of the word which had its origin in England, and spread to the United States. Do not say, "I want him to report to me directly he returns to the office." Say, instead, "I want him to report to me as soon as he returns to the office," or, "I want him to report to me immediately upon his return to the office."

In "Good English, Misused Words," by E. S. Gould, published in 1867, it is said: "Many English novelists use this word as the equivalent of 'as soon as'; hitherto, this use of the word has not gained currency in the United States; and, as it has been used in England since the days of 'Pelham,' that is, for nearly forty years, we may hope to escape it altogether." But a more recent authority tells us that this faulty use of "directly" has found some favor in the United States.

Disappointed, Agreeably, see *Agreeably Disappointed*.

Disassemble

The word "disassemble" is frequently used in commercial language, and means to take something apart after it has been put together, as to disassemble a machine for shipment. There are critics who dislike the word, and condemn it as poor English. It is not found in some dictionaries.

But the fact is that "disassemble" meets a common need, and there is no good substitute for it; therefore it is good English.

Discover and Invent

We should use the word "discover" when we mean to convey the idea of finding, or finding out, what existed previously, and the word "invent" when we wish to express making anything for the first time, in idea or visible form. Some writers and speakers use these words, "discover" and "invent," as though they had the same meaning. The

54

following are examples of correct use: "Columbus discovered America; Bell invented the telephone." "Priestly discovered oxygen," which, of course, existed already; he did not invent the element.

Disinterested and Uninterested

"I should like to advise you in the matter, but I have always been disinterested in the subject to which you refer."

This use of the word "disinterested" is incorrect. The word actually means "impartial, without undue interest in one side or the other of a controversy, dispute, etc." The writer should have expressed himself thus: "I should like to advise you in the matter, but I have always been uninterested (or have never been interested) in the subject to which you refer." It will be seen, of course, that the proper word to use when the question is one of lack of interest (in the sense of attention) is "uninterested," not "disinterested."

"A disinterested judge is impartial (without undue interest in one side and is accordingly praiseworthy); an uninterested judge is not interested in the case he is judging (and is accordingly at fault), says "Manual of Good English," by H. N. MacCracken and H. E. Sandison.

Disremember

There was a time when you could say, in English, with correctness, "I disremember," meaning that you forgot what occurred, or were unable to recall. But the English language has grown beyond the word "disremember," and the Standard Dictionary says that it is "archaic, provincial or humorous." Therefore, do not "disremember" anything; say that you forget it or fail to remember it.

To say that a word is "archaic" means that it was in good usage in a former time, but is now considered antiquated. Poets frequently employ archaic words, for effect. A "provincial" word is one that is used in the provinces; that is, a word that is in common use only in a certain part of a country and may be misunderstood if used elsewhere. To say that a word is "humorous" means that it is quoted by a speaker or writer with the intention of ridiculing a user of the word.

Dived or Dove

The form "dove" as the past of the verb "dive" —for example, "He dove from the side of the ship"—seems to have made its way into the language, and is found in newspapers, magazines and books. Therefore it is, perhaps, just as well to consider it an accepted term, although it is not to be found in many of the lists of irregular verbs. The Standard Dictionary gives "dove" as meaning the same as "dived," but calls it "colloquial"; that is, used in common speech, as distinguished from literary usage.

When a verb forms its past by adding "ed," as in "love, loved," etc., it is said to be a regular or weak verb. But when the past is expressed by changing the form of the word, as in "dive, dove," "sing, sang," etc., the verb is said to be irregular or strong. There are some verbs which are both regular and irregular, weak and strong, such as "build, built or builded," "burn, burned or burnt," etc.

Divide Up

The little word "up" is frequently used in connection with other words to which it should not be joined. Some of the words to which "up" is more commonly added, incorrectly, are the following:

"Divide, end, finish, open, polish, rest, scratch and settle."

incorrect usage that is criticized here is an example of what is called "tautology"; that is, the useless repetition of an idea, in part or entirely.

Dove, see *Dived*.
Drank, Have, see *Have Drank*.
Drunk, Have, see *Have Drank*.
Due to, see *Caused By*.

Dumb

Do not say "dumb" when you mean dull of intellect, or stupid. It is incorrect.

The use of "dumb" for "stupid" is a Germanism; that is, it shows that a German word of similar sound to our word "dumb" has been transplanted into English, although the meanings differ. In German "dumm" means stupid, but in English "dumb" describes a person who has never possessed the power of speech or has lost such power.

Duplicate and Repeat

Although the word "duplicate" (as a verb) is used sometimes by good writers in the same sense as "repeat," it is held by many authorities that it should be used only when there is one repetition, not more than one. For example, take the following sentence, from a New York newspaper:

"With a rapidly increasing population, this would mean that the conditions which are now a horror to everybody who uses the Canal Street station would be duplicated—and made even worse at Brooklyn Bridge, Forty-Second Street, Fourteenth Street, Flatbush Avenue and every other important station in the system."

It would be better to say "repeated," according to the authorities referred to. "Duplicate," according to Webster, means "To double; to fold; to render double; to make a duplicate of something; to make a copy or transcript of."

Each Other; One Another; Either, Any, Neither, None (see also Either)

Properly, the term "each other" is to be used of only one pair of persons or things which stand in relation to each other, and the term, "one another" only of more than two such persons or things. Thus, we may say, "The two friends presented gifts to each other," but not "to one another"; "all of the nations of the earth should dwell in amity with one another," not, "with each other." There are, however, authorities on grammar who hold that the two phrases may be used interchangeably; for example, Lindley Murray says, "two negatives in English destroy one another."

A similar distinction is made by grammarians between "either" and "any," and between "neither" and "none." "Either" and "neither" apply to two; "any" and "none" to more than two. Thus, do not say, 'I have not seen either of the three men"; "neither of the twelve jurors was convinced of the man's guilt."

Effect and Affect

These two verbs are sometimes confused by speakers and writers who are careless in their choice of words. The verb "affect" means "to act upon, to influence, to change," etc.; as in the sentences, "When the mind is depressed, the body is affected"; "the climate of their new home affected their health."

The verb "effect," on the other hand, means "to bring about, to cause, to carry to completion"; as in the sentences, "Having effected their purpose, the soldiers withdrew"; "we hope that the new law will effect its purpose."

Either, Each, Both (see also Each Other)

"On either side of the street there was a row of tall buildings." The speaker meant to convey the idea that both sides of the street were lined with tall buildings, not that there was a row on either side, for "either" means "one or the other." He might have used the word "each," and have said, "On each side of the street there was a row of tall buildings," and his idea would have been clothed in correct words.

In the English of the days of King James I the usage on which comment is made was correct, and the King James version of the Bible, written in the early years of the seventeenth century, (I Kings vii, 15) says, "A line did compass either of them about," but the dictionary calls such use at the present day "archaic"; that is, ancient and outworn, and not to be approved in modern writing or speaking.

Elder and Older

The word "elder," should be used when one refers to persons or objects of the same group; thus, "My elder brother left for Europe today," not, "My older brother." "The elder of the two churches." The same rule is applied to the words "eldest" and "oldest." One should say, if he has more than one brother, "My eldest brother left for Europe today," not "My oldest brother."

When direct comparison is made between two persons, use "older," as in the sentence, "My mother is older than my father." But when the comparison is not made directly, use this form: "My mother is the elder of my parents."

Elegant

"We had an elegant time at the birthday party," says the school-girl, giving the word "elegant" a use upon which grammarians frown. The word properly used means, "marked by refinement, grace or symmetry; exhibiting faultless taste and delicacy of finish; polished; refined; as, an elegant

61

apartment" (Standard Dictionary). It should not be used in the sense of "excellent," "enjoyable," etc.

Professor Meiklejohn, in his "Art of Writing English," a work published in England, makes fun of what he calls the incorrect use of the word "elegant" in the United States, saying:

"'Elegant' is still used in the United States as equivalent to 'very nice,' and people there talk of 'an elegant leg of mutton'; but on this side of the Atlantic its use is much more restricted."

A proper use of the word is found in the following quotation from Oliver Wendell Holmes' "Guardian Angel": "He had not expected to find so much taste for elegant literature in an old village deacon."

Elevator, see *Lift*.
Eligible, see *Legible*.

Else

A word that is frequently omitted when it should be used is "else." Sometimes even writers and speakers who are ordinarily careful are guilty of this error. An example was noted recently in the "society column" of a newspaper, in which the writer said:

"Mr. McAllister knew society, and was better equipped than any one to write about the smart set of his day."

The word "else" should be inserted after the word "one," in the foregoing sentence, to make good English of it. Without it the sentence is incomplete, and the writer contrasts Mr. McAllister with himself (he is, of course, included in "any one") which is absurd and illogical.

Emigrants and Immigrants

An "emigrant" is a person who leaves a country or part of a country to go to another, while an "immigrant" is one who enters. The two words come from the Latin root "migro," which means to move. But "emigrant" is formed by prefixing, or placing before, the root the prefix "e" which means "out," "out of," or "from," and "immigrant" is formed by prefixing "im," which means "in" or "into."

Therefore, it is incorrect to say, "The emigrants arrived here." Say, instead. "The immigrants arrived here." And do not say, "The immigrants sailed for this country a month ago." Use "emigrants" in the latter case.

Of course, it will be understood that a person emigrating from one country becomes a person immigrating into another. It is the same person, but the direction in which he moves makes him either an emigrant or an immigrant.

Eminent, see *Imminent*.

Enable or Permit

A newspaper headline said:

"'Asserts underground street would avoid congestion and enable removal of surface cars.'"

Should "permit" have been used instead of "enable"?

According to Webster the word "enable" is employed properly in the sentence quoted. Webster gives as one of the meanings of "enable" the following: "To make possible, practicable, or easy; as 'steam and electricity enable rapid transit.'"

Enclose, see *Inclose*.

Enjoin

Commenting on the use of the word "enjoin," the writer of a letter to a New York newspaper said that it is "lamentably misused" He declared:

"The lawyer misuses 'enjoin,' which means to

63

command, in the directly opposite sense, as if it meant to forbid. When you read, as I read once in a formal decision of a justice of very important position, that 'the collection of the tax must be enjoined,' what are you to understand? The phrase means, of course, that the collection must be commanded; the context shows that the learned jurist meant that it must be forbidden."

But, according to the Standard Dictionary, the writer of the letter is wrong. The word "enjoin" is used ordinarily in one sense, and in legal usage in a sense that is directly opposed. The book says that "enjoin" means "to lay command or injunction upon; to charge," but in law it means "to prohibit by judicial order or decree."

Enjoy Poor Health

It is absurd to say that a person "enjoys" poor health. "To enjoy" means "to experience joy or pleasure in; receive pleasure from the possession or use of or participation in; delight in." (Standard Dictionary).

Of course, it is quite proper to say, "I have enjoyed good health," since good health, being the greatest of human blessings, is to be appreciated and enjoyed.

A similar error is to be "agreeably" disappointed. If you are disappointed, the experience cannot be agreeable. Say rather, "I was agreeably surprised, or astonished."

Enormity and Enormousness

"Before passing sentence upon the convicted man, the judge dwelt upon the enormousness of his offense." This use of "enormousness" is incorrect; the proper word to be employed is "enormity," which means (Standard Dictionary) "the state or quality of being enormous, outrageous or extremely immoderate; especially, the quality of being extremely bad; outrageous wickedness; as, the enormity of his crime."

"Enormousness" means simply the state of being extremely large. It does not convey any idea of moral quality; it refers simply to size. The dictionaries tell us that the use of "enormity" to denote a distinction in size is erroneous, and should be avoided by all careful writers and speakers. The distinction that is made between "enormousness" and "enormity" is the same as that which is made between "monster" and "monstrous."

Enthuse

The verb "enthuse" or "enthuse over," used frequently in recent years, and especially in newspaper head-lines (its shortness giving the hurried head-line writer a word easily substituted for "to become enthusiastic over") is not good English. Indeed, some writers call it slang; and all writers on good English agree in calling it a vulgarism. One authority says, "The word is unknown to good usage."

One should not say, "She does not enthuse me," or "she does not enthuse." For these, substitute "She does not arouse any enthusiasm in me," and "she is not enthusiastic."

Envious and Enviable

In a newspaper article it was said:

"She is the first woman ever nominated for this office, and it is expected she will poll an envious vote."

The use of the word "envious" instead of "enviable" may have been due to a printer's error, but in any event the word should have been "enviable," not "envious." The latter word means feeling or holding envy; the former means ca-

pable of exciting or calling forth envy, or desire
for possession. It is true that formerly we used
"envious" in the present sense of "enviable," but
that was so long ago that the dictionary now calls
such use obsolete, which means out of date, dis-
carded, gone out of use.

Envious and Jealous

There is a distinction to be made in the meanings of the two words "envious" and "jealous,"
although the difference is ignored very frequently.

For example, a woman will say, "I showed her
my new dress, and she seemed to be very jealous
of me." The proper word to use in this case,
and in similar cases, is "envious," not "jealous."
The word "envious" means cherishing or holding
envy, which is ill will caused by the superior
possessions, accomplishments, etc., of another.
"Jealousy" on the other hand, is the ill will
brought about by the fear of losing the affection
or favor of another.

The Standard Dictionary says: "One is envious of that which is another's, and to which
he himself has no right or claim; he is jealous
of intrusion upon that which is his own, or to
which he maintains a right or claim."

Epitaph and Epithet

As in the cases of other words which look or
sound alike, these two words "epitaph" and "epithet" are sometimes used incorrectly. An epitaph is an inscription on a tombstone or tomb
or monument, in honor of a dead person; an epithet is a phrase or an adjective applied descrip-
tively to a person or object, as "a worthy man,"
"Father Tiber," etc.

The word "epithet" is misused sometimes by
persons who have a good command of language.
They believe that the term "epithet" means "in-

sult," and that to apply epithets to a person is to insult or vilify him. But, as explained above, an epithet is simply a word or phrase that expresses a quality, either good or bad. We read, for example, "these epithets stung him to the quick"; in this case the term "epithet" should be qualified by an adjective, as, "these insulting epithets stung him to the quick," or, "these unbearable epithets."

Equable and Equitable

These two words are sometimes confused, although there is a sharp and clear distinction in meaning.

"Equable" means, "even, uniform, not varying or going from one extreme to another"; in referring to temperament it means "calm, tranquil, not easily disturbed or ruffled." Wordsworth wrote: "He spake of love, such love as spirits feel in worlds whose course is equable and pure."

The word "equitable" means, on the other hand, "just, fair, reasonable, acting according to the rules of honesty and uprightness."

"All his dealings with his fellowmen were equitable and upright."

The word "equitable" is frequently mispronounced. Many persons put the accent on the "quit." That is incorrect. The accent is placed properly on the first syllable, pronounced "ek."

Errors, grammatical, see *Grammatical Errors*.

Et cetera

We frequently see (and less frequently hear) the expression, "and etc." (or "and et cetera," in speaking), as in, "I was provided with all the tools I needed—hammers, chisels, saws, and etc."

This is incorrect. It is just as though we should say or write, "hammers, chisels, saws and and others," since the little word "et" is Latin and means "and." The phrase "et cetera" means

67

"and other things" or "and the rest." Say or write, therefore, "I was provided with all the tools I needed—hammers, chisels, saws, etc."

Some critics assert that "et cetera" is used far too freely in ordinary English, and that its use should be restricted to business. We should use instead, they tell us, such phrases as "and others," "and the rest," "and the like." "Etc." is unnecessary after a series that is introduced by "such as," or other words used to indicate selected examples. Do not say, "He urged extreme measures, such as embargoes, blockades, orders in council, etc." Say, instead, "such as embargoes, blockades and orders in council."

Euphonius and Euphemistic

The two words, "euphonious" and "euphemistic," are sometimes used incorrectly for each other.

A case in point was that of a writer who commented on the recent paying of the income tax. He said: "A bookmaker who said his winnings for the year were $20,000 also offered to pay a tax. This man's money was accepted, too, his income being euphoniously listed as 'Commissions.'"

It should have been "euphemistically," which is derived from "euphemism," meaning "the use of an agreeable or non-offensive word or expression for one that is harsh, indelicate or otherwise unpleasant."

"Euphonious" means "pleasing or soothing in sound; pleasant to the ear."

Ever, see *Seldom Or Ever*.

Evidence and Testimony

Although these two words, "evidence" and "testimony," are sometimes misused and confused by careless speakers and writers, there is a decided

68

difference, which should be observed, in the meanings of the two words.

"'Evidence,'" says Alfred Ayres in "The Verbalist," "is that which tends to convince; "testimony" is that which is intended to convince. In a judicial investigation, for example, there might be a great deal of testimony—a great deal of testifying—and very little evidence; and the evidence might be quite the reverse of the testimony."

"At the trial for murder," says a well written newspaper article, "the hotel keeper gave testimony to the effect that the accused man passed the night at this house, and further evidence of this was brought forward by the fact that the bed had been slept in that night."

Testimony may be false, if given for the purpose of concealing the truth, but evidence can only be true.

Evident, Obvious and Apparent

The distinctions in the uses of these three words are made by the Standard Dictionary as follows:

"That is 'apparent' which clearly appears to the sense or to the mind as soon as the attention is directed toward it; that is 'evident' of which the mind is made sure by some inference that supplements the facts of perception; the marks of a struggle were 'apparent' in broken shrubbery and trampled ground, and the finding of a mutilated body and a rifled purse made it 'evident' that robbery and murder had been committed. That is 'obvious' which is directly in the way so that it cannot be missed; as, 'the application of the remark was obvious.'"

The same authority tells us that something is "manifest" which we can lay the hand upon; "manifest" is thus stronger than "evident," touch is more absolute than sight; that the picture was a modern copy of an ancient work was "evident," and on comparison with the original its inferiority was "manifest."

Except, Save, Other

"He had no coat except the one he wore"; "he had no coat save only the one he wore"; "he had no coat other than the one he wore."

"All are grammatical," says one authority, "and the first sentence is unexceptionable and in current good usage. The last is also in good form, but in present speech would preferably be slightly recast to read, 'He had no other coat than the one he wore.' The second is slightly archaic, for the reason that 'save' is now obsolescent in that sense. It is not quite in good Elizabethan English as it stands, yet it might be easily cast to pass muster in the speech of Raleigh and Drake, and one greater than either."

Except, Unless, Besides

"I will not go, except thou bless me," says a well known passage in scripture. The construction is found in Holy Writ, and was good English in the seventeenth century, when the King James version of the Bible was written. It is heard, nowadays, also, but it is obsolete—that is, outworn. For "except" substitute "unless" in all such cases. Say, "I shall not go unless I am ready," etc.

"Besides" is often used incorrectly in sentences in which "except" is required. An example of such incorrect usage is found in the following sentence: "No one besides the immediate family was present at the wedding." For "besides" in this sentence substitute the word "except."

There is a difference between "beside" and "besides." The former means "by the side of";

the latter is an abverb of excess and means "in addition to."

Excuse Me or Pardon Me

Some persons, who are "nice" in their use of English, raise objections to the apology that is made so frequently, "Excuse me." They believe we ought to say, "Pardon me," or "I beg your pardon."

Despite these careful persons, it is quite correct to say, "Excuse me." To excuse is "to pardon and overlook, as a fault." It means also to make excuses for.

Shakespeare says, in "King John": "And oftentimes excusing of a fault doth make the fault the worse by the excuse."

In the Standard Dictionary, the correct use of "pardon" and "excuse" is pointed out as follows:

"To excuse is to overlook some slight offense, error or breach of etiquette; 'pardon' is often used by courtesy in the same sense."

Executed

The use of "execute,' in application to a human being, has been criticized by some purists, but there is good authority for such use. It has made a place for itself in the language. In "Words and Their Ways in English Speech," it is said:

"'Execute, has long been used for putting to death by legal process, but is still perfectly familiar in its general meaning of 'carry out,' 'follow out,' or 'fulfill.' The judgment of the court is executed, that is, 'carried out,' when a murderer is hanged. Hence, the hanging is called an 'execution,' that is to say, a carrying out of the judgment pronounced; and, by transference, the man is said to be executed as well as the sentence."

Exorcised and Exercised

"There is no occasion for anyone to become exorcised over the criticisms that have been made of
the present state government," said a writer of a
letter to the editor of a newspaper in a large
city. The letter writer fell victim to a desire to
use a word with which he was not wholly familiar, and he did not take the pains to consult the
dictionary.

He confused the words "exercised" and "exorcised." The former word means "made anxious
or filled with worry; harassed in mind." Substitute it for "exorcised" in the sentence first
quoted, and you will have a good example of its
proper use. The word "exorcise" means to cast
out evil spirits by religious or magical ceremonies,
incantations and the like, as in the sentence, "The
natives believed that the phonograph was filled
with evil spirits which could be exorcised only
by casting the instrument into the river."

Expect and Think

Do not use the word "expect" in the sense of
"suppose," "believe" or "think." For example,
the use of the word "expect" in the following
sentence is incorrect: "I expect that your lessons
are done." The verb "expect" means "to look forward to as probable or certain; to await, to feel
assured of something before it occurs; to an-
ticipate"; as, "I expect to go to church next
Sunday, if the weather is fine." Usually we use
"expect" when we look forward to an event with
interest or desire. "One should not say, 'I expect it is,' still less, 'I expect it was.' We cannot
expect the present or the past," says one authority.

Expected to be Caught

In a description of the escape of a convict from

state prison, it was said that "although Jones got away during the night, and therefore had a long start on his pursuers, he was expected to be caught before another day passed."

This is an awkward use of the word "expected," and no authority for it can be found. Say, instead, "It was expected that he would be caught before another day passed," or, "His capture was expected before the passing of another day."

Expected to Have Written

The following conversation was overheard in a street car:

"Why didn't you write to me when you were in the country?"

"Oh, there was so much to do. I expected to have written to you every day, but something always happened to prevent my writing."

The speaker should not have said, "I expected to have written to you every day," but should have said instead, "I expected to write to you every day."

This is a very common error, and it occurs in the writings of many authors who are usually careful in their use of English. John Stuart Mill, the famous English economist, wrote: "To have prevented their depreciation, the proper course, it is affirmed, would have been to have made a valuation of all the confiscated property." He should have written: "Would have been to make a valuation of all the confiscated property."

Experiment, To Try, see *Try And*.
Facts, True, see *True Facts*.

Fair or Fairly

"It is well to treat the strikers fair, but it is also well to let them know the exact truth," says an editorial.

This use of "fair" for "fairly" is perfectly good

73

English, according to Webster and other authorities. Webster defines "fair" as follows: "In a fair manner; specifically, in an attractive or agreeable manner; gracefully; pleasantly; as, the sun shone fair; graciously, as to speak one fair; in an equitable manner; formerly, fitly; as, to play fair; auspiciously; promisingly; as, events promise fair; the day breaks fair; clearly, plainly; as, to write fair."

Fall or Autumn

The use of "Fall" instead of "Autumn" has been criticized by some writers who have not considered the matter carefully. There is excellent authority for holding that the word "Fall," to indicate the season, is quite as good as "Autumn." Some writers have said that "Fall" is an incorrect "Americanism," but that opinion is unfounded. A writer in "Country Life," of London, said:

"I wish that the old word 'fall' could be used again instead of 'autumn.' It is quite wrongly regarded as an Americanism. It may well have been taken to America in the 'Mayflower,' for it has always been used in our West country. I have a long memory, reaching to the fifties, and can certainly aver that the word 'autumn' was never used by the country folk at all; it was always 'last fall,' or 'come next fall,' and this in a neighborhood where Americanisms had never penetrated."

Farmer's "Americanisms" says that "fall" is "a good old English word erroneously thought by some writers to be American by origin."

Famous and Notorious

"Famous" is used of persons or things that are of good fame; while "notorious," on the other hand, is used of those that are of ill fame. Thus, we say of President Garfield that he was a famous

74

man, while Guiteau, who shot him, was notorious for his crime. We speak of a "famous" statesman, but of a "notorious" gambler.

"Though the word 'notorious' cannot be properly used in any but a bad sense," says Alfred Ayres in "The Verbalist," "we sometimes see it used instead of 'noted,' which may be used in either a good or a bad sense. 'Notorious' characters are always persons to be shunned; whereas, 'noted' characters may or may not be persons to be shunned."

Farther, see *Further*.

Father-in-Law for Stepfather

Probably readers of Dickens, besides the present writer, have been interested and puzzled by his use of "father-in-law" where the ordinary usage calls for "stepfather." Thackeray also employs "father-in-law" in this sense and so does Shakespeare.

Webster defines "father-in-law" as "the father of one's husband or wife," and says that "a man who marries a woman having children is sometimes, although erroneously, called their father-in-law."

One authority on good English says that this use of "father-in-law" for "stepfather" was common in England to the time of Dickens and Thackeray —that is, the first half of the nineteenth century, but that the term has now fallen into disuse.

It was seldom if ever used in America in writing, and was part of the common speech in out-of-the-way places only; if, indeed, it was ever employed at all in America.

Favor and Resemble

Although the word "favor," in the sense of "resemble," is frequently used, it is not regarded as good English by many authorities, and some of them call it "colloquial," which means in common, but not literary, use. Other authorities say that it is a provincialism; that is, a term that is used in some parts of America or England only.

The word "favor," used as a verb, has the meaning of "to show kindness to." Therefore, when you say, "The son favors his father," you mean, properly speaking, that the son shows kindness to his father, not that the son resembles his father. When you wish to express the latter meaning, use the word "resemble."

Provincial expressions are not always to be condemned. William Archer, a famous Scotch critic, said: "There can be no rational doubt, I think, that the English language has gained, and is gaining, enormously by its expansion over the American continent. It is not a source of weakness, but of power and vitality to the English language that it should embrace a greater variety of dialects than any other civilized tongue."

Fetch, see *Carry*.

Fetter and Fettle

These two words, "fetter" and "fettle," are sometimes confused, as in the following sentence:

"There had been rumors abroad during the earlier race that the horse was hardly in his best fetter."

This should have been written "fettle," which means, according to the dictionary, "The state of being fettled or made ready; trim."

"Fetter," on the other hand, means "anything that confines or restrains; a restraint."

Fewer, see *Less*.

Fictitious Writer

"Nathaniel Hawthorne, who wrote 'The Scarlet Letter,' 'The Marble Faun,' and other well

76

known works, is ranked as one of the leading fictitious writers of America."

So wrote a high-school student. He should not have called the author of "The Scarlet Letter" a "fictitious writer." He should have said, "one of the leading writers of fiction of America," or "one of the leading writers of American fiction."

"Fictitious" means "created or formed by the imagination; having no real existence." We may say, therefore, that Arthur Dimmesdale and Hester Prynne, the leading characters of "The Scarlet Letter," are fictitious characters, but Nathaniel Hawthorne, who created them, is not one. He was a very real and very great figure in American literature.

Fierce!

"Did you enjoy the moving picture?"

"No, it was fierce!"

The second speaker meant that he did not like the picture at all. A girl said: "She asked my opinion of her hat, and I told her I thought it was fierce!"

This slangy, indefensible use of "fierce" to express disappointment or intense dislike is a recent and very undesirable addition to the English language. Its use has become common in some parts of the country, especially in the larger cities and towns. It is so recent that no mention of it is found in dictionaries published twenty years ago. The word "fierce," according to the dictionaries, means "merciless; savage; having a desire to harm or kill; possessing a cruel nature."

Finished, see *Through*.

First married, see *When I was First Married*.

Firstly

Clergymen and others sometimes use the word

"firstly" in the sense of "first," but the latter word is itself an adverb, and does not need the suffix "ly" that is the sign or mark of adverbs. Some editions of Webster's Dictionary contain "firstly," but say that "many prefer the word 'first' in this use," and the Standard Dictionary says "'firstly' is used by some for the adverb 'first.'" General good usage, which is the only standard of language that we have, requires us therefore to say, "first, secondly, thirdly."

It is stated above that "first" is an adverb; that is, a word which modifies or affects the meaning of a verb. But "first" is also an adjective, or word that modifies a noun or name word. The word has come down to us almost unchanged from the Anglo-Saxon, the parent tongue of many words in common use. In its Anglo-Saxon form the word is "fyrst." It is derived from the word "fore."

To Fix

We Americans "fix" too many things. Originally, the word meant "to fasten, to secure in place, to establish," as, to fix a roof upon a house; to fix one's thoughts upon a subject, or to fix a charge upon a man. In the course of time the word has come to mean "to mend, to repair, to set in order." While some grammarians still condemn this use of the verb "fix" as incorrect, the majority are agreed that it has found a proper place in the English language. We may now fix a furnace, or a clock, and we may also "fix up" a matter of business.

But there are some uses of the word, as commonly employed, which are not correct and which will not find their way into the language if the grammarians can prevent it. One of these is the use of "fix" in the sense of disable or injure or

78

kill, as in the sentence, "I'll fix him for cheating me." If you must have your revenge, have it grammatically, at least, and say, "I'll become even with him," or "I'll have my revenge on him."

To Flee and To Fly

"These verbs, 'flee' and 'fly,' though near akin, are not interchangeable," says Alfred Ayres in "The Verbalist." "For example, we cannot say, 'He flew the city,' 'He flew from his enemies,' 'He flew at the approach of danger,' 'flew' being the imperfect tense of 'to fly,' which is properly used to express the action of birds on the wing, of kites, arrows, etc. The imperfect tense of 'to flee' is 'fled,' hence, 'He fled the city,' etc."

Do not say, "The inhabitants of the forest, menaced by the fire, flew to the city for safety," unless they actually flew. Say, instead, that they "fled" to the city for safety. Do not say, "The wild geese fled to the south early last year"; say instead, "The wild geese flew to the south early last year."

The principal parts of the verbs are as follows: "Fly, flew, flown; flee, fled, fled."

For That

The following sentence is quoted from a letter to a newspaper, "I wish I might claim the credit for it, but may not do so for that it was suggested by my friend."

While the words "for that" are used correctly in this sentence, in the sense of "because," and the dictionary upholds such usage, they are uncommon and smack of the obsolete or, at least, of the archaic. That is to say, the use of "for that" instead of "because" is like an echo of old-time English, and will sound strange to many ears. The words "for that" as meaning "because" are not to be found in Roget's "Thesaurus of English Words and Phrases," a standard work on English.

It is to be understood, of course, that the expression "for that" is not criticized simply because it is unusual. Every person with a vocabulary larger than the average must use words and phrases that are not in common use.

Forbear From

Even some writers and speakers of good English fall into the error of using the preposition "from" after the verb "forbear," which does not require the preposition. "The excuse he presented was so far fetched that I could not forbear from laughing," said a school teacher. "Forbear" means, in this sense, to refrain or abstain from, to avoid voluntarily; it is what is known as a transitive verb; that is, one that has a direct object. A correct use of the word is found in the following: "I have known many superstitiously and foolishly to forbear the making of their wills."

Forgetful Memory

"I can never remember things I ought to. I have such a forgetful memory!"

So said a young woman who was bewailing her inability to remember things which she should not forget. But while her meaning was clear, her wording of it was not quite correct. She should have said:

"My memory is not good," or, "I am forgetful," or "My memory is treacherous, or poor," etc.

In other words, a person may be forgetful, but his or her memory cannot be. According to the dictionary, "forgetful" means "apt to forget; having a poor memory." That is the first definition given; there are two others, as follows: "Heedless, careless, neglectful, inattentive," and "causing to forget, inducing oblivion, oblivious."

Fortuitous

In an account of a baseball game, it was said of a certain club that by a victory it "gained on both its nearest rivals, the even break between the other two teams being a fortuitous happening for the club all around."

Now, while writers on baseball are not masters of perfect English, as a rule, and often clothe their writings in phrases that are more picturesque than grammatical, they should not write, "fortuitous" when they mean "fortunate."

The word "fortuitous" is not one in common use, and is therefore not included in the vocabularies of most of us. It means "occurring or taking place by chance, not by design or intent; accidental." Scott wrote of "the happy combination of fortuitous circumstances."

Fraction

How much is a "fraction" of anything?

Very often one sees and hears the word "fraction" used as though it meant only a small portion, or a small fraction. A recent example is the following, taken from a newspaper article:

"It was stated that Mr. Robinson's trust fund from his grandfather, over which he had power of disposal, was worth about $100,000, and that his independent estate was but a fraction of this sum." Evidently, "a small fraction" was meant.

The word "fraction" means a part of something that has been divided or "broken" into parts. (It comes from the Latin word "fractio," a breaking.) Now, the part may be either large or small, so that "fraction" should not be used without indicating whether the part is large or small.

"Fractional currency" is small coin, or paper money, less in value than the unit.

Friend and Acquaintance

We should reserve the title "friend" for one whom we admit to the intimacy of our hearts, one who has been tried in adversity, and who shares in our joys and our sorrows. Only such a one can be our "friend"; anyone whom we meet casually now and then is merely an "acquaintance." Reserve the name "friend" for those who have earned it.

"A friend is one to whom we may say, 'Let there be eternal truth between us two forevermore,'" says Emerson.

Friend, Gentleman and Lady, see *Gentleman Friend.*
Friends, Bad, see *Bad Friends.*

Friend of Mine

Although it is questioned sometimes that the expression, "a friend of mine," and similar expressions, are correct English, they are correct, and good idiomatic English.

What would one use in place of "a friend of mine"? Would one say "a friend to me" or "my friend"? Neither of these has the force and expressiveness of "a friend of mine." "Mine," says the dictionary, means "of or belonging to me," and one dictionary quotes Thackeray, English novelist, as writing, "That unhappy sister of mine."

Commenting on this use of "mine," one writer on good English says that in this case, as in many others, "most of us are content to regard usage as the best warrant for good English." And usage certainly supports "a friend of mine."

From Whence, etc.

It is incorrect to say, "from whence," "from thence," "from hence."

"Whence" means "from what source," and therefore does not require "from." Say, "Whence does he come?" not "From whence does he come?" "Hence" means "away from this place," therefore say, "I am going hence." "Thence" means "from that place," and it is therefore incorrect to say, "He went from thence to Chicago." The proper form is, "He went thence to Chicago."

The use of the word "from" with these three words, "whence," "hence" and "thence," is an example of redundancy, or use of words not needed.

Full, Most, see *More Perfect.*

Funny

One of the funniest (meaning most ludicrous) errors in common usage is the employment of the word "funny" in the sense of odd or strange or curious, when the context shows that the occurrence to which reference is made is anything but funny.

"Funny" means "affording fun; provoking laughter; comical; ludicrous; facetious"; (Standard Dictionary), but frequently one hears such sentences as the following: "Isn't it funny that Robinson, who was born on Lincoln's birthday, should have died on the same day as the President?" and "It was funny that he escaped all dangers here, and was killed in another city." Certainly there was nothing "funny" in the tragedy. "It was curious that he escaped," etc., would be the proper form. Instead of the word "funny," use in such cases "curious, odd, strange, peculiar, unusual," etc.

Further and Farther

Probably the best way of showing the difference between these two words, in correct usage, is to give examples. The following two sentences will illustrate this:

"My time is limited, so I shall not be able to go further into the subject." "We shall have to travel ten miles farther before we reach our destination."

It will be seen from the foregoing examples that the word "further" is to be used when the writer or speaker intends to give the idea of quantity, or degree, and the word "farther" when the application is to actual distance. Thus, do not say, "San Francisco is further from New York than Chicago is," but "farther from New York." "Farther" is the comparative of "far," and "further" is derived from the old Anglo-Saxon word "fore."

Further and Furthermore

The question is asked sometimes whether it is better to use the word "further" or the word "furthermore" in sentences such as the following:

"Further, when peace is declared our war passport laws will die."

In reply, it may be said that the use of either word is correct. Each of them means "besides," "in addition to." The dictionaries make no distinction between them. There is another word, "furtherover," with the same meaning, which is called obsolete, but which may still be in use in some parts of the world where English is spoken.

Future

"Beginning life as a poor boy, the future general made a good record in the schools of his native town, and was nominated for a cadetship at West Point by the Congressman from his district."

The word "future" is used incorrectly in this sentence. "Future" expresses time to come, dating from the present, and not from any time in the past. Therefore, the sentence should be corrected to read, "Beginning life poor, the boy who later (or subsequently) became a general, made a good record," etc.

Another instance is found in the following: "Until she was eighteen years old, her life was marred by constant illness, but in her future life she was a healthy, vigorous woman." Instead of "future," use the word "later" or "subsequent."

" 'Future' looks forward from the present, and not from some time in the past," says one critic.

Future Tense expressed by present, see *I Am Going Next Week*.

Gentleman Friend, Lady Friend

"The terms 'gentleman friend' and 'lady friend,' not in themselves objectionable, have, through the use that has been made of them, become ambiguous and vulgar," says "Handbook of Composition," by Edwin C. Woolley. Say "a gentleman or a lady of my acquaintance," or "a man friend" or a "woman friend."

Despite the criticism, it seems certain that the terms "gentleman friend" and "lady friend" will remain in common usage, and in time may be recognized by grammarians. When a young woman says that she has a "gentleman friend," you know exactly what she means; and you know also what a young man means by his "lady friend." The terms are not elegant, but they are expressive, and they may be said to fill a need that is created by the absence, from English, of gender, or sex, endings for our nouns. In Latin "amicus" means a male friend, "amica" a female friend. But in English a "friend" may be of either sex.

Gents and Pants

Despite the fact that all critics—and even many writers who are not disposed to be very critical—have condemned the use of the word "gents," for "gentlemen," the former word is still used in common speech and in numerous advertisements. "Clothing for ladies and gents" is advertised, and in announcements of entertainments we are told that "gents' tickets are one dollar, ladies' fifty cents." The following was overheard recently: "Oh, Mary, did you see the man who picked up my purse?" "Yes; he looked like a perfect gent."

Never say "gent," say "gentleman."

The word "pants," as an abbreviation for "pantaloons," is also condemned by critics; but "pantaloons" is now seldom used, so the only word that is left when one wishes to describe a man's nether outer garment is "trousers."

General, see *Universal*.

Going to "The" College

Why do we say, "John goes to college," but "John goes to the university," and not "to university"? Also, why do we say "John goes to town," but "John goes to the city"?

In this case, as in many others, it is impossible to say why an English idiom has taken one form rather than another. We can say only that in the course of centuries the users of the language have come to prefer one form rather than another, without logical reason for the preference, and that the preferred form has come to be fixed in the language.

Good and Well

It is astonishing to note that many persons, educated and presumably able to speak English correctly, use the word "good" incorrectly in the sense of "well."

"I slept good last night," "I can play cards as good as he can." (Sometimes we hear, "I can play cards as good as him"; in this sentence there are two errors—"good" should be "well" and "him" should be "he.") The first sentence quoted, "I slept good last night," should be, "I slept well last night."

The grammatical rule governing this case is that a verb is modified by an adverb, and not by an adjective. "Good" is an adjective and "well" is an adverb. Therefore, in the sentences given, the adverb "well" should be used in connection with the verbs "slept" and "play," and not the adjective "good."

Gourmand and Gourmet

According to the latest edition of Webster's International Dictionary, there is in present usage no distinction between "gourmand" and "gourmet," the meaning being, in both cases, "one who is a luxurious eater, an epicure." But "gourmand," according to the same authority, formerly meant a ravenous or gluttonous eater, the word in this sense being now obsolete, or disused.

The authority quoted says that "gourmet" (pronounced "goormeh," the second syllable very short) is a foreign word. Both words come from the French.

Governor, see *My Old Man.*

Graduate or Be Graduated

Occasionally we find a modern authority on English who tells us that we should never say, "The man graduated from college two years ago," but should always say, "The man was graduated from college two years ago."

But as long ago as 1890 a well known writer on the proper use of words said that the expression, "He graduated from college," instead of "He was graduated from college," was well established. Some of the most recent and best books that deal with distinctions in the uses of words do not touch on this subject at all. It is probably correct to say that "he graduated" has made a place for itself, despite the objections of the older critics and grammarians.

Grammatical Errors

An interesting and amusing war has been waged over the question of the correctness of the expression, "grammatical error." It has been asked, "How can an error be grammatical?" and we are urged to say, instead, "An error in grammar." But equal, if not more serious, objection is made to the latter phrase.

"Of the two expressions, 'a grammatical error' and 'an error in grammar,' the former is preferable," says one authority. "If one's judgment can accept neither, one must give up the belief in the possibility of expressing tersely the idea of an offense against grammatical rules. Indeed, it would be difficult to express the idea. It need scarcely be added that, grammatically, no one can make a mistake, that there can be no bad grammar, and, consequently, no bad English; a very pleasant conclusion, which would save us a great amount of trouble if it did not lack the significant quality of being true."

Grand

The word "grand" has its proper place in English, but it is frequently misused. Used properly, it means "impressive, of imposing character or size, or large proportions."

But we hear frequently such ludicrous uses of the word "grand" as the following. "Did you enjoy your dish of ice cream?" "Yes; it was grand!" "We had a fine sail down the bay, the weather was grand." "We had a grand time at the picnic." In most cases of the incorrect use of the adjective "grand" the word "enjoyable" or "delightful" may be substituted; in other cases it is not difficult to find an adjective that expresses correctly the meaning of the writer or speaker.

Great, see *It Went Great.*

Grouch

"Grouch" is a very expressive word, and there seems to be no other in English to express the idea exactly. So we shall have "grouch" recognized, in time, as a member in good standing of the great family of English words.

But now such dictionaries as recognize its existence call it "slang," and therefore, by inference, warn their readers not to use it. Webster defines "grouch" as "a fit of ill temper or sulkiness," and gives also "grouchy," but has not come yet to the point of recording the verb "to grouch." That also will come in time, no doubt, as the word is in use among the people, who make the language.

It is interesting to note that in the Middle English period, when the English language was forming, there was a word "grucchen," or "grochen," which meant to grumble. So "grouch" is probably a word that has a long line of ancestry.

Grow Smaller

If persons who say or write that a thing "grows smaller" or "grows less" would pause to consider the meaning of the word "grow" they would see that a thing cannot "grow less." To grow means to increase in any manner—for instance, in size or in strength—or to pass from one state to another. Thus, we say, "the child grows in stature or in mental strength"; "the weather grows mild"; "the day grows dark."

Richard Grant White, in "Words and Their Uses," says: "What is large cannot be reasonably said to grow smaller; for example, 'after the full, the moon grows smaller.' It lessens, diminishes;

89

the opposite of growth. And in general even a change of condition is more accurately expressed by 'become' than by 'grow.'"

(It should be noted that this use of to "grow less" is defended by some authorities on English, but White's opinion is accepted widely.)

Guess

There are few words in common use in the English language so frequently employed incorrectly as the verb "guess." Even persons who pride themselves upon their ability to speak correctly permit themselves to fall into the common error of using "guess" instead of "think."

"I guess I'll go home now," says someone who knows that he intends to go home, and that there is no guesswork about the matter.

To "guess" means, according to the Standard Dictionary, "to judge from slight indications, or on merely probable grounds; as, to guess a person's age; to conjecture correctly; to judge at random." It should not be used in the sense of "believe," "decide," or "think," and is, in fact, seldom so used save in some parts of the Northern United States. Such usage is quite old, but that fact does not save it from condemnation by grammarians.

Guest, Invited, see *Invited Guest*.

Habit and Custom

The word "custom" refers generally to the repeated action or course of conduct of many persons, considered as the inhabitants of a community, a city, a state, etc. "Habit" refers to the actions of a single person. Thus we say, "It is the custom of the Chinese to pay all their debts at the New Year," not "It is the habit of the Chinese," etc. Speaking of a man, we say, "It is his habit to turn a certain corner each morning on his way to his office," or, "It is his custom," etc., either being correct, but the weight of authority inclines toward restricting the use of "custom" to reference to many, and to restricting "habit" to reference to one.

"'Custom' is chiefly used of the action of many; 'habit' of the action of one; we speak of 'customs' of society, the 'habits' of an individual," says the Standard Dictionary. "'Habit' always includes an involuntary tendency, natural or acquired, greatly strengthened by frequent repetition of the act, and may be uncontrollable, or even unconscious."

Had Ought To

The expressions "had ought to," and "hadn't ought to," are used frequently, but they should never be heard. They are not only incorrect, but all authorities agree that they are vulgarisms. Instead of saying, "He does not want to go home, but I think he had ought to go," say, "I think he ought to go," leaving out the word "had."

"He hadn't ought to do it," is incorrect English, It should be "He ought not to do it" or "He should not do it." "He hadn't ought to have done it" should be "He ought not to have done it" or "He should not have done it."

Had Rather or Would Rather

Should one say, "I had rather go home" or "I would rather go home?" The matter is in dispute among grammarians, but it seems to be fairly well established that "had rather" is as good English as "would rather." The former term has made its way into the English language; "it has the merit of being idiomatic and easily and universally understood," says one authority. A passage from the Psalms, "I had rather be a doorkeeper in the house of my God than to dwell in the tents of wickedness," is quoted frequently.

However, some grammarians believe that "would rather" is preferable. They say that "would rather" may always be substituted for "had rather," and that therefore it is preferable. But in this case, as in so many others, it is held that usage governs, and users of "had rather" should know that the expression has been employed for centuries, and has the approval of some of the greatest and most careful writers of English.

Half, Largest, see *Largest Half*.

Half Mast or Half Staff

On the morning of Memorial Day, May 30, and on occasions of mourning for the dead, the American flag is raised to half its usual height. Some persons say that the flag is displayed at "half mast"; others say that it is flown at "half staff." Which expression is correct?

If we accept the wording of the regulations of the United States Army covering the point, we must say "half staff," not "half mast." The dictionaries, however, give "half mast," and one of them cites "half staff" only as a "variant" of "half mast." So it would seem that either expression is correct.

It has been suggested, with considerable ingenuity, that the expression "half staff," as prescribed by the Army regulations, is correct on shore, where the flag is flown from a staff, but that on shipboard, where the flag is flown from a mast, it is better to say "half mast."

Handsome, Beautiful and Pretty

The differences in meaning of the words "handsome," "beautiful" and "pretty" must be "felt" by the mind. If such "feeling" is not present, it is very difficult, if not impossible, to put it there.

"Handsome" means, according to Webster, "agreeable to the eye or to correct taste; having a pleasing appearance, with symmetry and dignity; comely." The word expresses, according to the same authority, more than "pretty" and less than "beautiful"; as "a handsome man, a handsome garment, house, tree."

We say that a man is "handsome," but we seldom if ever refer to a man as "beautiful," and we never call a man "pretty." But a woman or a child may be pretty, beautiful or handsome, and so may an animal, a plant or an inanimate object.

Hanged and Hung

Should we say, "The man was hanged," or "The man was hung?" Both forms are used, and both are correct, grammatically, but usage among careful writers and speakers directs us to say, "The man was hanged"; not, "The man was hung." One critic writes: "Pictures, signs, bells and other inanimate objects are hung; men are hanged. While some writers ignore this distinction, the best authorities observe it." If you wish, you may say that a person is hung, and not hanged, and no one may accuse you of speaking ungrammatically; but you will be in better literary company if you say "the man was hanged."

Hanker

If anyone desires to cast the word "hanker" and its derivative, "hankering," out of his own vocabulary and into the outer darkness of forbidden words, he may do so, and may quote in defense of his action the editor of Webster's International Dictionary, who says that the use of "hanker" is chiefly colloquial or familiar. But he must be prepared to meet the reply that "hanker" is used by such good English scholars as James

Russell Lowell, J. A. Symonds and others. The word is given, as one in good standing, in Roget's "Thesaurus of English Words and Phrases."

It means "to long for something with a keen appetite and uneasiness." Trollope, the English novelist, wrote: "She still hankered, with a natural hankering, after her money."

Hard of Hearing

The expression, "hard of hearing," is good English and is recognized as such by high authorities. Objection to it is not justified, and discarding it would mean throwing away a long established idiomatic expression. It is found in Webster's Dictionary, Roget's "Thesaurus" and other authorities.

Webster says, however, that the use of "hard" to mean "able or capable only with difficulty," is rare except in the phrase "hard of hearing."

Hardly, see *Don't Hardly.*

Have a Right

An incorrect use of the word "right" is seen in expressions such as the following:

"If you break the law, you have a right to be arrested." The word "right" has for one of its meanings, "a just and proper claim or title to anything," and one can hardly say that a person has a just and proper claim or title to arrest.

In other words, it is incorrect to use "right" in the sense of "liability." The proper way in which to word the sentence commented upon is to say "If you break the law, you are liable to arrest," or "to be arrested"; or, perhaps, one might say, "you deserve to be arrested." One commentator says that a person is supposed to desire or claim what he has a right to, which is not the case when he is told, "You have a right to fall and break your neck."

94

Do not say, "You had a right to tell me." Say, instead, "You should have told me," or "You ought to have told me."

Have Drank

It is astonishing to note how many persons, including some who are well educated, are guilty of saying "have drank," instead of "have drunk." We hear someone say, "I would have drank that water, but I doubted that it was clean." He should say, "I would have drunk that water," etc. There is no excuse for "have drank." The principal parts of the verb "drink" are as follows: Drink, drank, drunk. In former times it was not improper to use "drunk" in the sense of "drank" in such sentences as the following, "I drunk the liquor," but it was never correct, so far as a study of authorities shows, to say or write "have drank."

Have Seen, see *Saw.*

Healthy and Healthful

There is a distinct difference in the meanings of these two words, "healthy" and "healthful," and the distinction should be made by all who desire to speak and write correctly. "Healthy" means possessing or enjoying health or its effects; as, "a healthy person" or "a healthy condition." But "healthful" means promoting health, or adding to it, or preserving it. Thus, we say that a healthy person is the product of healthful surroundings. "The finances of the country are in a healthy condition." "Healthful living is conducive to length of life."

A correspondent of a newspaper wrote, "Are plants in a sleeping room healthy?" It was evident that she meant, "Does the presence of plants in a sleeping room affect the health of the occupant of the room?" Of course, a plant, in a sleeping room or elsewhere, may or may not be healthy; and its presence in a room may or may not be healthful for the human occupant.

Heaps

"You seem to be very popular."

"Oh, yes; I have heaps and heaps of friends."

Although many authorities on English do not mention as incorrect this use of the word "heaps," in the sense of "many" or "a large quantity," others tell us that it is not good English, and should be avoided by anyone who wishes to speak and write correctly. One authority calls it a "colloquialism that approaches a vulgarism." This authority, The Standard Dictionary, says: "While it is true that this sense of the word 'heaps' was included in the word in the Anglo-Saxon period, it is also true that we have now 'quantity, number, crowd' and many other words of similar general application, and 'heap' has been well differentiated to mean 'a collection of things laid or thrown together in a body so as to form an elevation'; so that to speak of 'a heap of friends,' or of 'doing one heaps of good,' seems incongruous, and is unnecessary and inadmissible."

Hear To

Do not say, "hear to" when you mean "listen to," "hear of," "consent to," etc. It is a colloquialism.

For example, it is not well to say, "I asked him to go with me, but he would not hear to it." Say, instead, "I asked him to go with me, but he would not consent," or, more simply, "I asked him to go with me, but he would not go." "Hear of" is admissible, but is "colloquial."

Another use of the word "hear" that is incorrect—perhaps it was more commonly heard years ago than now—is in the expression "hear tell of." One hears occasionally, for example, some such expression as the following:

"Have you heard of the accident?" "Yes, I've heard tell of it."

The proper form is, "I've heard of it," or, "I've heard it talked about."

Hearing, Hard of, see *Hard of Hearing*.

Hebrew, Jew, Israelite

The three terms, Jew, Hebrew, or Israelite, differ in origin, but they are now used interchangeably save, perhaps, by scholars. Webster defines "Hebrew" as "a member of one of a group of tribes of the northern branch of the Semites, which group includes the Israelites, Ammonites, Moabites and Edomites; generally, specifically, an Israelite." An "Israelite" is said by the same authority to be "a descendant of Israel, or Jacob; a Hebrew; a Jew," while "Jew" is defined as follows:

"Originally, one belonging to the kingdom of the tribe of Judah; after the return from the Babylonish captivity, any member of the new Hebrew state; hence, any member of the Hebrew race or people or any one whose religion is Judaism."

Hectic

This word, "hectic" seems to have become, in recent years, a favorite with writers of many sorts, especially those who treat of baseball, football and other sports. But almost all of them, if not all, use it incorrectly. They believe it to mean "feverish," but they are wrong. One sporting writer said, not long ago:

"Football history of the sort that will not be forgotten easily was made on Saturday. When the other victories and defeats of that rather hectic

97

afternoon have been dimmed by time, football followers will still remember the hotly contested game."

"Hectic" means "habitual or constitutional; denoting a wasting habit or condition of the body; as, a hectic fever, one that consumes the body."

The incorrect use of "hectic," noted above as meaning "feverish," arose from the medical expression, "hectic fever."

Help To Do

There are some verbs after which the little word "to" is usually omitted as unnecessary; "The Institutes of English Grammar" by Goold Brown, states:

"The active verbs, 'bid, dare, feel, hear, let, make, need, see,' and their participles, usually take the infinitive after them without the preposition 'to'; as, 'If he bade thee depart, how darest thou stay?'"

To this list the verb "help" is generally added. In Webster's International Dictionary it is said that "an infinitive following 'help' is commonly used without 'to'; as in 'Help me scale yon balcony,' written by Longfellow."

It may be said, therefore, that it is generally considered correct to say, "I helped him do it," etc. To help one to something is, of course, another matter.

Hence, see *From Hence.*

Hire, Let, and Lease

There is a difference between the words "hire" and "let" that is often ignored. "I hire a house from a man, but I let it to him." In other words, the man who takes the house hires it, while the man who parts with it lets it to the other man. Do not say, therefore, "I let my office from Jones

& Co.," but "I hire my office," etc. Do not say, "I hired my house to my neighbor for the summer," but "I let my house to my neighbor for the summer."

Concerning the use of the word "lease," we find the following in "The Principles of Rhetoric," by Professor Adams Sherman Hill: "'To lease' is improperly used in the sense of 'to hire by lease.' It means 'to let by lease'; the lessor leases to the lessee. In consequence of the misuse of this word, one is often at a loss to determine from the language of an advertisement whether an estate is to be let or hired."

His, see *One.*

Hisn and Yourn

When a writer sets out to criticize such words as "hisn" and "yourn" he must assume, of course, that his readers know that the words are found only in the common speech and have no place in literary language, save as they are employed in recording dialect or provincial speech.

The writer has been asked, "Why should 'hisn' and 'yourn' be considered incorrect while 'mine' and 'thine' are recognized as good English?" The answer is to be gathered only from a study of the growth of the English language, such study as is found in Professor Lounsbury's "History of the English Language," for example. He says: "In the Middle English period, a custom sprang up of using 'min' and 'thin' before words beginning with a vowel or silent 'h,' and 'mi' and 'thi' before consonants. This was observed, with a fair degree of regularity, up to the latter half of the sixteenth century, after which it became largely a matter of individual choice." Later, the forms in "s" were created, "and," says Lounsbury, "the forms in 'n' speedily disappeared from the language of literature, although they have exhibited a marked vitality in the language of low life."

Home, see *House*.
Honorable, see *Reverend*.

Hope and Trust

"I hope that your fall on the ice did not injure you." This expression, and similar expressions, are heard frequently. But some authorities declare that the verb should be "trust," not "hope." The latter word, according to the Standard Dictionary, means "to desire with expectation of obtaining"; for example, "We hope for better weather to-morrow." In other words, "hope" refers to a future event, to which the speaker looks forward with anticipation or desire; "trust" refers to the present time.

This rule, like many others in English grammar, is subject to modification. Some good authorities approve of the use of "trust" as applying to a future event; for example, "I trust that he will come" is cited by one authority as an example of good usage. Tennyson in his poem, "In Memoriam," says, "Oh, yet we trust that somehow good will be the final goal of ill."

House, Home and Residence

When should we speak of a man's dwelling place as his "home" and when as his "house" or his "residence"?

Let us bear in mind that the word "home" has been called "the most beautiful word in the English language." It conveys, or should convey, the idea of a place in which the affections are rooted; the abiding place of those whom we love and who love us. On the other hand, a "house" has merely a physical meaning; for example, "I made my home in his house." It is not incorrect, of course, to use "residence" in the sense of "house,"

present English is derived, there was no future tense, and the present was usually employed to express the future. This peculiarity of Anglo-Saxon was shared by all the Teutonic languages, and it continues to exist in them to the present day. Phrases like "To-morrow is Sunday" and "I am going to the city next week," and many others, are found in every period of the English language and are employed by every great writer of English.

We may say, therefore, that the use of the present tense to express the future has always been recognized as good English usage.

Idea and Opinion

"I am afraid that our party will not be successful in the coming election; what is your idea?"

It is better to use the word "opinion" in the foregoing sentence than the word "idea," although some authorities hold that "idea" is not incorrect. The word "idea" has, among other definitions, the following, which is taken from the Standard Dictionary: "Any product of mental apprehension or activity, considered as an object of knowledge or thought; knowledge in the loosest and widest sense." For the word "opinion," the following definition is given: "A conclusion or judgment held with confidence, but falling short of positive knowledge"; also, "a settled judgment or conviction on some subject, such as religion or politics." Note that forming a judgment enters into the matter of holding an opinion.

It may be thought by some readers that drawing distinctions like that between "idea" and "opinion" is splitting of hairs. But it should be remembered that the variety and richness of a language depend largely upon the maintenance of the distinctions in the meanings of words.

Identical To

"You may not like a suit that is identical to the one we show in this advertisement; if so, we have plenty of other models," says a clothing advertisement.

The use of "identical to" affords another instance of poor "commercial" English. It should be "identical with." "Identical" means, according to Webster, "the same in kind, quality or characteristic; exactly alike or equal; as, many were sick with an identical disease."

The same authority says that "same" may be exactly synonymous with "identical"—that is, may have exactly the same meaning—but is often used more loosely. "Identical," however, is the strictest term for entire and absolute agreement, or negation of difference. "No two leaves are identical."

If and Whether

Although some dictionaries and writers on grammar tell us that we may use the word "if" in the sense of "whether," it is better to make a distinction in the uses of the two words. "I shall go and see if the milkman has brought the milk," expresses the meaning of the speaker, and the sentence is therefore defensible on the ground that language is correct if it conveys the meaning of the speaker or writer. But from the viewpoint of the grammarian the sentence is, at least, open to criticism. It should be, "I shall go and see whether the milkman has brought the milk."

"If" expresses a supposition, as in the sentence, "I shall go if I am well." The word "whether" expresses an alternative, as in the sentence, "I shall go whether I am well or not." Therefore, grammarians hold that it is best to make a distinction between the two words, and not to use "if" when the meaning calls clearly for "whether." Some say that the failure to use "whether" when it is needed, and the habit of using "if" instead, are due to the indolence or laziness that leads to the use of a shorter word instead of one that is longer.

Ignorant, see *Illiterate*.

Ilk

"Jameson, like others of his ilk, was dissatisfied with the conditions in the office, and planned to change them as soon as possible."

The use of "ilk" in the sense of "kind," "class," etc., as in the sentence quoted (taken from a popular magazine), is condemned by all or most of the writers on good English. Webster's International Dictionary says:

"Ilk—family, kind; breed; class; an erroneous use arising from misunderstanding of the expression, 'of that ilk.'"

The word "ilk" is used correctly nowadays only in the phrase, "of that ilk," meaning "of the same name, surname, place, or territorial designation; as 'Grant of that ilk'"; that is to say, "Grant of Grant."

The use of "ilk" in the sense of "kind" or "class" is, however, quite common in writing, and it is not unlikely that in the course of time it will be recognized as good English.

Illiterate and Ignorant

The difference in meaning between the two words, "illiterate" and "ignorant," is made clear in "English Synonyms, Antonyms and Prepositions," by Fernald, as follows:

"'Ignorant' signifies destitute of education or knowledge, or lacking knowledge or information; it is thus a relative term. The most learned man is still ignorant of many things; persons are spoken of as ignorant who have not the knowledge that has become generally diffused in the world; the ignorant savage may be well instructed in matters of the field and the chase, as he is thus more properly 'untutored,' than ignorant.

"'Illiterate' is without letters and the knowledge that comes through reading. 'Unlettered' is similar in meaning to 'illiterate,' but less absolute; the unlettered man may have acquired the art of reading and writing and some elementary knowledge; the uneducated man has never taken any systematic course of mental training. Ignorance is relative; illiteracy is absolute; we have statistics of illiteracy; no statistics of ignorance are possible."

Imaginary and Imaginative

A letter written to the editor of one of the New York newspapers contained the following sentence:

"I hope storekeepers will pardon suspicions of their long-suffering customers that 'price cutting' is still largely imaginative."

Now, while the meaning of the writer of this sentence is clear, his English is faulty, in that he uses the word "imaginative" instead of "imaginary." He should have said, "price cutting is still largely imaginary," not "imaginative," since "imaginary" means, according to the Standard Dictionary, "existing or occurring only in imagination; fancied; unreal; visionary"; while "imaginative" means, according to the same authority, "having capacity for imagining; given to imagining; producing or creating the things of imagination."

When two words resemble each other so closely as do these two, "imaginary" and "imaginative," it is well to be on one's guard against the possibility of confusing them.

Immigrants, see *Emigrants*.

Imminent and Eminent

The words "imminent" and "eminent" must not be confused. The former means "threatening to occur immediately; impending; near at hand," and, therefore, "full of peril or danger; threatening; menacing."

The word "eminent" means standing out as prominent, distinguished, famous. We may speak of an eminent author, statesman, general, etc., not of an "eminent situation."

Imply and Infer

Many grammarians hold that there is a difference in the meanings of these two words, "imply" and "infer," although some dictionary makers say that they mean the same thing.

One authority tells us that the word "imply" refers to the speaker or writer; while the word "infer" applies to the hearer or reader. Thus, a speaker or his statement implies something which is inferred by the hearer.

"Imply" means to signify or intimate something which the speaker or writer does not express openly or directly; as in, "In bidding farewell to his constituents, the representative implied by some of his words that he intended to run for office again when a good opportunity presented itself." And the reporter, using proper English, added: "At least, this was what some of his hearers inferred from his words."

In Bad, see *In Good*.

"In" Behalf Of, or "On" Behalf of

If one may judge from the usage of good writers, it is proper to use, in connection with the word "behalf," any one of the four prepositions, "in," "on," "upon" and "for." Shakespeare used "in behalf of" thirty-nine times, and "on behalf of" only four times. The King James version of the Bible uses "on" eight times, "in" twice, and "for" once. It may be said, therefore, on the authority of Shakespeare and the Bible, that it is proper to use any one of the three, "on," "in" or "for," and "upon behalf of" is also found.

In Good and In Bad

"Do you think you'll get your raise?"

"Sure! I'm in good with the boss."

"Well, see that you don't get in bad with him."

"In bad," "in good," "in Dutch," and similar phrases, are slang, and therefore to be avoided. They have not reached the latest dictionaries.

Probably we should not expect the office boy to say, "The boss approves of me," but he might say, "I stand well with the boss." ("Boss," by the way, is still considered "slang" or "colloquial English.")

In Our Midst

Is it correct to write or say "in our midst," "in your midst," "in their midst," meaning "among us, you or them"? Here is a question that has been argued pro and con by grammarians for many years, and no conclusion has been reached. It is probable, however, that the expressions, "in our midst," etc., will never be accepted by most authorities as good English, because the meaning is conveyed as well or better by the use of the phrase, "among us."

Possibly no other phrase in common use in English has been criticized and ridiculed so much as this one, "in our midst." "One of the visitors in our midst is Senator Jones," writes the reporter for a small newspaper, and the city column conductor seizes the opportunity to poke fun at him. If he writes, "one of the visitors to our town is Senator Jones," or, simply, "Among our visitors is Senator Jones," he escapes censure.

In the Neighborhood Of

Don't say "in the neighborhood of" when you mean "about," as in the sentence:

"I paid in the neighborhood of five thousand dollars for the house."

It is a poor expression, marked in the dictionary as "local United States." It violates the rule against the use of too many words to express an idea and, besides, it is not needed, since the meaning is expressed as well by the word "about" or the word "approximately."

Inaugurate, see *Initiate*.

Inclose or Enclose

Either "inclose" or "enclose" is correct; some dictionaries prefer the one, while others give the preference to the other. In Great Britain and the colonies the preference seems to be for "enclose"; in the United States, "inclose" is used more generally. Webster's International Dictionary gives "enclose," but sends the reader to "inclose" for definitions.

Individual

Like the word "party," used frequently and incorrectly to mean a "person," the word "individual" does not mean a person, a man, a woman, a child. It means simply a single person, or animal, or thing, as in the following sentences: "The orator addressed the convention, and spoke to the delegates in general; his remarks were not directed toward any individual in the vast assemblage." "I can distinguish the individual stars in the constellation."

The foregoing illustrate the correct use of the word. The following gives an example of incorrect usage: "The man who was speaking was a short, stout individual." In this case say "fellow" or "person" or "man."

Infectious and Contagious

The Standard Dictionary says that "infection" is frequently confused with "contagion," even by medical men. The dictionary declares that the best usage now limits "contagion" to diseases that are transmitted by contact with the diseased person, either directly by touch or indirectly by use of the same articles, by breath, effluvia, etc. "Infection" is applied to diseases produced by no known or definable influence of one person upon another, but where common climatic malarious or other widespread conditions are believed to be chiefly instrumental.

It is held, therefore, that "contagious" and "contagion" should be used only in connection with certain diseases which are communicated by contact, direct or indirect. Infection acts gradually and indirectly through the medium of clothing, etc., when infected.

Infer, see *Imply*.

Infinitely Small

"He believed that he would gain a fortune in foreign trade, but his friends declared that his chances of doing so were infinitely small."

This use of the word "infinite" is taken from a magazine article. It affords an example of what are known as "contradictions in terms," for the words "infinitely" and "small" contradict each other. A thing cannot be "infinitely small," because "infinite" means "so great as to be immeasurable or unbounded in quantity, number or duration; limitless; measureless; countless." The word is taken from the Latin, and, translated literally, means "without end or limit."

The antonym, or opposite, of "infinite" is "infinitesimal." We may say, "His chances of doing so were infinitesimally small," but possibly, if we do so, we shall be accused of being "high brow."

Initiate and Inaugurate

These two words are frequently used instead of the simpler words, "begin" and "commence," by writers or speakers who thereby lay themselves open to the charge of being pretentious and given to the unnecessary use of "big" words.

"Use 'initiate' and 'inaugurate' in the sense of 'begin,'" says the "Manual of Good English," by MacCracken and Sandison, "only when there is a distinct implication of formality or dignity (often deliberate) in the act of beginning; we inaugurate a campaign with an impressive meeting; we initiate a formal inquiry; we cannot be said to initiate or inaugurate a discussion, for example, with a tactless allusion, or an informal party with dancing.

"The pretentious use of these words instead of the simple 'begin,' is very common in reports of political and commercial transactions, and the like."

Intelligent and Intelligible

From a book which deals with ancient magic, astrology, etc., the following passage is taken:

"In rewriting these pages, it has been deemed wise to change the language somewhat from the ancient reading, so as to render the wording more intelligent to the modern mind."

The word "intelligent" is used incorrectly in this statement. "Intelligent" means "marked or characterized by intelligence; quick to understand; reasoning," etc.

The word that should have been used is "intelligible," which means "capable of being understood," as in the sentence, "Although he spoke in a foreign tongue, his meaning was quite intelligible from his gestures."

Intrigue

The verb "intrigue" has not yet made a place for itself in our spoken language, in the sense in which it is used so frequently in popular fiction, but it may soon do so. Writing on this subject, an editor said:

"I wonder if any of our noted advocates of the purity of English, have expressed themselves in print lately with regard to the word 'intrigue' in the sense of 'to excite curiosity and interest.' It seems about 50 per cent of the manuscripts submitted to me contain the word used in that sense. According to the Standard Dictionary, the verb, 'intrigue' means 'to accomplish by intrigue; to plot or scheme.' According to the Century Dictionary, used transitively it means 'to entangle, involve, cause to be involved or entangled (the last being given as a Gallicism); to plot or scheme for.'"

The writer declares that he does not like the use of the word in the sense in which it is creeping into our language.

Introduce, see *Present.*
Invent, see *Discover.*

Invited Guest

A "guest" is, according to the dictionary, a person to whom the hospitality of one's home, club, etc., is extended. Necessarily, therefore, a guest must be invited, so the phrase "invited guest" is incorrect.

Some authorities call "invited guest" a vulgarism, but that seems too harsh a term to apply to it. It is better to call it an example of tautology, that is, needless repetition of words.

Is, see *Was.*
Israelite, see *Hebrew.*

It Went Great

Two young women were overheard discussing a dance which one of them had attended the night before. "How was it?" asked the other one of the girls. "Oh, it went great!" was the answer, in a tone that left no doubt in the mind of the hearer that the speaker had enjoyed the dance greatly.

Now, according to those who hold that we should have in English as few rules of grammar as possible—or none, perhaps—the young woman's expression, "It went great," is not to be condemned, because it expressed her meaning. But those who believe that we should have and should maintain some standard of correct speech, hold that this use of the adjective "great," instead of the adverb "well" or "very well," must not be passed by lightly.

The speaker could have said, "It went very well," or "It was very enjoyable," or she could have used some other expression that would have conveyed her meaning quite as well as "It went great" and would have had the added merit of being grammatical.

Its and It's

In speech, of course, it is impossible to tell apart these two words, "its" and "it's," since the pronunciation is exactly the same. But in written English there is a difference between "its" and "it's."

The former is a pronoun, the possessive form of "it." For example, "The cat raised one of its front paws." The latter word, "it's" is really two words, being a contraction of "it is." The apostrophe, or little mark between the "t" and "s," is placed there to show that a letter has been left out. This is called by grammarians the "elision" of the letter.

It's Up To You

Is the expression, "It's up to you," good English?

That is a question which, like so many others pertaining to grammar, cannot be answered by a simple "yes" or "no." Some authorities condemn the expression; others hold that it has a place in language, and that there is no equivalent for it. Webster calls it "colloquial," and gives as a definition, "to be incumbent on," but surely the latter phrase will never be accepted by lovers of strong, vigorous English as the equivalent of "up to."

Jealous, see *Envious.*
Jew, see *Hebrew.*

Jolly and Fix

"An intelligent Englishwoman, coming to America to live, told me," says Henry L. Mencken in "The American Language," "that the two things which most impeded her first communications with untraveled Americans, even above the gross differences between English and American pronunciation and intonation, were the complete absence of the general utility adjective 'jolly' from the American vocabulary, and the puzzling omnipresence and versatility of the American verb 'to fix.' In English colloquial usage, 'jolly' means almost anything; it intensifies all other adjectives, even including 'miserable' and 'homesick.' An Englishman is 'jolly tired, jolly hungry or jolly well tired; his wife is jolly sensible,' etc.

"He has no verb in such wide practice as 'to fix.' In his speech it means only to make fast or to determine. In American it may mean to repair, to prepare, to bribe, to finish, etc." Mencken gives a large number of cases to show how Americans use "fix" in many ways that are not dreamed of in England.

Judge or Justice

The question is asked sometimes, "Is there any difference in meaning between 'judge' and 'justice'?"

It is difficult to reply to this question. Sometimes the term "judge" is applied to the holder of a judicial office, sometimes the term "justice." For example, in New York State the highest court, known as the Court of Appeals, is composed of a chief judge and a number of associate judges. In the Supreme Court of the state, however, the proper term to use is "justice." The United States Supreme Court is composed of the Chief Justice of the United States and eight associate justices.

On the other hand, we have "justices of the peace" and "police justices," holders of inferior judicial offices. It will be seen, therefore, that both in legal usage and in common use the terms "judge" and "justice" are frequently used interchangeably.

Keeping Company

If you wish to be precise in your choice of words, you must not use the expression, "keeping company." So say the grammarians and the purists.

But they do not provide us with a good substitute for the expression. How shall we describe the state of affairs when a young man is paying attentions to a young woman, and she is accepting them, but they are not engaged to be married? One recent writer says:

"In fact, there is no way of expressing this idea very definitely. One says that a certain young man has been 'going about' with a certain young woman, or that he is a 'frequent caller.'"

It seems probable, therefore, that the phrase,

"to keep company," will survive, and will eventually be received into good language. Some of the dictionaries recognize it, but they call it "provincial."

Kind of, Kinder, Sort of, Sorter

"I wanted to visit my cousin, but I felt kind of (or sort of) ashamed, not having been there for so long."

This use of "kind of," and "sort of" in the sense of "somewhat, somehow, rather," etc., is not good English. In the sentence quoted say, "I felt somewhat ashamed."

More often than "kind of," and "sort of," perhaps, we hear the expressions, "kinder," and "sorter," as "I felt kinder (or sorter) ashamed." This is, of course, only a careless way of saying "kind of," or "sort of" and may therefore be called one error imposed upon another.

It should be remarked, of course, that there is a use of the words "kind of" and "sort of" that is perfectly proper and grammatical. For example, we say, "I felt a kind of (or sort of) weakness"; that is, "I felt a weakness of some kind." However, one should not say, "I felt a kind of a weakness," or a sort of a weakness. The second "a" should be omitted.

To Knock

The word "knock," in the sense of criticizing adversely, or speaking unfavorably of a person, affords a very interesting example of the manner in which the English language grows. Dictionaries published twenty or thirty years ago contain no mention of the word "knock" in this sense; it is a recent addition to the language. So recent a work as "The American Language," by H. L. Mencken, contains no comment on the word; the book was published in 1919.

The latest edition of Webster's Dictionary contains the word and defines it, but calls it a slang term.

There is, or there seems to be, no exact synonym or equivalent for "knock," as the word is used and understood by the people of the United States. It fills a need, and therefore justifies its use. So although purists may call it slang and condemn it, the great jury of the American public has decided in its favor, it seems.

Knockdown

"I was awfully anxious to meet him," a girl in a big city was overheard saying, "but I didn't know no one who could give me a knockdown to him."

Very poor English—three errors in one sentence. In the first place, "awfully" is used incorrectly for "very." In the second, "didn't know no one" is an example of the double negative which most readers will recognize as incorrect. And in the third place "knockdown," instead of "introduction" is extremely slangy.

The young woman should have said: "I was very anxious to meet him, but I knew no one (or, didn't or did not know anyone) who could give me an introduction to him (or, who could introduce him to me.)"

Knots

When speaking or writing of the rate of speed which a ship makes, do not say, "knots an hour." Say, simply, "knots." For example, do not say, "The gunboat proceeded up the river at the rate of eight knots an hour." Say, instead, "The gunboat proceeded up the river at the rate of eight knots," or "at an eight-knot speed." The words "an hour" are not needed, since the word "knot" means "a speed of a nautical mile in an hour."

Another definition of the word "knot" gives it as "a distance of one nautical mile covered in a period of one hour."

Know and Be Acquainted With

Do not say that you "know" a man, when you mean that you are merely "acquainted" with him. In fact, according to some good authorities on English, we should never say that we "know" a man or a woman, unless we are so intimately acquainted with a person that we know his or her very thoughts. Therefore do not say, "I know John Jones"; say, rather, "I am acquainted with John Jones."

Lack, Plentiful, see *Plentiful, Lack.*
Lady, see *Woman; see Saleslady.*
Lady Friend, see *Gentleman Friend.*

Largest Half

Two of the pupils in a class for the study of English grammar, rhetoric and composition set a trap for the teacher. One of them asked:

"Which is correct—the 'larger' half, or the 'largest' half?"

The teacher fell into the trap. His mind was filled only with thoughts of grammar, and failed to perceive the question of fact involved. He was intent on the rule of grammar which tells us that when two things are compared we must use only the comparative degree, not the superlative. So he said:

"Why, the 'larger' half, of course!"

Whereupon the other pupil said:

"How can one half be larger than the other?"

And the teacher had to admit that he was wrong—that one half is exactly as much as the other half. If the question had been, "Which is correct—the 'larger' part or the 'largest' part?" of course the answer would have been, the "larger" part.

Last and Latest

"Last" means the end of a series, "latest" indicates the most recent. For example, we say: "This is the latest issue of this magazine," when we mean that the issue is the most recent one. But if we say, "This is the last issue of this magazine," we mean that the publishers have discontinued the issue of the magazine, and no more numbers are to come.

An illustration that is frequently given, to show the proper use of the two words, tells us that a young lady requested the autograph of a celebrated author. "Have you read my last book?" he wrote to her, and she responded with the prompt and brief reply, "I sincerely hope not." It is recorded that her keen wit brought the desired autograph.

Last, at, and At Length, see *At Length*.

Law, see *Bill*.

Learn and Teach

The pupil "learns" something which the instructor "teaches." The teacher does not "learn" the pupil; the latter "learns" the lesson. As an example of the error, one authority cites the following: "The ladies at the college settlement learned many poor girls to make their own clothing."

Lease, see *Hire*.

Leave Instead of Let

Do not use "leave" when you mean "let," as in the following sentences: "Leave me be"; "leave it alone"; "leave her be"; "leave me see it." Writers on English call such use of the word "leave" vulgar, which means, in this sense, inelegant, unrefined, commonplace, opposed to what is approved by good authorities, offensive to good taste, etc.

Legible and Eligible

Although these two words are quite different in

meaning, they are sometimes confused. This is due, of course, to the similarity in pronunciation.

"Legible" and "eligible" are both adjectives. The former means, "That may be read; especially, read easily," as in the sentence "His handwriting is cramped and therefore not legible." The adjective "eligible" means "suitable for choice or election; worthy of being chosen or elected," as in the sentence, "The senate seat becoming vacant, the party sought an eligible candidate."

Lengthways and Sideways

The following is taken from a recent description of a novel method of launching ships:

"Instead of moving lengthways down the ways, as is usual, the vessel moved sideways into the water, when the blocks were removed."

The use of the words "lengthways" and "sideways," as in the sentence quoted, is not condemned by writers on English, but some of them express a preference for "sidewise" and "lengthwise." The latter forms are given as preferable in "Better Say," issued by the publishers of the Standard Dictionary.

Less and Fewer

When you are speaking or writing of something that may be considered as a mass, use "less," but when speaking or writing of a collection, or gathering, or assemblage, use "fewer." "Less" refers to quantity, "fewer" refers to number. Thus, it is incorrect to say, "When he came out of the orchard, he had less apples than I had." Say, "He had fewer apples than I had." Do not say, "There were no less than a thousand persons in the crowd." Say, "There were no fewer than a thousand."

Let, see *Hire*; see *Leave*.

Let On

"I don't mind telling you this," said a man to his friend, "but don't let on that I told you."

Did he use poor English when he employed the expression, "let on"? The question was raised some years ago by the writer of a letter to a New York newspaper. He said he had been informed that while the words were generally understood, they were considered slang.

"Let on" affords one of those interesting cases of the acceptance of a word or phrase by the common people, while the grammarians and dictionary makers condemn it. If it is slang, it is of respectable age. It dates back at least as far as the year 1725, before some words and phrases now in good standing were born. It is fairly safe to say that if you want to use "let on" you may do so, and be understood generally, although Webster's Dictionary and other authorities call it slang.

Liable, see *Likely*.

Lift or Elevator

Americans say "elevator," while their British cousins employ the word "lift." Webster says that this use of the word "lift" is "chiefly English."

Professor Brander Matthews, who has written much on the subject of good English, comments on the words "lift" and "elevator," and asserts that the British word is better than the American.

Like (verb), see *Love*.

Like, As

The word "like" is used properly when it may be followed by "to," as in the following sentence, "The boy looks like his father." In this case, and in similar cases, the word "to" is understood. But "like" is used incorrectly in the following: "The boy does like his father does"; the proper usage requires that "as" be used, and the sentence should read, "The boy does as his father does." In the language of grammarians, "like" in the first case is an adjective, and in the second case "as" is an adverb.

The word "like" is frequently used incorrectly instead of the word "as." Do not say, "Do like I do"; say, instead, "Do as I do." "That Anthony Trollope, Hugh Conway and other writers are chargeable with this offense does not justify the use of 'like' for 'as,' but rather proves the need of constant vigilance in order to avoid such errors." says Bechtel in "Slips of Speech."

Like As How

"Looks to me like as how Ty Cobb was still doing a pretty good job of it out there," said a baseball "fan," commenting on the work of the famous Detroit ball player.

His admiration of the famous "Ty" should have been expressed in better English. "Like as how" is not correct. Instead, "as if" or "as though" should be used, making the sentence: "Looks to me (or, it looks to me) as if Ty Cobb," etc., or "Looks to me as though Ty Cobb," etc.

Like For

"Before you decide to invest elsewhere, we would like for you to see our machine in action." Thus runs an advertisement printed in an American magazine.

It is not good English. The word "for" should have been omitted. "We would like you to see our machine in action" conforms to present usage.

The dictionary says that such use of "for to" is obsolete or illiterate.

Like I

"You could not expect a busy man like I to

waste so much time," or, "You could not expect a busy man like me to waste so much time"?

The second form is correct. The word "like," when used in this manner, is an adjective—that is, a word which modifies a noun—meaning "resembling," "similar," and the word "to" is "understood" as coming after it. The sentence, therefore, would read, with the word "to" expressed instead of understood, "You could not expect a busy man like to me" (not "like to I") "to waste so much time."

Likely, Liable

"Will you disobey the law?" "It is not likely that I shall do so." "Well, if you do, you will be liable to arrest."

The foregoing sentences may be used to illustrate the distinction that is made by careful writers and speakers between the words "likely" and "liable." The former word is used properly of an event that is regarded as very probable, and usually, but not always, favorable. "Liable" is not used properly in the sense of "likely" except to indicate an undesirable or injurious event which may befall a person or thing.

An eminent lecturer was asked, at the conclusion of an address on "The Moral Tendencies of the Times," whether he did not consider it probable that all men, being trained properly in youth, would pursue the paths of honesty. He replied, "Yes, it is likely that they will do so; but all men are liable to err."

Limited

Do not use the word "limited" in the sense of "low" or "poor," as in the sentence, "I have a limited opinion of his ability." Such use is incorrect, and is not recognized by authorities, although it is common.

"Limited" means "confined within limits; narrow, restricted." You may use the word, if you wish, in such sentences as the following, "His admiration of the President's achievements was limited by his personal dislike of the man," and "The amount of aid that can be sent to the famine stricken districts is limited by the lack of railroad equipment." But do not say "I have a limited opinion of his ability" when you mean that your opinion is low.

Line

The word "line" is frequently misused by ill-educated or careless writers and speakers. Examples of the errors and corrections thereof are given herewith:

"Besides being a poet, John Hay was famous along the line of statesmanship." Corrected: "Besides being a poet, John Hay was famous as a statesman."

"What line of business are you now engaged in?" Corrected: "In what kind of business are you now engaged?"

"I like anything in the line of fruit." Corrected: "I like any kind of fruit."

"Let me give you some advice along that line." Corrected: "Let me give you some advice in connection with that subject."

Love and Like

To confound these two words is especially poor usage, since English is perhaps the only language in which one can make the distinction between "loving" and "liking." Love is an emotion which, as everyone knows, involves the deepest relations of human beings, and the use of the word "love" should be restricted accordingly. On the other hand, "like" is a word which conveys the idea or suggestion of feelings of a distinctly lower order.

"I love strawberries and whipped cream," says the schoolgirl; "I love to skate," says the schoolboy, but to "like" such things is quite sufficient. In other words, we "love" that which appeals to our affections very deeply, and we "like" that which seems to us worthy of a lower degree of admiration. A woman "likes" a fine gown, a piece of jewelry, a good recipe, but she "loves" her husband and children.

Lovely

"Did you enjoy the play?" "Yes, I had a lovely time." The person who used the word "lovely" in this sense did not know, or forgot, that "lovely" should be used only to describe something which is adapted to or worthy of being loved—that is, of inspiring the highest esteem of which the human being is capable. The word "lovely" means, according to the Standard Dictionary, "possessing mental or physical qualities that inspire admiration and love; winsome, charming, lovable, as 'a lovely face.'"

The word "lovely" has, therefore, a distinct and valuable place in English diction, and should not be debased by use in connection with common or ordinary matters, or trifles. Instead of "lovely," in most cases some such word as "attractive," "agreeable," "pleasant," "enjoyable" should be employed. Here is a correct use of "lovely": "She's adorned amply that in her husband's eye looks lovely."

Low Priced, see *Cheap*.

Luxurious and Luxuriant

Although these two words are sometimes used as though they had the same meaning, it is proper to make a distinction between them.

"The line is drawn much more sharply between these two words than it was formerly," says Alfred Ayres in "The Verbalist." "'Luxurious' was once used, to some extent at least, in the sense of 'rank growth'; but now all careful writers and speakers use it in the sense of indulging or delighting in luxury.

"We talk of a luxurious table, a luxurious liver, luxurious ease, luxurious freedom. 'Luxuriant,' on the other hand, is restricted to the sense of rank or excessive growth or production; thus, luxuriant weeds, luxuriant foliage or branches, luxuriant growth."

The poet Cowper wrote: "But grace abused brings forth the foulest deeds, as richest soil the most luxuriant weeds."

Mad and Angry

Few words are more frequently misused than "mad" and "angry." It must be confessed, however, that there is some excuse for the misuse of the words, since many psychologists hold that it is difficult to tell, when the emotions of a person are aroused, just where anger ends and madness begins. But in grammar there is a sharp distinction between "angry" and "mad." The former means to be vexed or out of patience, while the latter indicates madness, insanity. A person who is insane is mad, but a person whose mail is delayed is not mad, but merely angry. There is a figurative use of the word "mad"— that is, a use in which the words are not to be taken literally—such as "mad with pain," "mad with terror," etc.

"I am mad at that fellow"; says a man, "he cheated me in a stock deal." He should say, "I am angry with that fellow," etc.

Majority

In a review of a play, the following was noted:

"The comedy honors, however, go to William Jones. With Joseph Brown he shoulders a majority of the real comedy of the piece, and in their lines one could see a strong satire on life, society and politics."

The error in the language quoted lies in the use of the word "majority." The word should be used only in reference to number, and not in reference to quantity. For example, say, "He received a majority of the votes in the recent election"; "the majority of the company left the room."

In the criticism of the play that is quoted, the writer should have said, "With Joseph Brown he shoulders the greater part, or the larger part, or the major part, of the real comedy of the piece," etc.

Majority and Plurality

After every election of importance, especially if there have been more than two candidates, the question is raised, "What is the difference between a 'majority' and a 'plurality'?" Many letters are written to the newspapers about it, and the distinction is pointed out frequently, but the question recurs.

"Majority" means more than half; "plurality" means the greatest of more than two numbers, whether or not it is a majority of the whole; also, the excess of the highest number of votes cast for any one candidate over the next highest number. The Standard Dictionary says:

"When a candidate for office, out of 10,000 votes cast, receives 4,000 and two other candidates receive respectively 3,500 and 2,500, the first is elected by a plurality, though he has received less than a majority of the whole vote, and he is said to have a plurality of 500 votes. If the numbers are 6,000, 3,000, and 1,000, the majority is 2,000 and the plurality is 3,000."

Make Wages

Is it correct to say that a person "makes" wages or a salary?

Consultation of several standard works on English fails to find any objection to the use of the verb "make" in connection with wages or salary, and it seems to be a good, strong, idiomatic English phrase that has been used for many years, and is therefore approved by the people.

Manner Born, see *To the Manner Born.*

Mannerisms and Manners

"Mr. Jannings studied extensively the mannerisms, customs and conditions of ancient Egypt, before attempting the role," said an advertisement of a moving picture play.

What it meant was that Mr. Jannings had studied the manners, customs and conditions, not the mannerisms, etc.

"Mannerism" means, according to the dictionary, "excessive adherence to a peculiar style or manner; a characteristic mode of action, bearing or treatment, carried to excess, especially in literature or art."

Thus we cannot speak of the "mannerisms" of a country or a people, as in the sentence quoted, but we can speak of the "mannerisms" of an individual writer, painter, musician, etc. When speaking of a country, a people, etc., we mention their "manners," not their "mannerisms."

Manor Born, see *To the Manner Born.*
Married, First, see *When I Was First Married.*

Marry

There has been considerable discussion, at one time and another, in regard to the proper use of the verb "marry." Should we say "John Smith marries Miss Jones," or "is married to her"? Likewise, does Miss Jones "marry" Mr. Smith, or is she "married to" him?

Inasmuch as the dictionary defines "marry" as "to accept in marriage, or to take in matrimony," it is generally accepted that either of the two forms discussed is correct. Nevertheless, some authorities on English hold that as the woman loses her name in that of the man to whom she is wedded, and becomes a member of his family, not he of hers—that is, it is her life that is merged in his—it would seem that, properly, Miss Jones is married to John Smith, and that this would be the proper way to make the announcement of their having been wedded, and not John Smith to Miss Jones.

In other words, some grammarians hold that the man marries the woman, but the woman does not marry the man, but is married to him.

May, see *Can.*

Meeting and Session

A common error is made in the use of the words "meeting" and "session."

"The legislature met, and began its annual session," said a newspaper report. The verb "meet" is derived from the Anglo-Saxon "metan," with the same meaning as our modern word; the word "session" is derived from the Latin word "sedeo," sit. A meeting means a coming together, or assemblage, as in a congregation or convention. A session means the sitting of an organized body, as a legislature or a court, for the purpose of transacting business, or the state of such a body as assembled and engaged in its deliberations.

Memory, Forgetful, see *Forgetful.*

Messrs.

Is it correct to use the word "Messrs." in addressing a business house, such as Smith, Jones & Co., or Foley & Co., for instance? Irrespective of the proper use of the word, has not "Messrs." in connection with addressing firms practically passed into disuse in the United States in business correspondence?

"Messrs." is correctly used in addressing a firm,

but the tendency is to eliminate all unnecessary words from business correspondence.

In this connection it may be interesting to note the advocacy, by many persons, of the abolition of such phrases as "Very truly yours," "Sincerely yours," etc. The phrase "We remain" has gone already, to a large extent, and the others may soon follow it.

Midst, In, see *In Our Midst*.
Mind, To Doubt In, see *Doubt*.
Minority, Vast, see *Vast Minority*.
Miss Smiths, see *Two Miss Smiths*.

Mollycoddle

"Mollycoddle" is a word of good standing in the English language, and has been in use for more than a century. Webster defines "mollycoddle" as: "A person who coddles himself or is coddled; an effeminate man or boy; one who lacks spirit or courage; a person who takes excessive or unnecessary care of his health." "Mollycoddle" is used also as a verb, in the sense of "to coddle" or "to pamper." The word "mollycoddle" gained renewed vogue some years ago when it was used by the late Theodore Roosevelt. It has been condemned by some authorities.

Monstrous and Monster

"Nearly every American athlete within many hundreds of miles of the city who will compete in the Olympic games will take part in a monstrous carnival to be held in the near future."

So read an announcement in a city newspaper. Note the use of the word "monstrous." It is incorrect, as the word is generally employed, although some authorities do not condemn "monstrous" when used as meaning "enormous" or "unusual in size or number." What the writer meant to say was that the carnival would be a "monster" one, not a "monstrous" one. In general usage, the word "monster," as an adjective, means "very great in size or number; huge," while "monstrous" means departing greatly from the natural or normal; unnatural; shocking, hateful, hideous, as "a monstrous crime." Therefore, it will be noted that in the use of "monstrous" there is something of feeling or emotion, while "monster" refers simply to size.

More Angrier

The following sentence is quoted from a description of a baseball game:

"In the third inning the outfielder became still more angrier at another close ball which he just failed to catch."

There is no excuse for "more angrier." The meaning of the writer could have been expressed by either "more angry" or "angrier," but "more angrier" is not English.

"Angry" belongs in the class of words called adjectives, which modify the meanings of nouns. Adjectives of one syllable, and many adjectives of two syllables, are compared by adding "er" to form the comparative, and "est" to form the superlative, as "tall, taller, tallest." Sometimes it does not sound well to add "er" and "est" and then we compare the adjectives by using the words "more" and "most." For example, "more beautiful" and "most beautiful," instead of "beautifuler" and "beautifulest." But never use both "er" and "more," or both "est" and "most" in connection with the same word.

More Perfect and Most Perfect; Most Complete; Most Full

Probably grammarians will dispute this point as long as the English language lasts. Those who argue against "more perfect" and "most perfect" are the strictest of the strict; they assert that if a thing is perfect it cannot be improved upon, it cannot be "more" perfect or "most" perfect. But they are, or seem to be, in a minority, and many good writers use "most perfect" and even "perfectest." The foregoing applies also to "most complete," "most full."

In commenting on this matter Maetzner, in his "English Grammar," remarks: "Here an absolute rule does not suffice. The superlative, especially, in spite of the censure of grammarians, is used to strengthen the meaning conveyed by the positive, and even comparisons are not wanting which seem to mock the literal conception."

If, therefore, you wish to say "more perfect" or "most perfect" you may do so, and rest secure in the knowledge that you can find authority for such use. But some writers tell us to say "more nearly perfect."

More Than You Can Help or Cannot Help

"'Do not exaggerate more than you cannot help.' Is this good English?" wrote a correspondent to the editor of a New York newspaper.

To this the editor replied:

"None better. It has the overwhelming authority of Dr. Samuel Johnson. The Oxford Dictionary classes as a 'common but erroneous' usage the omission of the negative. Ayres, however, condemns it." The Ayres to whom reference is made is Alfred Ayres, who wrote a book called "The Verbalist," a manual devoted to brief discussions of the right and the wrong use of words, and also to other matters of interest to those who would speak and write with propriety. The book was published forty years ago.

Most and Almost

The distinction between "most" and "almost" is made thus in Lockwood's "Lessons in English": "Use 'almost' whenever 'nearly' may be used in its place; use 'most' in the sense of the greatest number or quantity." The book gives as an example of the incorrect use of "most," twice in one sentence, the following: "My work is most done, and I am most tired out."

Too Many "Mosts"

"Everybody abuses this word 'most'," says "Good English," by Edward S. Gould, and then, in another paragraph, he adds:

"If a man would cross out 'most' wherever he can find it in any book in the English language, he would in almost every instance improve the style of the book." He gives many examples from good authors, some of which are the following:

"A most profound silence"; "a most just idea"; "a most complete orator"; "this was most extraordinary"; "an object of most perfect esteem"; "a most extensive erudition"; "he gave it most liberally away."

Another authority says: "'Most' is often loosely used in the sense of 'very,' as 'This is a most interesting book.' Aim to use 'most' only as the superlative of 'much' or 'many.' Do not use the indefinite article before it, as 'This is a most beautiful picture.' We may say, 'This is the most beautiful picture,' for here comparison is implied."

Mrs. Professor

Calling a wife by her husband's title, as "Mrs. Doctor Brown," "Mrs. Professor Robinson," etc., is not so common as it was formerly, since it has been subjected to much ridicule, in newspapers and elsewhere. "The combination of 'Mrs.' with a husband's title is a vulgarism," says one writer. "Mrs. should be followed by the woman's surname, as 'Mrs. Jones'; by her husband's Christian name or initials and surname, as 'Mrs. John B. Jones';

or, if the woman is a widow, by her own Christian name and her surname, as 'Mrs. Mary Jones.' If the title of the husband is used at all in connection with the name of the woman, it should be placed in another part of the sentence, as, 'Mrs. Jackson, wife of Dr. Jackson.'"

Murder, see *Assassinate*.

Mushmelon or Muskmelon

In some parts of the United States the fruit that is known elsewhere as muskmelon or cantaloupe is called "mushmelon" by less learned folk. It is not possible, of course, to condemn this without qualification, since a matter of usage is involved, but it should be said that the authorities do not uphold "mushmelon," calling it "dialect" or "illiterate." Better say "muskmelon," therefore.

Muss

If you desire to be careful in your use of words, don't use "muss" in the sense of "fight" or "squabble." The dictionary calls it slang. When used in the sense of confusion or disorder or jumble, the word "muss" is not quite so bad, being termed merely "colloquial," but it is better to avoid it.

My Dearest Wife

"My dearest wife," wrote a man beginning a letter to his spouse. To which the wife replied:

"My dear husband: I am shocked by the way in which you begin your letter to me. There is something wrong with either your morals or your grammar. You call me your 'dearest' wife; is it possible that you have other wives?"

Of course, she was hypercritical of her husband's grammar. He did not mean that she was his dearest wife; merely that she was dearest of all to him. But there is no doubt that to the mind of a very strict grammarian the expression "My dearest wife" is incorrect.

My Old Man

Many a young man—and perhaps many a young woman—refers to a father as "the old man," and to a mother as "the old woman," without meaning to be disrespectful. All authorities on English agree in condemning the use of the terms, not only as showing positive disrespect for parents, but also as indicating a lack of refinement and disregard for the proper use of words. Besides, the term may not be an accurate description; many a father, still in middle age, has had his feelings hurt by being referred to by his son or daughter as "My old man." Why not say, simply, "My father"? Of course, the same criticism applies, and with even greater force, to the use of "my old woman" for "my mother."

The same criticism is made of the use of the word "governor" instead of "father." The dictionary calls such use slangy.

Naught, see *Aught*.

Necessaries and Necessities

The question is sometimes asked whether the word "necessities" is used correctly in the following sentence, and whether it should not be "necessaries": "The powers that be would be well advised to turn their attention to the reduction of the prices of the necessities of life."

While a few writers on grammar have made a distinction between the words "necessities" and "necessaries," and have said that in sentences such as the one quoted the word should always be "necessaries," their statement is not supported by other writers, and the dictionary defines both "necessary" and "necessity" as "an essential requisite; something that is indispensable." Therefore, it is correct to use either word.

"Buy what thou hast no need of, and ere long thou shalt sell thy necessaries," is one of the sayings of Poor Richard, by Benjamin Franklin.

Née

The French word "née" means exactly the same as the English word "born." But in English, "born" is applied to either sex, while in French "née" is applied only to women, the masculine form being "né," with one "e."

In English the word "née" is used only in the phrase, "Mrs. Jones, née Brown." But it is frequently used incorrectly, as in the following sentence:

"The American wife of the Bavarian minister, Count Lerchenfeld, née Edith Wyman."

To be correct, the writer should have omitted the given name of the countess, and should have written:

"The American wife, née Wyman, of the Bavarian minister, Count Lerchenfeld."

She was born Wyman, not Edith Wyman; the name Edith was given to her some time after her birth.

Neighborhood of, see *In the Neighborhood of.*
Neither, see *Each Other.*

New and Novel

Although both of the above words convey the idea of newness, there is a distinction to be made between them.

The word "new" means, according to the Standard Dictionary, "recently come into existence; fresh; lately made, produced or modified"; while the word "novel," according to the same authority, means "of recent origin or introduction; not ancient; new; hence, strange or unusual, as 'a novel idea.'"

A pair of shoes may be new, having been made recently, and it may also be novel, if it embodies original ideas in material, in shape, in construction, or the like.

"That which is novel is unprecedented in kind," says the Standard Dictionary; "that which is new is just produced, but may be of a familiar or even of an ancient sort, as a new copy of an old book."

New Beginner

"New beginner" is an example of what grammarians and rhetoricians call "redundancy," which is one form of the use of more words than are needed to express the thought of the writer or speaker. The expression cited is in the same class of error as the sentence, "Collect together all the fragments." Omit the word "together," and it will be seen readily that the sense is expressed perfectly without it.

A beginner in anything must necessarily be new —that is, unless he has begun something, has dropped it and has taken it up anew.

Nice

Among the words that are greatly overworked by many persons, and made to do duty in all sorts of places, is "nice." The word "nice" is as good a word as any other in its place, but its place is not everywhere, says one authority.

Archdeacon Hare, a well-known English writer, pokes fun at the habit of using "nice" on every occasion, and says that the English speak in the same breath of a nice cheese-cake, a nice tragedy, a nice sermon, a nice day, a nice country.

Alfred Ayres, in "The Verbalist," declares that we talk very properly about a nice distinction, a nice discrimination, a nice calculation, a nice point, and about a person being nice and over-nice and the like; but we certainly ought not to talk about "Othello" being a nice tragedy, about Salvini being a nice orator, or New York being a nice harbor.

No More Than I Got There

"No more than I got to her house I had to go home."

This use of "no more than" is not uncommon among persons who are not careful in their speech. It seems to have escaped the notice of the writers on good English. Very few of them, if any, comment on it.

The meaning is, of course, clear, but that does not justify the use of the phrase, since it is not generally accepted. "No more than" means, in this sense, "as soon as," "scarcely," "hardly." Since there are, therefore, a phrase and at least two words in good standing to express the meaning, there is no reason for the use of the phrase "no more than." Sometimes "no more than" is contracted to "no more'n," which is, of course, worse.

No Other Alternative

Do not say, "I had to accept the offer; there was no other alternative." Say, instead, "I had to accept the offer; there was no alternative," omitting the word "other." The word "alternative," which comes from the Latin word "alter," meaning "other," means "something that may or must exist, or be chosen, or taken, in place of something else." Consideration of the matter will show, therefore, that the use of "other" in connection with "alternative" is really a repetition of the word "other."

There has been controversy over the question

whether or not the word "alternative" may be applied to more than two choices. Some hold that it must be restricted to two; that to speak of three or more alternatives is absurd. Others say that the making of such a distinction is an example of hair-splitting in grammar, and they cite good authorities in support of their contention that an alternative may be one of three or more.

No Sooner When

Sometimes we hear a person say:

"We had no sooner arrived in the city when we were taken to our hotel." This is not correct. It should be, "We had no sooner arrived in the city than we were taken to our hotel," using the word "than" instead of "when." A little reflection will show the reader that the word "sooner," which is the comparative of "soon," should be followed by "than" and not by "when." "I would a thousand times sooner believe that man made himself what he is than that God made him so," said Guthrie.

No Use Of Asking

"I wanted to leave the office early today, but I knew it was no use of asking the manager's permission."

The phrase or expression used in the foregoing sentence, "no use of asking," is quite common, but it is not considered good English. Say, instead, "I knew there was no use in asking."

In this connection, it may be noted that the expression, "to have no use for," meaning to feel a contempt for, or to wish to have nothing to do with, is not considered good English, and is frowned upon by grammarians and other authorities, who call it slang.

None, see *Each Other*.

Nothing Like

We often hear such expressions as the following:

"You are a tall man."

"Yes, but I am nothing like as tall as my brother."

This use of "nothing like," in the sense of "not nearly," is condemned by good authorities, who call it a "careless colloquialism." Say, therefore, "I am not nearly as tall as my brother."

Notorious, see *Famous*.
Novel, see *New*.
Novice, see *Amateur*.
Number, see *Quantity*.

O and Oh

The distinction between "O" and "Oh" is not made in speech, since the two monosyllables are pronounced exactly alike. But in writing there is a difference.

"Oh" is simply an exclamation, and should always be followed by some mark of punctuation; either a comma (,) or an exclamation point (!). For example, write, "Oh, what a good time we had!" "Oh! You have come at last!"

"O" is not used as an exclamation alone, but as an invocation, in formal, solemn addresses; as in, "O God, our help in ages past," "O Grave, where is thy victory?" "Hear, O Heavens, and give ear, O earth!" It will be seen that "O" is never followed by a punctuation mark.

Ayres says that it is only the most careful writers who use these two interjections (exclamations) with proper discrimination, and he asserts that the distinction between them is said to be modern.

Obvious, see *Evident*.
Occur, see *Transpire*.

Off Of

The use of the phrase "off of" leads often to

errors that are seen to be ludicrous, when analyzed. For example, one will hear the question,
"Where did you buy that steak?" The answer
comes: "I got it off of the butcher." To get a
steak "off of" the butcher might suit a cannibal
very well, but the very idea should shock anyone
else. In proper usage, omit the "off"; say, "I
got it of (or from) the butcher."

There are cases of the misuse of the phrase
"off of" that are not ludicrous as in the instance
already cited, but in which the "of" is not needed
and should be omitted. "He jumped off of the
car." Say, "He jumped off the car." A man
who expects to open a store says, "Will you buy
something off of me?" He should say, "Will you
buy something from me?"

Old, see *Ancient*.
Old Man, see *My Old Man*.
Older, see *Elder*.
On Behalf of, see *In Behalf of*.

One and His

If you begin by using "one" in a sentence, do
not continue by using "his." For example:

"Suppose one were to lose his control of the
machine, what would happen?"

Change this to read, "Suppose one were to lose
one's control of the machine, what would happen?"
Referring to this matter, Professor Bain says, in
his "Composition Grammar": "This pronoun (one)
continually lands writers in difficulties. English
idiom requires that, when the pronoun has to be
again referred to, it should be used itself a second
time. The correct usage is shown by Pope: 'One
may be ashamed to consume half one's days in
bringing sense and rhyme together.' It would be
against idiom to say, 'half his days.'

"The better acquainted one is with any kind
of rhetorical trick, the less likely he is to be

misled by it,' should be, 'The less likely one is to be misled by it.' "

One Another, see *Each Other*.
Only, see *Alone*.

Onto

The word "onto" affords an interesting example of the manner in which words make their way into the language in spite of purists. "Onto" seems to be fixed firmly in usage, despite the authorities. "It is the result of a desire for a preposition formed from 'on,' in the same way that 'into' is formed from 'in,'" says one writer. And he proceeds to say that "if it were accepted, we should say, 'I lay on the bed but I jumped onto the table.' It is, however, usually regarded as a vulgarism. 'On' has long been used with verbs of motion."

However, there is a difference, easily seen, between "I jumped on the table" and "I jumped onto the table." Since the word "onto" meets a need of the language, and there is no other word that can take its place, it has been accepted by the public, and is in common use, and it is an old saying that "usage makes language."

Operate

You cannot operate a person, but you can operate "on" or "upon" him. In this use, the verb "operate" is an intransitive verb; that is, it does not have a direct object. When a verb has a direct object, as in the sentence, "I love my mother," it is said to be a transitive verb; the action is "carried over" directly from the verb to the object.

In some other senses, the verb "operate" may be transitive, as when we say, He operated the machine, the elevator, the automobile, etc. But you cannot operate a person.

Opinion, see *Idea*.
Opinion, Consensus of, see *Consensus*.
Oral, see *Verbal*.

Orderly

The word "orderly" is an adjective, and should be used as an adjective only, never as an adverb, in spite of the fact that it ends with "ly," which letters are usually the mark of an adverb. (An adjective is a word that is used to modify or tell something about a noun or name-word, while an adverb is used to tell something about a verb, or action-word.)

In a recent newspaper article it was said, "After the excitement of the sudden finish had simmered down, the crowd left slowly and orderly." The word "slowly" is correctly used, but the word "orderly" is not. The sentence should have read:

"After the excitement of the sudden finish had simmered down the crowd left slowly and in order," or, "slowly and in an orderly manner."

Other (see also Except)

Be careful not to omit the word "other" when it is needed to express your meaning correctly. Do not say, for example, "John is more studious than any of the pupils." Say, instead, "John is more studious than any other of the pupils." Since John is one of the pupils, if the word "other" is left out the comparison is made between John and himself, which is absurd. You cannot compare a person or thing with himself or itself.

"The Woolworth Building is higher than any building in New York City." This should read, "The Woolworth Building is higher than any other building in New York City."

On the other hand, the word "other" is used sometimes unnecessarily. In the sentence, "Of all other creatures, man is the most intelligent," leave out the word "other," since man is included among all creatures.

"Of all other Americans, Washington and Lincoln are first in the hearts of their countrymen."

Sentences such as the foregoing are frequently seen. But it says that Washington and Lincoln are numbered among the "other" Americans, which is, of course, incorrect. The sentence should read:

"Of all Americans," etc. Or we may say, "Before other Americans, Washington and Lincoln have a place in the hearts of their countrymen."

An example given in "The Verbalist" says:

"'The vice of covetousness, of all others, enters deepest into the soul.' This sentence says that covetousness is one of the other vices. A thing cannot be another thing, nor can it be one of a number of other things. The sentence should be, 'Of all the vices, covetousness enters deepest into the soul'; or 'The vice of covetousness, of all the vices, enters,' etc.; or 'The vice of covetousness, above all others, enters,' etc."

Ought, see *Aught*.

Out Loud

A schoolboy was studying his lessons at home. He repeated some of the figures to himself, but audibly.

"Don't do your lessons out loud," said his mother. "You disturb the rest of the family."

"Mother," asked the boy, "is it correct to say 'out loud'? Shouldn't you have said 'aloud'?"

Some authorities hold that "out loud" and "aloud" are really the same expression, "out loud" being the older, and "aloud" being derived from it through "at loud."

There is good authority for the use of "out loud," the Standard Dictionary giving the phrase as a synonym for "aloud."

Pair of Stairs

We have good authority for "a pair of stairs," which is defined by the Standard Dictionary as follows:

"Pair of stairs, a set of stairs from one story to another; sometimes restricted to a flight."

The same authority gives the following as one of the definitions of the word "pair":

"A set of like or equal things making a whole; now restricted in use, but formerly widely applied, as to chessman, chaplets, playing cards, organ pipes, or beads."

Pants, see *Gents*.
Paradox, Seeming, see *Seeming Paradox*.
Pardon me, see *Excuse Me*.
Part, see *Portion*.

Party

"How do you know that that is so?" "A certain party told me."

The foregoing conversation was overheard recently. The second speaker should have said, "A certain person told me," not, "a certain party."

This use of the word "party" for "person" is common, but it is condemned by all authorities on English grammar as being incorrect. Some, indeed, go so far as to call it vulgar.

It should be remembered, however, that the word "party," meaning an individual, has a proper place in English. We may speak of "a party to a contract," or "the party of the first part" or "the parties to the marriage." Woolley's "Handbook of Composition" gives the following sentence as an example of the correct use of the word: "The parties to the marriage were both young." The following is given by Woolley as incorrect: "The party who wrote that article must have been a scholar."

Pathos and Bathos

There is a wide difference in meaning between the word "pathos" and the word "bathos." The former, which is used much more frequently than the latter, means, according to Webster:

"That quality of human or animal experience or of its representation in art which awakens feelings of pity, sympathy and tender sorrow."

"Bathos," on the other hand, has the following meaning:

"A ludicrous descent from the elevated to the commonplace, in writing or speech; anticlimax."

Patronage, see *Custom*.

Peer

In telling of a race that had been arranged to take place between two horses, a writer on sporting topics said: "If only the two horses go to the post, the question which is the peer will be settled."

The word "peer" is used incorrectly in this case. When used correctly it means an equal, especially in rank, position, qualities, etc. If the word "equal" be substituted for the word "peer" in the sentence quoted, the absurdity of the use of "peer" will be seen—"if only the two horses go to the post, the question which is the equal will be settled."

"Better" or "faster" or "superior" is the word that should have been written.

Peeve

If you want to poke fun at the highly dignified art or science of grammar, you may say that the word "peeve" peeves the grammarian. Therefore, don't peeve him by using it.

"Peeve" is slang. There's no doubt about that. Only the very latest dictionaries contain the word, and they call it slang. Webster's New International Dictionary defines it thus, "To make or become peevish or ill-tempered," and says it is probably derived from "peevish," which is a word in perfectly good standing.

In using seven or eight words to define the slang word "peeve," the dictionary foreshadows the probable acceptance of the word. If there is no single word that is a synonym for "peeve"— since "vex" or "irritate" does not seem to convey exactly the same meaning—the English language will almost certainly, in time, adopt it. But in the meantime it is not accepted by good authorities, and if one desires to be very choice in his use of words, he will not use "peeve."

Pell Mell

From a short story, the following sentence is taken:

"Hearing her exclamation, he was greatly astounded, and rushed pell mell down the stairs after the fleeing visitor."

This illustrates a common but incorrect use of the expression "pell mell." A person cannot rush downstairs pell mell, because "pell mell" means mingled or mixed together, as in the expression, taken from a book on ancient history, "Men, horses, chariots, crowded pell mell to the front of battle."

To say "He rushed down the stairs pell mell" is as incorrect as it would be to say, "He rushed down the stairs mixed together." Evidently the speakers or writers who use "pell mell" incorrectly believe that it means "hastily" or "in confusion." But they are wrong.

People, see *Persons*.

Per Day, Per Year, Etc.

Grammarians agree in asserting that the Latin word "per," meaning "by means of, through," should be used only with Latin words, and not with English words; that is, the critics object to the mixture of the two languages in one expression or phrase.

Therefore do not say, "The man receives fifty dollars per week," but say, instead, "The man receives fifty dollars a week." Do not say, "That cloth is worth two dollars per yard," but say, "That cloth is worth two dollars a yard." The word "per" may be used correctly with Latin words such as "annum," "diem," etc., as, "The governor's salary is ten thousand dollars per annum"; "the naval officers received a per diem allowance for food."

One authority on English refers to the use of the Latin "per" with English words as "slang phrases or commercial vulgarisms." This criticism is probably too harsh; the error is too widespread for such condemnation.

Perfect, More and Most, see *More Perfect*.

Perfectly Miserable

Speaking strictly "by the book," it is correct to say, "I feel perfectly miserable," since "perfectly" means "completely; thoroughly, entirely." But there is good authority for holding that the word "perfect" should not be so used—at any rate, such use should be avoided by those who wish to use only the best English.

Better say, therefore, "I feel utterly miserable," or "I feel thoroughly miserable," or "downright miserable." Instead of saying "He is a perfect wretch"—which seems somehow, to contain what is known as a "contradiction in terms"—say, "he is a thorough wretch" or "an utter wretch."

Permit, see *Enable*.
Persecution, see *Prosecution*.

Persons and People

The word "persons," used to indicate a number or a gathering of human beings, is numerical; the word "people" is collective. The difference

148

in the uses of the words may be illustrated more easily by giving examples than by discussing the grammatical principles involved.

We say, correctly, "Three persons entered the theater," not, "Three people entered the theater." But we should not say or write, "There was a crowd of persons in the theater"; say, "There was a crowd of people." The rector was asked, "How many can be seated in your church?" He replied, "We can seat comfortably about one thousand persons, but if an unusual crowd of people wishes to attend the services we can accommodate more than a thousand." The Standard Dictionary says, "It would be quite out of place to say, 'The pastor desires to meet the young persons of the church.'"

Pitiful and Pitiable

Although some authorities hold that the words "pitiable" and "pitiful" have the same meaning, others make a distinction between them. Webster defines "pitiable" as follows:

"Deserving or exciting pity; miserable; lamentable; piteous; arousing pitying contempt, wretchedly insignificant." The meaning of "pitiful" is given as follows: "Full of pity; tender-hearted; compassionate; piteous; lamentable; eliciting compassion; to be pitied for littleness or meanness; miserable; paltry; contemptible."

Thus we may say, "Her plight was pitiable, and the beholders looked upon her with a pitiful eye."

"The Lord is very pitiful, and of tender mercy," we are told in the Bible.

Play, see *Show.*

Pleaded or Plead

Is it proper to say 'The prisoner pleaded guilty,' or 'The prisoner plead guilty?" (In the latter case the word is pronounced as if spelled "pled").

Either form is correct; there is good authority for both "pleaded" and "plead."

When a verb forms its past tense by adding "ed," it is called a "regular" or "weak" verb. When it forms its past by changing the form of the verb, as in "grow" and "grew," "weep" and "wept," "shake" and "shook," etc., it is called an "irregular" or "strong" verb. Some verbs are both "strong" and "weak."

It is strange that in common speech we find frequently that verbs which the grammarians say should be regular are changed into irregular verbs, while irregular verbs become regular. Thus, we hear, "The girl growed up nicely," instead of "grew up nicely," and "He dole the cards," instead of "dealt."

Plentiful Lack

Can a "lack" be "plentiful"?

A lack is a deficiency, a want, a need. "Plentiful" means "copious, abundant, ample." It would seem, therefore, that the expression, "a plentiful lack" would be, clearly, what is known as a "contradiction in terms."

And yet one of the leading newspapers of America said, in an editorial:

"There is no lack of courageous and honest men in American trade unions, but there is a plentiful lack of honest and courageous leadership."

We know what the writer wishes to say, but there is some difficulty in finding just the proper form of words. Perhaps one of the best ways in which to express it is as follows:

"There is a dearth of honest and courageous leadership."

Plenty and Plentiful

"The times are bad, and money is not plenty now." "Our cherry trees were covered with blossoms, and we expect that the fruit will be plenty."

The use of the word "plenty" in sentences such as the foregoing, instead of the word "plentiful," is incorrect, and is condemned by authorities on English. One of them says that the use of "plenty" for "plentiful" is a common fault, even among the fairly educated. One writer tells us that although Shakespeare says, "If reasons were as plenty as blackberries," etc., words have settled into more definite grooves since Shakespeare's time.

The word "plenty" should not be used as an adverb, as in the sentence, "This house is plenty large enough for us." Say, "This house is quite large enough for us," or, simply, "large enough."

The word "plenty" is a noun, and should be used as such only.

Plural with "fuls," see *Spoonfuls.*

Plurality, see *Majority.*

Polite

Do not use "polite" in the sense of "kind," as in the following incorrect sentence:

"I have received your polite invitation to your party, for which I thank you."

Commenting on this matter, Alfred Ayres, in "The Verbalist," writes:

"The word 'polite' is much used by persons of doubtful culture, where those of the better sort use the word 'kind.' We accept 'kind,' not 'polite' invitations and, when anyone has been obliging, we tell him that he has been 'kind'; and, when an interviewing reporter tells us of his having met with a 'polite' reception, we may be sure that the person by whom he has been received deserves well for his considerate kindness. 'I thank you and Mrs. Pope for my kind reception,' Atterbury.'"

Poorly

"He was better yesterday, but he is poorly again today."

Such use of the word "poorly" as an adjective is an example of what is called dialectal English; that is, English that has local forms and is therefore different from the standard in use generally. It consists, in many cases, of survivals of ancient forms and words.

"Poorly," in the sense of "somewhat ill; indisposed; slightly ailing" is used in the mountains of eastern Tennessee and the bottom lands of Arkansas, and probably in other sections of the United States and England. In some places the term "poorlyish," with the same meaning, is also heard.

In Australia some ignorant users of English say of a sick person who is like themselves, "he is bad," and of a person in a better station in life, "he is poorly."

Portion and Part

There is a difference between the meaning of the word "part" and that of the word "portion," although some persons use the words as though they meant the same thing. For example, one should not say, "In which portion of the country did you live before you came here?" but instead, "In which part of the country did you live," etc.

"Part" means simply "a certain amount of anything," while "portion" means a part that it alloted to some person, etc., or set apart for a specified purpose; a share, a division. The verb "to portion" means to divide, to parcel, to endow.

In the sentence "A large portion of the land is untilled," the right word would be either "part" or "proportion," according to the intention of the writer; whether he meant to say, simply, that much of the land was untilled, or that much of the land was untilled when considered in relation to the land that was tilled.

Posted

To be "well posted" is, according to many persons who do not use their native tongue carefully, the same as to be well informed. But grammarians are offended by such use of the word "posted." It is incorrect. Therefore do not say, "If I had been well posted concerning him, I should not have done business with him." Say, "If I had been well informed," etc. Do not say, "He is thoroughly posted in the affairs of the day."

Practical and Practicable

"Practical" means having reference to actual use or experience, as opposed to theoretical or ideal; as in, "Although the engineer was well trained in college, he had had little practical experience." The word "practicable," on the other hand, means "that can be put into effect or practice; capable of execution"; or "serviceable, capable of being used for an intended purpose." We say, "It seemed that he had planned well; but when the time for execution came, it was seen that his plans were not practicable." Another example: "The road was blocked with snow, and was therefore not practicable."

One authority pokes fun at business signs, which are seen sometimes, such as "Practical Haircutting," and asks what theoretical haircutting would be. A man calls himself a "practical" carpenter or a "practical" tailor, meaning that he practises one of those crafts, but the passerby would know it if the sign bore simply the word "carpenter" or the word "tailor."

Practically or Virtually

Is it incorrect to use the word "practically" as in the sentence, "This machine is practically useless for the purpose for which it is intended," and should one use "virtually" instead?

153

There is no reason for holding that the word "practically" is used incorrectly in the sentence quoted, since two of the definitions of "practically" are, according to Webster, "in actual practice or use; really." Other definitions are as follows: "In a practical way; not theoretically; really; by means of practice; by experience or experiment."

"Virtually" is defined as the adverb of "virtual," which means: "Being in essence or effect, but not in fact; as, the virtual presence of a man in his agent or substitute."

Present and Introduce

Do not say "present" when you mean "introduce." If you say, "Mr. Jones, permit me to present Mr. Brown," you imply that Mr. Jones is superior to Mr. Brown.

"Few errors are more common, especially among those who are always straining to be fine, than that of using 'present' in the social world, instead of 'introduce'" says Alfred Ayres, in "The Verbalist." "'Present' means to place in the presence of a superior; 'introduce' means to bring to be acquainted. A person is presented at court, and on an official occasion to our President; but persons who are unknown to each other are 'introduced' by a common acquaintance. And in these introductions, it is the younger who is introduced to the older; the lower to the higher in place or social position; the gentleman to the lady. A lady should say, as a rule, that Mr. Blank was introduced to her, not that she was introduced to him."

Pretty, see *Handsome.*

Prevent To

Do not say, "prevent to" instead of "prevent from."

"By preventing the opposing team to score for

154

eight innings, the pitcher made certain of his game," said a sporting writer. He should have written, "By preventing the opposing team from scoring for eight innings," etc. The proper preposition to use after "prevent" is "from," not "to."

"'Prevent' is the general term for hindering, checking or stopping," says Webster. "To 'preclude' is to hinder by excluding, or especially, to prevent by anticipative action. To 'avert' is to prevent or turn aside, especially, some threatened evil."

Preventive or Preventative

For many years this has been one of the "pet" errors of grammarians and writers on correct English—that is, hardly a work on the proper use of words fails to tell us that "preventative" is incorrect and "preventive" is correct. Despite all the criticism, the word "preventative" is seen frequently, in books and in newspaper and magazine articles.

There is no reason for putting the extra syllable into the word "preventive," making it "preventative." To form an adjective or a noun from the verb "prevent," as in "preventive medicine has made great strides in recent years"; "good drainage is a preventive of disease," it is necessary to add only "ive," not "ative."

Arguing backwards, as it were, it might be said that "preventative" would be correct if there were such a verb as "preventate" from which to form it. But as there is no such verb, and as the verb is "prevent," the proper form of the noun and the adjective is "preventive," not "preventative."

Principal and Principle

These two words, "principal" and "principle"

are not confused in speaking, of course, since the pronunciation of the two is almost the same. (There is a slight difference in pronunciation; in the former the "a" is sounded, but very little; in "principle" there is no sound of "a".)

But it is not uncommon to find the two words confused in writing. They are entirely distinct. "Principal" may be either a noun (name word) or an adjective (a word describing a noun); "principle" is a noun and in rare cases a verb (action word), but never an adjective. The word "principal" has many meanings as a noun, too many to be reprinted here; as an adjective it means "highest in rank or authority; chief; main, etc." "Principle" has several meanings; two of them are "a fundamental truth" and "a settled rule of action."

Promise and Threaten

"The weather man promises unfavorable weather to-morrow," and "Magistrate promises workhouse term for violators of city ordinance." These two newspaper headlines contain instances of the incorrect—or, at any rate, undesirable— use of the word "promises." The word should be "threatens."

The dictionary defines the verb "promise" as "to engage or covenant, in a manner binding in honor, to do or not to do for another, especially something desired or desirable." To threaten means "to express an intention or intentions of evil or mischief against; utter menaces or threats against." Therefore, when the thing that is to come is to be favorable in its nature, use the word "promise" in referring to it; but when it is unfavorable, the proper word is "threaten."

One authority on English writes of the odd effect that is produced on the reader when he sees a headline like "Assassination promised to all officials," "that would be an ominous 'promise,' indeed!"

Propose and Purpose

These two words are often confused, even by careful writers and speakers, although there is in the meanings a difference which has often been commented upon.

"Propose," when used according to good authority, means to put forward or to offer for the consideration of others; hence, a proposal is a scheme or design offered for acceptance or consideration, a proposition. "Purpose," means to intend, to design, to resolve; hence, a purpose is an intention, an aim, that which one sets before one's self. Examples: "What do you purpose doing in the matter?" "What do you propose that we shall do in the matter?"

Macaulay wrote: "I purpose to write a history of England from the accession of King James the Second down to a time which is within the memory of men still living." The Standard Dictionary says that in the majority of cases what we purpose is more general, what we propose is more formal and definite; "I purpose to do right; I propose to do this specific thing because it is right."

Proposition

In recent years the term "proposition" has been applied by careless writers and speakers to anything and everything. Almost anything is a "proposition," although there is no authority for the use of the word as it is commonly employed. Correctly speaking, a proposition is a subject for debate or a basis of negotiation; a scheme or measure proposed or brought forward for consideration, acceptance or rejection. One authority says, "To apply the term indiscriminately to a girl, a golf ball, a dress suit, or a transatlantic liner, is either slang or the result of ignorance."

Here is an instance of the incorrect use of the word: A man was observed looking at a new automobile which he admired very much. "That's a sweet little proposition!" he said.

This incorrect use of "proposition" is a recent introduction into the English language. So new is it, that standard books twenty years old contain no reference to it.

Prosecution and Persecution

Owing to the similarity in spelling and pronunciation of these two words, "prosecution" and "persecution," they are sometimes confused and mistaken for each other.

"Prosecution," in its most common use, means "the institution and continuance of a criminal proceeding; the exhibition of formal charges against an accused before a legal tribunal and the pressing of them to a conclusion." (Standard Dictionary.)

The same authority defines "persecution" as "the act of persecuting, or the state of being persecuted; harsh or malignant oppression, the infliction of pain, punishment or death upon others unjustly, particularly for adhering to a religious creed or mode of worship, either by way of penalty or to compel them to renounce their principles."

Thus we say, "The district attorney prosecuted with vigor the charges against the accused man," and "The Jews were persecuted in Russia."

Protest

According to the best authorities on English, we should not say, "I protested the holding of the meeting," but should say, instead, "I protested against the holding of the meeting."

Such use of the verb "protest" without the preposition "against" has become common in recent years, especially in newspaper headlines, where it is sometimes inconvenient to use the word "against" because of its length.

Proud and Vain

"She is very proud of her good looks, isn't she?" asked one girl of another. She should have said, "She is very vain of her good looks."

Commenting on the difference between pride and vanity, the Standard Dictionary says: "Vanity is eager for admiration and praise, is elated if they are rendered, and pained if they are withheld, and seeks them; pride could never solicit admiration or praise."

The difference in meaning of the two words is well illustrated by the following quotations, the first from Jane Austen and the second from Robertson: "Pride relates more to our opinion of ourselves, vanity to what we would have others think of us." "No man will acknowledge that he is vain, but almost any man will acknowledge that he is proud."

Proved or Proven

Shall we say that a matter is "proved" or is "proven"? It is a disputed point in English grammar, and the authorities are divided on the question. But the most modern opinion is that we should say "proved," not "proven."

"'Proven' is an obsolescent word; it is not actually incorrect, but it is undesirable," says "The Use of Language," by Lomer and Ashmun. ("Obsolescent" means "going out of use; becoming out of date.")

In this case, as in very many others, anyone may, if he wishes—use the word that is criticized, and be in good company. The word is used by Bulwer, Lowell, Thackeray, Tennyson, Herbert Spencer and others. Other good writers avoid it, however, and write "proved" for the past tense

159

of the verb "prove." The word "proven" is a dialect form of "proved," and comes from the northern English and Scotch speech.

Proves

The expression, "The exception proves the rule" has puzzled many generations of users of English who have not been students of grammar, rhetoric, idioms, etc. "How can an exception, which is something that falls outside a rule, prove or demonstrate the truth of the rule?" they ask.

They do not know, or they overlook the fact, that the word "prove" has two meanings. One is to demonstrate, as stated in the foregoing paragraph; the other is "to put to a test or trial." When viewed in the light of this second meaning of "prove," the expression, "The exception proves the rule," becomes clear. The exception tests the rule, to tell whether or not it is of general application.

The Government "proves" or tests a gun; the place where the test is made is known as the "proving ground."

Providing or Provided

The use of "providing" instead of "provided" is a very common error, even persons who pride themselves upon their correctness in speaking and writing being guilty of it. They say, for example, "I will give a thousand dollars to the hospital building fund, providing twenty others each give a like amount." The proper word to be employed is "provided," which means, according to the Standard Dictionary, "on condition; it being stipulated or understood."

Provoked, see *Aggravated*.
Pupil, see *Scholar*.
Purpose, see *Propose*.

Quantity and Number

The word "quantity" is sometimes used incorrectly as in the sentence, "What quantity of railroad cars can you spare?" Corrected, the sentence reads, "What number of railroad cars can you spare?" or, "How many can you spare?"

The rule is that "quantity" should be used in speaking of what can be weighed or measured, as in the sentence, "He had a large quantity of sugar on hand," and the word "number" should be used of what can be counted, as in the sentence, "A large number of persons was present," not "a large quantity."

Another writer puts the correction thus: "'Quantity' refers to the 'how much'; 'number' to the 'how many'," and gives the following example: "He purchased a large quantity of wheat, corn, apples, lime and sand, and a number of houses, stores, chairs and books."

It is incorrect to say, "There was a large quantity of bicycles in the yard, or "He sold a large quantity of books at auction." In each of these cases substitute the word "number" for the word "quantity."

Quite a Number

When you say, "Quite a number of persons were present," just how many do you mean? The phrase is too indefinite; it does not convey a clear, sharp idea to the mind of the hearer, and therefore it should be avoided by all who desire to speak and write correctly. If you mean, "There was a large number of persons present," why not say so?

Similarly, there is objection to the expression, heard in some parts of the United States, "quite a few." We hear, "How many were in the church today?" and the answer, "Quite a few." The speaker does not mean that a few were there, but many. "'Quite' means 'completely, entirely, in a finished manner.' The common phrase, mis-

called an Americanism, 'quite a number,' is un-
justifiable. 'Number' is indefinite in its signifi-
cation, and therefore cannot be properly qualified
by 'quite,' says White in "Words and Their
Uses."

Quite Some

How much is "quite some"?

The question was suggested by a letter to a
newspaper, in which the writer told how the
late Melville W. Fuller, chief justice of the United
States, became so absorbed in "The Three Mus-
keteers," by Dumas, that he failed to notice that
his room was on fire, and, still clutching in his
hand the famous masterpiece, had to be carried
from his bed. "Quite some advertising for the
great French author's work," said the letter
writer.

This use of the words "quite" and "some" is
not recognized by grammarians, and the meaning
of the writer could have been expressed more
grammatically by some other form of words; for
example, by "good advertising for the great
French author's work."

Rabbit, Welsh, see *Rarebit*.

Raise Children

The verb "raise" is applied with propriety only
to crops or cattle, never to human beings. "She
raised a family of eight children," says a charity
report; it should have said, "she reared" or "she
brought up." The Standard Dictionary ridicules
the expression, attributed to a Southern aunty,
"She raised thirteen head of children."

The term "brought up" is the more modern of
the two; the term "reared" is older. This misuse
of the term "raised" is a colloquialism that is
common in some of the Southern and Western
states.

Some authorities criticize the use of the verb "grow" in connection with crops, asserting that we should not say, "We grow wheat on our farm," but should say, "We raise wheat."

"Raise" in Wages or "Rise"

The question is sometimes asked, "Should we say 'He received a raise in wages,' or 'a rise in wages'?"

If we desire to speak with strict regard for accuracy in language, we should use neither of these expressions, a "raise in wages" and "a rise in wages." There is good authority for condemning both. However, the term "raise" has come into colloquial use recently, and is therefore defended by some authorities, on the familiar ground that usage makes language. But it is better, in any case, to say "an increase in wages," about which expression there cannot be any doubt. It expresses the meaning quite as well as either "raise" or "rise."

"The tendency to introduce 'rise,' commonly employed in England when referring to wages, may be due to the influence exerted by the newspaper press," says one authority.

Rarebit or Rabbit, Welsh

Some bills of fare call it "Welsh rarebit," while others spell it "rabbit." Which is correct?

The matter is of no great importance, of course. The weight of authority favors "rabbit" rather than "rarebit." The book, "Words and Their Ways in English Speech," says:

"Welsh rabbit is often spelled 'rarebit' (and even so pronounced) from a whimsical notion that it is compounded of 'rare' and 'bit.' In fact, however, 'Welsh rabbit' is merely a joke, like 'Cape Cod turkey' for codfish, the Australian 'colonial goose' for a leg of mutton with savory

herbs, and the old 'French of Norfolk' for the
Norfolk dialect of English."

Rarely and Rare

The word "rarely" is frequently misused for
"rare," as in the following sentence:

"It is very rarely that a statesman is so devoted to the public good that he loses all thought
of self."

Commenting on this point, "The Verbalist,"
by Alfred Ayres, says:

"It is no uncommon thing to see the adverb
'rarely' improperly used in such sentences as 'It
is very rarely that the puppets of the romancer
assume,' etc. 'But,' says the defender of this
phraseology, ' "rarely" qualifies a verb—the verb
"to be." ' Not at all. The sentence, if written
out in full would be, 'It is a very rare thing
that,' etc., or 'The circumstance is a very rare one
that,' etc., or 'It is a very rare occurrence that,'
etc. To those who contend for 'It is very rarely
that,' etc., I would say: 'It is very sadly that persons of culture will write and then defend—or
try to defend—such grammar.' "

Real

"So you have come to visit my sick mother!
That is real kind of you!"

The good feeling of the speaker is apparent,
but his grammar is faulty. He should not say,
"real kind," but, instead, "really kind" or "very
kind." In view of the fact that this error is
widespread, and many persons who speak and
write good English are guilty of it, we should
probably not call it a vulgarism, as some critics
do. Others do not go so far as to condemn it
entirely, and call it a "colloquialism." However,
the use of "real" in this sense is certainly not

according to the best usage, and it is better to avoid it.

Of course, the word "real" has its proper place in English, as a synonym for "genuine," as in "real lace," "real antiques," "real sympathy," etc. The word is frequently mispronounced, being sounded as one syllable, "reel"; the correct pronunciation is in two syllables "re-al."

Reason Because

We sometimes hear a person say:

"The reason I ask you to tell the story is because you can do so better than I." This is incorrect. The meaning of the word "because" is "for the reason." Therefore, if we use the sentence as quoted, we really say, "The reason I ask you to tell the story is for the reason that you can do so better than I," which is, of course, absurd. Instead of using the word "because" in the sentence, use the word "that," making the sentence read, "The reason I ask you to tell the story is that you can do so better than I."

The following incorrect use of the word "because" is also heard frequently: "Because Mary went to college is no reason why her sister should do so." It is much better to say or write: "That Mary went to college is no reason why her sister should do so."

Recipe and Receipt

Although it is asserted by some authorities on English that the word "receipt" should never be used in the sense of "recipe"—that is, a formula or list of ingredients of a mixture, with directions for compounding or using—other good writers uphold such use. Among others, George Eliot uses "receipt" in the sense of "recipe." However, it may be said, that "receipt" means, generally, an acknowledgment of something that has been received, while "recipe" is used generally as defined above.

Therefore, while we may speak of "a receipt for a cake" or a "recipe for a cake," the former may mean an acknowledgment that a cake has been delivered, while the latter can mean only the directions for making the cake.

Reckon

Probably the use of the verb "reckon," in the sense of "think," "believe," "suppose," etc., is too widespread and too firmly established, especially in parts of the Southern states, to be dislodged, but it is well to record that it is incorrect, from the grammarian's point of view. The authorities condemn it, as they do the use of the word "guess" used in a similar manner in parts of the Northern states.

"I reckon we are going to have fair weather tomorrow." Say, rather, "I think," or "I believe." "I reckon you're a stranger in this town, else you would know that that is the postoffice." Say, "I believe you must be a stranger."

Grammarians object to the provincial employment of "guess" and "reckon" because these words have correct uses, and it is well to reserve them for such.

Recourse and Resource

These two words are sometimes confounded, or used incorrectly, even by persons who possess good vocabularies, owing to the similarity in spelling and pronunciation.

"Recourse" denotes resorting or applying to a means for the accomplishment of an end or purpose; as "When the funds of the colonists were almost exhausted, they had recourse to a loan from France."

"Resource," on the other hand, means supply

or support, or anything to which resort is made for help or support, as in the sentence, "The lawyer called upon his last resource, an appeal to the Governor, in his effort to save his client." The two words, "recourse" and "resource" are employed properly in the following sentence; "When his own last financial resource was gone, the merchant had recourse to loans from his friends."

Refer, see *Allude*.
Refuse, see *Decline*.

Regarded and Regard (See also As Regards That)

The word "regarded" is sometimes used incorrectly as meaning "believed, thought, considered," etc. An example of this error is found in the following sentence: "Among the officials here it is regarded that the matches are most timely."

An expression that is frequently heard, and is considered incorrect by many authorities, is "in regard to that." It is better to say, "with regard to that," or one may say, if one wishes, "as regards that," or "regarding that."

Reiterate, see *Repeat*.

Relent or Relax

The word "relent" is sometimes used for "relax," as in the following sentence:

"The boxers have attained that stage in their preparation for the bout where they can afford to relent a little in their training." Now, although the dictionary seems to look with favor on this use of "relent," in giving to the word a secondary meaning, "to abate; slacken," the word is thus used very seldom, if ever, by good writers or speakers. It is much better to use "relax," making the sentence read, "They can afford to relax a little in their training."

Remainder, see *Balance*.

Repeat and Reiterate (See also Duplicate)

If you "repeat" something, you simply say or do it over, as, to repeat a question or a command, to repeat an operation, an attempt, etc.

But if you reiterate something you say or do it over and over again, or repeatedly. In other words, as Webster tells us, "to 'repeat' is to do or say something over again; 'reiterate' applies to words more frequently than to actions, and sometimes suggests repetition again and again; as, to repeat a successful performance, to repeat a question; reiterated protestations of regret."

"The lawyer repeated the question, to which the accused man replied with reiterated assertions that he was innocent."

There is a word "iterate," which is contained in the larger dictionaries and which has much the same meaning as "reiterate," but it is not used so frequently as "reiterate."

Replica

"Nashville is building a replica of the Parthenon; Tennesseans plan an exact to-the-inch reproduction of the famous Grecian temple," said a headline in one of the leading newspapers of America.

The English is questionable; the word "replica" should not have been used, perhaps, since, in its strict sense, "replica" means "a duplicate executed by the artist himself and considered, with the first, as an original." Of course, it will be seen, when one keeps this preferred use of "replica" in mind, that it is impossible for Nashville or any other place to have a replica of the Parthenon. The newspaper might have said that Nashville is building a "copy," a "duplicate" or a "reproduction" of the Parthenon.

However, the use of "replica" in the sense of "copy" or "duplicate" is permitted by some authorities, including Webster, and is becoming general.

Reply, see *Answer.*
Reputation, see *Character.*
Resemble, see *Favor.*
Residence, see *House.*
Resource, see *Recourse.*
Rest, see *Balance.*
Revenge, see *Avenge.*

Reverend and Honorable

Neither of these titles of honor should be used unless the writer uses also with it the word "The." It is also incorrect to use the title, even when "the" is used, and put the title immediately before the name. Thus, it is improper to say "Rev. Jones" or "The Rev. Jones," or "Hon. Smith" or "The Hon. Smith." You should say, "The Rev. Mr. Jones" or "The Rev. Arthur Jones," "The Hon. Mr. Smith" or "The Hon. Richard Smith."

Of course, when the degree of doctor of divinity has been conferred on a clergyman, it is proper to use "Dr." instead of "Mr." But it may be remarked that in many cases a pastor's flock, or other persons, call him "doctor" when he really has no right to the title. In the same way, many men are called "Hon." or "Honorable" to whom the title does not belong.

Right, To Have, see *Have a Right.*
Rise in Wages, see *Raise.*

Rotten

We hear the word "rotten," used in the sense of "bad" or "very bad," applied to many things. "How do you feel to-day?" we ask a friend; and if he does not feel well and is not careful in his use of words, he answers, "I feel rotten." Of another one we inquire, "Is business good with you?", and we are told that it is "rotten."

This use—or misuse, rather—of the word "rotten" is slang, and should have no place in the speech of the educated person. Everyone knows the proper meaning and use of the word, and it is not necessary to go into it in detail here. The word should be restricted to such meaning and use, and should not be employed in the sense of "bad," or "very bad," "poor" or "very poor."

Salary, see *Wages.*

Saleslady (see also Woman)

Don't use the word "saleslady." Say "saleswoman," instead.

Of course, no slur is intended upon a woman whose occupation is selling goods. She may be just as much of a lady, in one sense of that word, as any other woman. But when she is engaged in her occupation she is, in proper English, a "saleswoman," not a "saleslady."

The man who follows the same occupation is never referred to as a "salesgentleman," however gentlemanly he may be in demeanor, action, speech and principles. When he is selling he is a "salesman."

Same, The

In business correspondence, we frequently find the word "same" used as in the following examples: "We have received your letter of the 20th, and note what you say in same"; "your order for two hundred barrels received, and we shall give prompt attention to same."

This use of the word "same" is condemned by all authorities on English grammar. The two sentences quoted would be worded in much better English if they read as follows: "We have received your letter of the 20th, and note what you

170

say in it"; "your order for two hundred barrels has been received, and we shall give prompt attention to the matter."

Same and Similar

These two words, "same" and "similar," differ in meaning, although they are used sometimes, by writers and speakers who are careful ordinarily, as though they had the same meaning. "I called on that woman, and found her wearing the same hat as I," was heard not long ago. A moment's thought would have shown the speaker how ridiculous the statement was. What she meant to say was, "I called on that woman, and found her wearing a hat similar to mine."

"Same" means "identical in nature; not different; similar in kind or quality," and "similar" means "bearing resemblance to one another or to something else; like, but not completely identical" (Standard Dictionary). The "Literary Digest" said, in illustrating the proper uses of the two words: "A gale blowing to-day with a velocity of sixty miles an hour is similar to, but is not the same as, one that blew with a velocity of sixty miles one year ago, although it has the same amount of velocity."

Sanitarium and Sanatorium

Which is correct, "sanitarium" or "sanatorium"? Both are correct, and either may be used. They are both derived from the Latin—"sanatorium" from "sanatorius," meaning "health giving," and "sanitarium" from "sanitas," meaning "health."

However, the latest edition of Webster's International Dictionary makes a slight distinction between the two words. It says that both "sanatorium" and "sanitarium" mean "health resort; an establishment for the treatment of the sick," but that "sanitarium" is sometimes restricted to "an establishment where the treatment is wholly, or almost wholly, prophylactic"—that is, preventive, preservative or protective.

In other words, you go to a "sanatorium" to be cured, and to a "sanitarium" to be preserved from illness.

Save, see *Except.*

Saw or Have Seen

Should one say, "It is the best play I ever saw," or "It is the best play I have ever seen?"

Both expressions are correct, and either may be used without violation of any rule of grammar. The former is in the imperfect or past tense, sometimes called by grammarians the preterit, which is used to indicate simply past time; that is, time that is not continued into the present. The second expression, "It is the best play I have ever seen," is in the perfect tense, which signifies action or being that is past but is continued into the present time.

Say, see *State.*

Says

"I says to him, says I, 'How long have you had that suit?' and he says to me, 'Oh, I got it last week.'"

The foregoing sentence was overheard in a city street car. It illustrates an error of speech which is quite common, the use of "says" instead of "said," combined often with the unnecessary repetition of "says." So frequently is this error heard that many professional humorists take advantage of it to fill their writings with "I sez," "he sez" and "she sez." In the example quoted, the speaker should have expressed himself as follows: "I said to him, 'How long have you had that suit?' and he said to me, 'Oh, I got it last week.'"

"Says" is the present tense of the verb "say"; "said" is in the past tense.

Scholar, Pupil, and Student

Although these three words are frequently used as though they bore the same meaning, there is a distinction to be made.

A pupil is one who is under the personal supervision of a teacher or tutor. A scholar is one who is being schooled, or who has attained to high scholarship; thus, we may say that a lawyer who has reached a high rank in his profession is a scholar, while it would be incorrect to refer to him as a pupil. A student is one who is still studying, but who has not reached the proficiency of a scholar. "The student is one who is learning, the scholar one who has learned," says the Standard Dictionary. "On the other hand, 'student' suggests less of personal supervision than 'pupil'; thus, the college student often becomes the private pupil of some instructor in special studies."

Screed

The word "screed" is seldom used correctly, even by writers who generally exercise care in their selection of words. It does not mean, as they seem to believe, a long writing of any sort, or something that has been hastily scribbled.

It means "a long tirade on any subject, oral, written or printed," according to Webster. "Tirade," means "a long drawn speech or declamatory passage, especially one marked by intemperate and, usually, vituperative or harshly censorious language."

Sculp

Is it proper to say that a sculptor "sculps" a statue, a bust, a memorial, etc.? A heading in a

173

prominent newspaper says: "Trotzky Revealed by Woman Artist Who Sculped Him."

It is difficult to reply with positiveness to this question. The use of the verb "sculp" is not incorrect, but the word is passing out of literary usage. Probably it looks and sounds "queer" to many educated persons. The Standard Dictionary says of it that it was once in literary use, but is now chiefly colloquial or humorous, and Webster's Dictionary calls it "obsolete, colloquial or humorous." The word is not found in Roget's "Thesaurus of English Words and Phrases."

As in the cases of many other words concerning which there is dispute, it may be said of "sculp" that while it may not be incorrect to use it in speech, it is better to avoid it in writing.

Secure

Although the word "secure" is used by almost everybody in the sense of "obtain," "procure," "get," etc., it differs slightly in meaning from those words. The Standard Dictionary says: "One obtains a thing commonly by some direct effort of his own; he procures it commonly by the intervention of someone else; he procures a dinner or an interview; he secures what has seemed uncertain or elusive, when he gets it firmly into his possession or under his control."

As has been said above, almost everybody uses the word "secure" in the same sense as "obtain," etc., and therefore this usage may be said to have made a place for itself in the language, no matter what some dictionary makers and grammarians say. In this case, as in so many others, it may be said that in language "whatever is, is right." A living language grows and changes constantly, adding new words, using old words with new meanings, casting off old expressions, and doing

174

other things that make it impossible for grammarians to set up fixed standards. Indeed, by some writers it is held that English changes so much and so frequently that it is a "grammarless tongue."

Seeing as How

Don't use "seeing as how," as in the following extract from a newspaper article:

"Seeing as how Ruth will not be permitted to appear in a game for thirty days, we imagine that both he and his companion Yankees will spend the first month of the season praying for rain."

"Seeing as how" is not good English. However, it is correct to use the word "seeing" in the sense of "considering; in view of the fact, taking into account; inasmuch as; since; because," followed by "that" or without "that." In the Bible (Genesis xxvi, 27) we find:

"Wherefore come ye to me, seeing ye hate me?"

This shows that the use of "seeing" in this sense was common and good English as far back as the time of the translation of the Bible into the King James or Authorized Version, in the early part of the seventeenth century.

Seeming Paradox

We hear or read, sometimes, the expression, "a seeming paradox," employed by persons who generally use good English and pride themselves upon their command of the language. But when they say "a seeming paradox" they are in error; they use too many words.

This is so because a paradox is a statement that seems to be absurd or false, at first sight, but which when examined is seen to be true. For example, a writer says: "Though it sound like a paradox, it is no less true that up to a certain point familiarity with a book causes it to be

175

quoted inaccurately." Do not use "seeming" with "paradox."

Seen, Have, see *Saw*.

Seen

Frequently we hear a person say, "I seen him do it." It is not always a person who has not been well educated in the use of English. In the language of the grammarian, the speaker does not make a proper distinction between "saw," the preterit, or past, form of the verb "see," and the perfect participle of the same word. The principal parts of "see" are as follows: Present, "see"; past, "saw"; imperfect participle, "seeing"; perfect participle, "seen." Therefore, the sentence should have been worded, "I saw him do it," not "I seen him do it."

We hear a person say, "I have saw" or "I would have saw"; in those cases, of course, the expressions should be, "I have seen," "I would have seen," since "seen" is the participle to be used after any form of the auxiliary or "helping" verb "have."

Seldom or Ever

Do not say, "I seldom or ever do so and so." It is incorrect. The idea which you intend to express may be worded in either of two ways. You may say, "I seldom if ever do so and so," that is, if you do so at all, you do so seldom. Or you may say, "I seldom or never do so," that is, you do so very seldom at the utmost, or probably never, in your opinion.

Session, see *Meeting*.
Set, see *Sit*.

Sewage and Sewerage

Although these two words are sometimes used interchangeably by the unthinking, they should not be confused, since their meanings are quite different. "Sewage" is the waste matter of a city, town, etc., that is discharged through the sewers or system of sewers. "The city disposes of its sewage by modern sewerage."

One authority gives "sewerage" as meaning the same as "sewage," but calls such use "a loose usage," which means, of course, that it is not approved.

Professor Hill, in his "Principles of Rhetoric and Their Application," lists these two words among those which are so much alike in appearance and sound as to be mistaken one for another.

Shall and Will (see also Would and Should)

No other two verbs are so frequently misused as "will" and "shall." We say "I will go" when we mean "I shall go," and vice versa. In the first person (which means the person or persons speaking and is expressed by the use of "I" and "we"), the simple future is expressed by "shall." Determination is expressed by "will." Thus, "I shall go," means "I am going to go," while "I will go" means "I am determined to go." In the second and third persons, meaning the persons or objects spoken to or referred to, "shall" express a command, while "will" expresses the simple future. Thus, "You shall go," means, "I command you to go," while "You will go," means, simply, that you are going to go. There are other rules governing the use of "will" and "shall," but the foregoing explanation shows the errors commonly made.

"The choice between 'should' and 'would' is based on the distinctions between 'shall' and 'will'" says Webster.

Shall or Should (see also Would)

Several years ago a correspondent of a New

York newspaper put the following question to the editor:

"Which is preferable: 'We prefer that all payments shall be made in thirty days,' or 'We prefer that all payments should be made in thirty days'?"

To which the editor replied:

"To use the form 'should be paid' implies 'If it be convenient' or 'if you have the money.' To say 'We prefer that all payments shall be made in thirty days' suggests a somewhat peremptory demand for payment."

In other words, in the opinion of the editor the form, "We prefer that all payments should be made in thirty days" is a much softer wording of a request or demand for payment.

Show or Play

According to the Standard Dictionary, "show" should not be used instead of "play." The dictionary says, in defining "show": "That which is shown or exhibited; specifically, a public spectacle or exhibition, as a pageant or a play; now usually of petty exhibitions, except as slang or in special usage; as, a traveling show."

Note that the word "show," when used instead of "play," is considered an example of slang, and slang is not good English. The difficulty in avoiding slang lies in knowing what is slang and what is not.

Showed or Shown

In the editorial columns of a newspaper the following sentence appeared: "Suspicion and abuse have at once showed their heads, even as against the highest dignitaries of the church."

Either "have showed" or "have shown" is correct, according to good authority. It is difficult to say which is in more common use. Probably persons who pay attention to the matter of speak-

ing and writing correctly say "have shown," while
the ordinary speaker says "have showed." But
he must not be accused of error for doing so.

Professor Lounsbury, in his "History of the
English Language," comments on this point and
says that "the three weak verbs 'show,' 'strew,'
and 'saw' showed a tendency, long ago, to adopt
the forms 'shown,' 'strewn,' and 'sawn.'"

Sickly

"Sickly" is an adjective, although it ends in "ly,"
which is the common sign of an adverb, being
added to adjectives to form adverbs, as in "quick,
quickly," "brave, bravely," etc. Now, if we add
"ly" to "sickly," we get "sicklily," which does not
"look right" or "sound right," although it is
recognized in some dictionaries as a perfectly
proper word. They give "sickly" as an adverb,
but call it "obselete," which means worn out,
no longer in use. Probably the best thing to do is
to avoid "sicklily," and the use of "sickly" as
an adverb, and to say "in a sickly manner," as in
the sentence, "He seemed to be well, but he acted
in a sickly manner."

Sideways and Sidewise, see *Lengthways.*
Similar, see *Same.*
Sin, see *Crime.*

Since and Ago

It is a difficult task to draw the line between
the proper use of the word "since" in the sense of
"ago" and that of the word "ago" itself. James
C. Fernald, author of "A Working Grammar of
the English Language," "Synonyms, Antonyms and
Prepositions," and other works, says:

"'Since,' used in the sense of 'ago,' refers to
quite recent past time, while 'ago' covers past time
in general; as, 'A messenger was here to see
you.' 'How long since?' or 'How long ago?'
But, if one says, 'The Spanish Armada was de-

stroyed off the coast of England,' to ask, 'How long since?' instead of 'How long ago?' would have a grotesque effect, as if the event had happened lately."

To illustrate the proper use of "since" he quotes from Shakespeare, "I brought you word an hour since"; to illustrate the use of "ago" he says, "He died a century ago."

Sit and Set

Probably it is impossible to teach the great majority of Americans the difference between the two words "sit" and "set," but grammarians have been trying to do so for many years. "Come in and set down," says one's host. He should say, "Come in and sit down."

Whether a hen sets on a nest or sits on it is not certain, in grammar, since the point is disputed, but it is quite certain that you do not "sit" a hen on her nest; you "set" her there. It is not correct to say, "The vase sets on the table"; say, instead, "The vase rests, or stands, on the table." Do not say: "The flagpole sets firmly in its socket," but, "The flagpole is set firmly in its socket." If you prefer, you may say, instead, "The flagpole sits firmly in its socket."

Small, Infinitely, see *Infinitely Small.*

So, see *As;* see *Such;* see *That.*

Some

The use of the word "some" for emphasis, as in the sentences, "That was some play I saw last night!" and "He had some disagreeable expression when he came in this morning," is vulgar and slangy, and therefore to be avoided. Its use has become widespread among careless or uneducated persons. In most cases, if not in all, the meaning can be expressed by the word "very." In the sentence first quoted say, "That was a very enjoyable play I saw last night." The second may be altered to, "He had a very disagreeable expression," etc.

The word "some" has, of course, its proper uses. One of the uses which is not exactly condemned by the grammarians, but which is called "colloquial," is in the sense of "about; as nearly as may be estimated"; as in the sentence, "There were some three hundred persons present at the meeting."

Some, Quite, see *Quite Some.*

Some Place

"Do not stop me; I must go some place."

This use of "place" instead of "where," is not regarded as good English by grammarians. Some of them call it "inadmissible," meaning that it is not to be approved by those who consider themselves the watchdogs of the language.

One authority says that such expressions as the following are solecisms: "She is always wanting to go some place"; "Can't I go any place?" "I must go some place"; "I can't find it any place."

A solecism (pronounced in three syllables, sol-e-cism) is a construction of words that violates grammatical rules or the approved idiomatic usage of a language. McElroy, in "The Structure of English Prose," says: "Solecisms are errors in (1) concord (agreement or government); (2) grammatical arrangement, the ordering of the sentence to express grammatically the thought intended; (3) grammatical propriety, the use of the proper grammatical element; (4) grammatical precision, the use of the precise number of words required to express the thought."

Somebody Else's or Somebody's Else

Here we have a question about which grammarians have disputed for many years, and about which they will continue their arguments for many years, no doubt. When we go back to the authorities that are older, comparatively, we find them insisting that we should say "anybody's else, nobody's else, somebody's else." But the more modern writers tell us that the common usage, "anybody else's, somebody else's, nobody else's," is correct, and as proper as the other form.

Therefore we may say, "That book is somebody else's," instead of, "That book is somebody's else." To many persons, no doubt, the latter form will seem incorrect. The former is in more common use in many places, and it probably "sounds right" to more speakers of English than the other form.

"The possessive of 'anybody else' is either 'anybody else's' or 'anybody's else.' The former has been much objected to by some critics, but is perfectly correct," says Professor G. R. Carpenter in "Rhetoric and English Composition."

Sorter, Sort of, see *Kind Of.*

To Speak "To" or "With"

The question is sometimes asked, Is it proper to say "I wish to speak to Mr. Smith," or "I wish to speak with Mr. Smith"? Which form shall we use when calling up someone on the telephone, and the person to whom, or with whom, we wish to speak does not reply himself or herself?

The rule as given in the Standard Dictionary is as follows:

"One speaks to a person when one addresses him, speaks with a person when one converses with him; speaks of or about a person or thing as the subject of remark; speaks on or upon a subject; in parliamentary language, speaks to the question."

Speciality, see *Casuality.*

Specie and Species

"The mouse is a specie of rat, isn't it?" said one speaker.

"No," said the other; "I believe it belongs to a different specie."

The speakers used the word "specie" incorrectly. They should have said "species," which is the same in the singular as in the plural, and means "a group of individuals having common attributes and designated by a common name" (Webster). It is, therefore, incorrect to speak or write of "a specie." The word "species" is derived directly from the Latin, in which language it has various meanings.

There is a word "specie," with a meaning entirely different. It means coin, or hard money, usually of gold or silver, and was much heard in the years following the Civil War. The United States Government had discontinued payment in specie, and the resumption of payment was discussed.

Spectators, see *Audience*.

Splendid

"Splendid" means, when used properly, brilliant, magnificent, inspiring, imposing, etc., but it does not mean, in the best usage, "very good," "excellent," "fine," etc. You may say, for example, "The sun setting behind a range of mountains is a splendid sight," or, "The poetry of Milton affords a splendid example of grandeur in writing," but if you are asked whether the apple you are eating is good, you should not say that it is "splendid," and you cannot, in good English, have a "splendid" time at a picnic.

Spoonfuls

In considering the proper form of the plurals of such words as "spoonful," "cupful," "armful," etc., it must be borne in mind that the unit considered is not the spoon, the arm, the cup, etc., but the material which fills the spoon, etc. Thus, the unit is the spoonful, not the spoon, and as "spoonful" is the name of a thing in itself, the proper form of the plural is found by adding an "s" to the word "spoonful," and not to part of the word, "spoon."

Of course, there are times when the unit is the spoon itself; that is, when two or more spoons are filled. When, for example, you have before you two spoons filled with sugar, you should say "two spoons full," and not "two spoonfuls." But when you take a spoon, fill it with sugar and empty it into your coffee cup, and repeat the process, you have taken two "spoonfuls" of sugar, and not two "spoons full."

Stand For

Although we frequently hear the expression, to "stand for," in the sense of "to agree to, to approve, to permit, to endure," no authority for its use is to be found. It is an expression that has crept into the language in recent years. Of course, as English is a living, growing language, the expression "to stand for" may in time win recognition. But at present it is incorrect.

The Standard Dictionary gives as the test of a new word or phrase that it must fill an "antecedent blank"—that is, if it is to win a place in the language it must supply a need. Now, judged by that test, why should we say "He wouldn't stand for that," when the meaning of the speaker is expressed quite as well by saying, in English that is recognized as being correct, "He would not stand or tolerate or endure or approve that?"

Start

Rossiter Johnson, well known as an author and
184

as a critic, commented not long ago on the misuse of the word "start." He asserted that it is made to do duty for "prepare," "attempt," "begin," "make ready," "set out." Mr. Johnson wrote:

"You do not say that Major Putnam attempted to speak. You say he 'started' to speak. You do not say the tenant prepared to move. You say he 'started' to move. You never say the merchant has begun to reduce his prices. You say he has 'started' reducing prices. You never say that Uncle John set out for Mexico. You say that he 'started' for Mexico.

"Some months ago, when one of our great papers was about to publish an interesting serial story, we were confronted by a great poster on which a conspicuous line advised us to 'start reading it next Sunday.' Some persons 'start in' to do a thing, while others 'start out' to do the same thing."

State and Say

The use of the verb "state" instead of "say," when the latter would express the meaning of the writer or speaker, is considered an affectation. To state is to set forth something in detail, or formally, or with the desire to explain fully. " 'State' properly means to make known specifically, to explain particularly, and is often misused for 'say,' " according to Alfred Ayres in "The Verbalist." "When 'say' says all one wants to say, why use a more pretentious word?" Another authority objects to the expression, "He states that he is going fishing tomorrow," and asserts that "states" is too formal a word, and should be used of some important assertion only. Say, "He says he is going fishing."

Still and Yet

Although these two words, "still" and "yet," have several meanings that are alike, so that they may be used interchangeably, there are also a few meanings that are different. For example, we may say, "While I was still a child, I lived with my aunt," or "While I was yet a child, I lived with my aunt." But in referring to the future the word "yet" has a meaning which is not shared by "still." We say. "He may be successful yet." meaning that success may come to him despite past failures. But if we say, "He may be successful still," we mean that the success which he has enjoyed in the past may be continued in the future.

This is an example, and an especially good example, of the fine distinctions in the uses of words made by careful writers and speakers.

Stop and Stay

How frequently do we heard some one say, or read in a newspaper, "He is stopping at the hotel." A moment's reflection should tell the writer or speaker that a person does not "stop" at a hotel unless he walks or drives to the hotel and halts his progress there. It is proper to say, "The parade stopped at the hotel," meaning that the parade ceased its motion when it reached the hotel. But the parade could not "stay" at the hotel. A person makes a "stay" at a hotel, not a stop, and he stays there. One should not say, "I stopped at the summer resort six weeks," but "I stayed there six weeks."

The true meaning of the word "stop" was well understood by the man who did not invite his professed friend to visit him. He said: "If you come at any time within ten miles of my house, just stop."

Student, see *Scholar*.

To Succeed Himself

In a recent discussion of current politics, the following question and answer were overheard:

"Do you think the Governor will succeed himself?" "Yes, I think the people will elect him to be his own successor."

Now, "to succeed" means (Standard Dictionary) "to be the successor of; especially, to be the heir of or to occupy an official position just after; as, Victoria succeeded William IV; he succeeds his brother by will," and a man cannot succeed himself, or be his own successor. He may succeed another person, who has held an office or position, or one of his terms of office may succeed his own previous term. In the example given at the beginning of this article, the question and reply should have been:

"Do you think the Governor will get another term of office?" "Yes, I think he will be re-elected by the people." Or, "Do you think another man will be elected to succeed our present Governor?" "No, I think he will be re-elected."

Such and So

Do not say, "I never knew such an honest man as my friend Mr. Robinson." Say, instead, "I never knew another man so honest as my friend Mr. Robinson." Do not say, "We had never before seen such a stately house," but say, "We had never before seen so stately a house."

The rule is that the adjective "such" should not be used instead of the adverb "so" to modify an adjective. In other words, it is incorrect to say "such honest" or "such stately" instead of "so honest" or "so stately."

However, when the word "such" means "like this" or "like these," it may be used before another adjective. The following sentence, therefore, is correct: "In such arid regions as border upon the desert, rain seldom falls." This means that rain seldom falls in arid regions like those that border upon the desert.

Sure!

"Are you going to the game to-day?"
And the answer is "Sure!"

The expression "Sure!" employed to mean "yes" or "certainly," has the merits of shortness and of conveying exactly the meaning of the speaker. Perhaps, therefore, it should not be denounced severely. Nevertheless, it is not grammatically correct, save as usage has made it so.

Poets often omit the suffix "ly" from adverbs, and we find "sure" used by them frequently when strict adherence to rules of grammar would require them to write "surely." Dryden wrote, "But sure a general doom on man is past, and all are fools and lovers, first or last."

Surprised, see *Astonished*.

Suspicion

Do not say, "When I saw his face, I suspicioned that all was not well at home." Say, instead, "I suspected that all was not well at home." The word "suspicion," used as a verb, as in the sentence first quoted, is held to be incorrect English by authorities on the language. They call its use a "barbarism," which means that it is employed by the ignorant or uneducated only.

Swell

"I had a swell time at the dance last night."
This use of the word "swell" in the sense of pleasant, agreeable, delightful, etc., is slangy, and disapproved by all authorities.

The same criticism is made of the word "swell" when it is used in the sense of beautiful, fashionable, refined, attractive, elegant, luxurious, expensive, etc. "I met a swell fellow in the country when I had my vacation," said a city girl. She meant that the young man had attracted her greatly; but, of course, she could have said, "I met a fine fellow."

As a noun, the word "swell," to indicate a person of fashion or importance, is also slang, and should not be used.

Taste Of and Tastily

It is not correct, according to many authorities, to say "taste of" a thing, instead of simply "taste" it. Alfred Ayres in "The Verbalist" says, "The 'of' often used in this country in connection with the verbs, 'to taste' and 'to smell' is a Yankeeism." We taste and smell a thing, not taste of, and smell of a thing. It is quite correct, however, to use the word "of" in such expressions as the following: "The butter tastes of garlic" and "the handkerchief smells of the roses among which it has lain." But do not say, "Taste of this jelly"; say, simply, "Taste this jelly."

The use of the word "tastily" in the sense of "tastefully"—that is, "with taste"—is not approved. Do not say, "The contents of the window are tastily arranged"; say, instead, "The contents of the window are tastefully arranged," or, "are arranged in good taste." The books do not condemn this use of the word "tastily" as incorrect, but say that it is a "colloquialism."

Teach, see *Learn*.

Teethache

We hear sometimes that a person is suffering from "teethache." The idea in the mind of the one who says so is that the ache is caused not by one tooth alone, but by two or more, and therefore he should say "teethache," not "toothache."

But the proper term is "toothache," even if the pain has its seat in many teeth.

The rule is that when two nouns are joined, or united, to form a compound noun, the first of the two is never put in the plural form. You may put both feet on a stool, but that does not make it a feetstool, merely a footstool. A man may be—or he may profess to be—a hater of all of the members of the opposite sex, but it is not proper to refer to him as a women-hater, but only as a woman-hater.

When a compound word consists of a noun following a numeral, or number word, the noun is not put in the plural form, but in the singular; thus, it is not proper to speak of a twelve-feet pole, but of a twelve-foot pole, a three-mile race, not a three-miles race.

Terribly, Awfully

While the use of "terrible" and "terribly," in the sense of "severe" and "extremely," is not condemned by some authorities on English, who call such use "colloquial"—that is, frequent in common speech and writing—it is not approved by grammarians. Examples of such use are found in the following sentences: "Last winter the cold was terrible." "I was terribly disappointed when I found that I could not go to the theatre." Say, instead, "the cold was severe"; "I was extremely disappointed."

The same remarks may be made concerning the use of "awful" and "awfully."

Testimony, see *Evidence*.

Thanks or Thank You

Shall we say, in acknowledgment of a favor received, "Thanks" or "Thank you"?

"There are many persons," writes one authority, "who think it questionable taste to use 'thanks' for 'thank you,'" and in one standard dictionary it is asserted that "thanks," meaning "my thanks to you," is a curt expression, while "thank you" or "I thank you" is a form of courteous acknowledgment of a kindness or service."

The writer is acquainted with one man who never says "Thanks" or "Thank you," but always "I thank you," and in such a way that the hearer cannot believe that he really means it. It seems an affectation, even when it is not one.

The question is not one of grammar, but of taste. Some persons can say "thanks" and convey the impression that they are sincerely grateful; while others, as in the case cited, can say "I thank you" without seeming to mean it.

That Instead of So

The word "that" should not be used instead of the word "so," as in the following examples:

"I intended to travel to the Coast, but I did not go that far." Say, instead, "I intended to travel to the Coast, but I did not go so far," or "I did not go so far as that."

"If the case is that bad, we shall have to take other measures." Say, "If the case is so bad," or "If the case is so bad as that."

"He needed a thousand dollars, but he did not ask for that much." Corrected, the sentence reads, "He needed a thousand dollars, but he did not ask for so much," or "for so much as that."

The and A (see also A, An)

"What is your favorite flower?" a girl was asked. She answered, "A rose is my favorite flower." She should have said, "The rose is my favorite flower," not "a rose." The word "the" in this case is employed to distinguish or mark off a class. We should not say, "A seal lives in the ocean," or "A lion is found in the African forests," but, instead, "The seal lives in the ocean" and "The lion is found in the African forests."

The little words "a" (or "an," before a vowel) and "the" are called articles, but some grammarians include them among the adjectives, the words which describe nouns or names of things. "A" or "an" is the indefinite article; that is, it points to or denotes one thing of a kind, but not any definite or particular one, as, "A boy, an orange."

"The" is called the definite article, because it points to or denotes some particular object or objects.

"The," Emphatic Use of

Is the word "the" used correctly in the following sentence?

"He was now recognized by the general public as being the great lawyer, the great orator, the great statesman; and the common folk rejoiced in the high official honors that were showered upon him."

Should the writer not have said, "He was now recognized by the general public as being a great lawyer, a great orator, a great statesman, etc.?"

Such use of the word "the" is correct, but is not common. The writer intended the reader to supply, in his mind, the words "that he was," after the word "statesman," making the sentence read, "He was now recognized by the general public as being the great lawyer, the great orator, the great statesman, that he was," etc. The sentence is more emphatic than if he had used "a" instead of "the."

"The Pair," Etc.

Such expressions as "These shoes are ten dollars the pair," instead of "ten dollars a pair," are seen frequently in advertisements and signs. They are disapproved of by writers on grammar, who tell us that we should use "a" and not "the." To many persons "ten dollars the pair," etc., and similar phrases, seem an affectation.

The dictionary affords no warrant for the use of "the" in such sense. It gives the following as one of the definitions of "a."

"'A' is used in such phrases as one dollar a bushel, with the distributive sense of 'each,' and equivalent to 'per' or the old English preposition 'on.'" The following is cited as an example of the correct use of "a," from "The Deserted Village," by Oliver Goldsmith:

"A man he was to all the country dear,
And passing rich with forty pounds a year."

Them

The use of such expressions as "I saw them boys" is not limited by any means to those who are uneducated or careless in other respects. Perhaps this is due, as are so many other examples of inelegant or faulty speech, to the effect of constant repetition. A person of education hears others employ the expression, "them boys," "those kind," and similar ungrammatical expressions, and falls unconsciously into the same errors.

"Them" is a pronoun, third person, plural, objective case form of "they," and should never be employed as an adjective, before a noun, instead of "those" or "these." Therefore, "I saw them boys," should be "I saw those boys," or, "I saw these boys."

Thence, From, see *From Whence.*
Think, see *Don't Think So;* see *Expect.*

Think For

Do not add an unnecessary "for" after the verb "think," as in the sentence, "You will find that he knows more about that affair than you think for."

Say, simply, "You will find that he knows more than you think." This error is quite common in some parts of the United States, and is probably the survival of an ancient usage that is no longer recognized as good English.

This Here

"Which hat is yours?"

"This here hat is mine."

We hear such expressions often, even among educated people. But the word "here" is not needed. The meaning of the speaker is expressed quite as well, and even better, by saying, "This hat is mine," because he employs one word less to convey his idea.

In some parts of the United States, and among certain classes, the words "this here," "these here," "that there," are frequently run together, becoming one word, as, "thish-yur," "these-yur," "that-er."

Some writers hold that in the breakdown of English grammar in America which they foresee and foretell, such expressions as "this here," and the like, will win places in recognized English. But others maintain that the diffusion of education among the people, now going on at a more rapid rate than ever before, will eliminate such expressions from the speech of all save the most unlearned.

Those Kind, etc.

A very common error, and one that grates with especial harshness on the ear of a person who has been trained in the correct use of English, is the use of such phrases as "those kind" and "these sort." How often we hear, "I cannot bear those kind of people"!

The words "these" and "those" are plural in number—that is, they denote more than one; the words "sort," "kind," etc., are singular in number, indicating one group, one class of persons or objects. According to a simple rule of grammar, the adjective and the noun, when used together, must agree in number—that is, when the noun is singular or plural, the adjective must be singular or plural. Therefore, do not say "I do not like those kind of people," but say, "I do not like that kind of people," or, better, "I do not like people of that kind."

Threaten, see *Promise*.

Three Hundred Per Cent Cheaper

"The vast stock of canned goods left in France by the American Army and now being sold to the public is proving a boon to the French housewife," said a news despatch. "She is now able to go to her grocery and buy canned goods at a price which is sometimes 300 per cent cheaper than the price of the same variety of food canned by the French."

This despatch contained an absurd error in arithmetic as well as one in grammar.

If a thing is 50 per cent cheaper than another, it is sold for one half of the price of the second article. If it is 100 per cent cheaper, the purchase price is abated 100 per cent; that is, the article is not sold at all, but given away. By the same reasoning, if a thing is 300 per cent cheaper, the person who acquired it receives it for nothing, and with it twice what would have have been the purchase price.

Evidently, the writer meant to say that the French housewife bought the American canned goods for one-third the price of the French goods.

Three "Twos"—A Catch Question

Some years ago a correspondent of a leading newspaper wrote to the editor as follows:

"There are a number of words in the English language of the same pronunciation, spelled differently and having various meanings; for example, 'to,' 'too' and 'two.' In writing the sentence, 'There are three "twos" in the English language,' is it correct to use the word 'twos' as I have?"

To this the editor replied:

"But there are not three 'twos' at all. There are three words in the English language which have the sound of the word 'two,' which is an entirely different matter."

Through and Finished

The use of the word "through" in the sense of "finished" or "completed" is condemned by virtually all authorities on English, as a vulgarism. One writer on the proper use of words says:

"Unless you have fallen through a trap door and have finished your career, do not say, 'I am through,' when you mean, 'I am finished.' The school boy says, 'I am through with that lesson,' when he should say, 'I have finished that lesson.' The farmer asks the man in his employ, 'Are you through with that field?' when he should have asked, 'Have you finished plowing that field?' You ask your friend, 'Are you through with that book?' when you should ask, 'Have you finished reading that book?'"

"I am through," meaning "I have finished eating," or "I have dined," is a vulgarism, according to the Standard Dictionary.

To and Too

The rule for the use of these two words, "to" and "too," is given as follows, in "Written English," by Dr. Edwin C. Woolley:

"The word 'to' is correctly used in only two ways: (1) As a preposition; for instance, 'He wrote to me,' 'I object to your words'; (2) as the sign of the infinitive form of the verb; for instance, 'Do you want to ride?' 'No; I don't want to.'

"With an adjective or an adverb, do not use 'to' in the sense of 'more than sufficiently'; use 'too.' Write, 'It is too sour,' 'there are too many people here,' 'he went too fast.'

"Do not use 'to' in the sense of 'also'; use 'too.' Write, 'He laughed, and I laughed too.' "

To the Manner Born

Which is correct, "to the manner born," or "to the manor born?" Both are used in books and magazines.

This is one of the "stock" questions that is certain to confront, sooner or later, every writer on English. It is settled, according to most if not all authorities, that "to the manner born" is the proper form. Webster's International Dictionary treats of this matter and says:

"To the manner born; born to follow or obey a certain practice or custom; also, having lifelong acquaintance with given conditions, customs, etc.; apparently naturally fitted for some occupation, work, or position. The phrase as used by Shakespeare in 'Hamlet' (I, iv., 15) has by some been wrongly understood to refer to a manor, of which manner is an old variant spelling, and hence the phrase, 'to the manor born,' is sometimes used in the sense, 'accustomed to the usages of a locality, or of high or polite society.' "

Transpire and Occur

To "occur" means to take place, to happen, to come to pass; to "transpire" means to become known, to escape from secrecy, to be made public. It is quite common, especially in ordinary speech and in writings in newspapers and magazines, to hear and see the verb "transpire" used instead of "happen" or "occur." Such use is, however, quite incorrect, and is condemned by critics in England and America. "It transpired yesterday, at the meeting of the common council, that permission was withheld," etc., wrote a reporter, but he should have written, "It happened yesterday." etc.

Following is a case of the proper use of the verb "transpire": "At the meeting of the common council yesterday it transpired that last week's action on the street-railway franchise was not final"—that is, it became known that the action was not final.

True Facts

Much ink has been spilled over the question, Is it proper to use the adjectives true, correct, real, etc., with the noun "facts"? Someone says or writes, "The real facts in the case are so and so," and a critic arises to remark that the word "real" is not needed and that the meaning is expressed just as well by saying "The facts in the case are so and so." If we consider a fact simply as something that is done or exists, we may agree with the critics.

But the case is not so simple. The word "fact" has a secondary meaning. According to the Standard Dictionary, it means "something that is asserted to have occurred or existed."

Therefore, we may have facts that are not real or correct or true, given by a person in describing something, and the only way in which we may distinguish these facts from the genuine circumstances of the case is to describe these latter facts as real, true, genuine, correct, etc.

Trust, see *Hope*.

Truth and Veracity

"I cannot vouch for the veracity of his statements, since I do not know him well," said a gentleman who is proud of the correctness of his speech. He should have said, "I cannot vouch for the truth of his statements."

The word "truth" is applied, properly, to the statement; the word "veracity" to the person who makes the statement. Thus, we may say, "I have no doubt of the truth of his assertion, since I know him to be a man of veracity."

We may say "a man of truth," but we should not say, as is sometimes said, "a man of truth and veracity." Alfred Ayres writes: "The loss would be a small one if we were to lose this word, 'veracity,' and its derivatives. 'Truth' and its derivatives would supply all our feeds. In the phrase so often heard, 'A man of truth and veracity,' the word 'veracity' is entirely superfluous, it having precisely the same meaning as 'truth.' The phrase, 'A big, large man,' is equally good diction."

Try And; Try An Experiment

"Try and do it," is not correct. The proper form is, "Try to do it." To say, "Try and do it," means that the person addressed should try and then do; whereas the meaning of the speaker's words is that the person addressed should make an attempt to do something.

A related error is the use of the phrase, "To try an experiment." A little reflection will show the reader that an experiment is not tried; it is made. The experimenter tries to do something by means of the experiment, but, as said, the experiment itself is not tried, but is made.

The Tumult and the Shouting Dies

When Rudyard Kipling published his famous poem, "The Recessional," the greatness of the work was acclaimed by readers and critics, but it was not long before some grammarians arose to say that in the line "The tumult and the shouting dies," the poet had been guilty of an error in grammar.

This was disputed immediately by those who asserted that the line was correct; that the "tumult and the shouting" were one thing, and must therefore take the singular verb, "dies," and not the plural verb, "die."

The controversy raged for a time, and then died down. It is revived occasionally, but it is fairly well agreed now, however, that Kipling was right in saying "dies." One recent writer says: "The two things named are component parts of a whole which, by the union of these two, becomes something different from either, something more hypnotic and terrifying. One fairly feels the silence pictured by the line. What existed a moment ago was more terrible than anything produced by the shouting alone or the tumult alone. It was some one thing, and the singular verb testifies to its many-sided force."

The Two Greatest

When a man pre-eminent in electrical science, one whom the scientific world delighted to honor, died, a newspaper said in an obituary notice:

"On this occasion Lord Kelvin said of him: 'He is one of the world's two greatest electrical engineers.'"

Lord Kelvin's grammar was faulty. He should not have said, "One of the world's two greatest electrical engineers." There could be only one greatest.

The proper way in which to word it is: "He is one of the world's greatest two electrical engineers." Or, if objection is made to this on the ground of awkwardness, one might say: "Of the world's leading electrical engineers, he is one of the greatest two."

Two Miss Smiths or the Two Misses Smith

If we were to decide this question strictly by the rules of grammar, there would be little doubt that we should say, "The Misses Smith," "The Messrs. Brown," etc., instead of "The Miss Smiths," "The Mr. Browns," since the title becomes plural, when reference is made to more than one person, and the name remains the same. But most persons find it easier to form the plural by adding the "s" to the entire phrase or title, rather than to the actual title itself. So they say, "The Miss Smiths," "the Mr. Browns," etc.

They should continue to do so, for there is good authority for the use of "the Miss Smiths," etc. Goold Brown, in "The Institutes of English Grammar," says: "When a title is prefixed to a proper name so as to form a sort of compound, the name, and not the title, is varied to form the plural; as 'The Miss Howards, the two Mr. Clarks.' But a title not regarded as a part of one compound name must be made plural, if it refer to more than one; as 'Messrs. Lambert and Son, The Lords Calthorpe and Erskine.'"

Typewriter or Typist

The machine on which the original of this article was written is called a "typewriter." What is the proper term to apply to the person who uses the machine?

In America we call him or her (generally her) a "typewriter." In England he or she is known more commonly as a "typist."

Ugly

Although there is some authority for the use of the word "ugly" in the sense of vicious, malicious, ill-tempered, etc., it is condemned by many writers, who call it a provincialism or colloquialism. They hold that the word means, when properly used, only "unsightly, displeasing to the eye, distasteful in appearance," etc.

Therefore, we may say "That horse is an ugly animal," meaning that his appearance is not good, but we should not say, "That horse has an ugly temper," but should say instead "That horse has a vicious temper."

An error that is common, and for which no excuse can be found in grammar, is the use of "ugly" as an adverb, as in the following sentence: "When I asked the conductor for a ticket, he acted ugly."

It must be said, however, that it is difficult to find an exact substitute for this use of the word, and in time it may gain a place in the English language. One writer suggests that we say, "The conductor acted very discourteously, or incivilly," but neither of these expressions is as forcible as, or has the same meaning as, "He acted ugly."

Uninterested, see *Disinterested*.

Unique

The word "unique" is frequently misused, being employed in the sense of odd, queer, rare or strange. A person will say, for example, "He is a very unique man; he lives by himself and he will not receive visitors." In having these characteristics, the man described is strange or unusual, but he is not unique. The word "unique" describes something or someone that is the only one of a kind. It is derived from the Latin word "unicus," meaning "single," from "unus," meaning "one."

It is true that some dictionaries and grammarians assert that the word "unique," by extension of its original meaning, has come to signify uncommon or rare; but it is generally held that it is better to confine its use to the original meaning of "only one of a kind."

For example: "Only one copy of the book is known to exist, and this unique volume is now the property of the British Museum."

Universal and General

A recent writer said:

"The custom is universal throughout the United States."

He should have written. "The custom is general throughout the United States."

The word "universal" means, "Of or pertaining to the universe; pertaining to the whole or all, either collectively or distributively." Webster's Dictionary says the following concerning "common," "general" and "universal": "'Common' suggests primarily that in which many share, and hence, that which is usual or often met with; 'general' denotes that which pertains to all, or almost all; 'universal' to all without exception, of the individuals or element, concerned; as, 'a general practice,' 'a universal belief.'"

Unless, see *Except;* see *Without.*
Up To, see *It's Up to You.*

Upward Of

There are in English many words and phrases which are condemned by some authorities, while others take no exception to them. One of the phrases about which there is doubt is "upward, or upwards, of," in the sense of "more than." "This phrase is often used, if not improperly, at least inelegantly, for 'more than,'" says Alfred Ayres, in "The Verbalist"; "thus, 'I have been here for upward of a year'; 'for upward of three quarters of a century she has,' etc., meaning for more than three quarters of a century." But if the reader is accustomed to using the phrase, he may continue to do so, and tell his critics that there is good authority for it, to be found in the Standard Dictionary and elsewhere.

Us Girls

"Father wanted us to go to college, but us girls decided we would rather go to work and earn our living."

The young woman who used the foregoing sentence might have derived benefit from a college training in the expression of English. She should not have said "us girls" but "we girls," since "we girls" is the subject of the verb "decided" and should therefore be in the nominative case, which is "we girls," and not "us girls." If she had said, "Father wanted us girls to go to college," she would not have added, "but us decided to go to work."

Used to Could

The following was overheard in a city trolley car:

"I used to could talk French pretty good—pretty near as good as I could talk English."

"Used to could" is not good English now, and probably never was good English anywhere. There is a similar expression, "used to was" which was in use centuries ago and is now archaic—that is, antiquated—but is still heard in some parts of England and America.

The reader will note, no doubt, the use of "pretty good" by the speaker instead of "pretty well."

Usen't

The verb "use," in one of its senses, is peculiar, in that it is employed properly only in the past tense. It means to do a thing customarily or habitually, or to be accustomed or wont to do something. "Usen't" is, of course, a contraction of "use not." It is incorrect to say, "He use not to do it," or "He usen't to do it." Say instead, "He used not to do it."

We hear frequently an expression that sounds like "yusta" or "yuster," the "u" having the long sound, as, "He yuster go to the beach every day in summer." This is, of course, a careless way of saying "He use to go to the beach," and it is ungrammatical, as pointed out above. The proper expression is, "He used to go to the beach," etc., with full value given to the "d" in the word "used."

Usurp

An opponent of the prohibition law said in a public utterance that "it will never be enforced, because it usurps the rights of everyone."

His use of the word "usurp" was incorrect. To "usurp" means, according to the dictionary, "to seize and hold in possession by force, or without right; applied only to seizure of office, place, functions, powers, rights, etc., as, to usurp a throne."

"Violate" or "infringe upon" would be proper in the sentence quoted. Thus we may say that a law, the act of a person, etc., violates the rights of another or of the public, or infringes upon the rights, not that it "usurps" the rights.

Vain, see *Proud.*

Valuable and Valued

These two words are not exactly similar in meaning, although they are sometimes employed as though they could be used for each other.

"Valuable" means precious, costly, having value; "valued" refers to our estimation of the worth. Bechtel, in "Slips of Speech," says: "'He is one of our most valued contributors,' not 'valuable,' unless you are thinking of the value of his contributions and the smallness of the compensation."

Another authority writes: "The following sentence, which recently appeared in one of the more fastidious of our morning papers, is offered as an example of extreme slipshodness in the use of language: 'Sea captains are among the most valuable contributors to the park aviary.' What the writer probably meant to say is, 'Sea captains are among those whose contributions to the park aviary are the most valuable.'"

Various, see *Different*.

Vast Minority

Not long ago, in describing the opposition that had been made to the holding of a certain sporting event, a writer on sports said:

"Opposition was to be expected, but those who oppose it are in a vast minority."

What he meant to say was that the opposition was confined to a very small minority, not that it was expressed by a "vast" minority. The word "vast" means "very large, immense, huge, massive, boundless, etc." A minority, being the smaller portion of something, cannot, in the very nature of things, be "vast."

Venal and Venial

Although these two words, "venal" and "venial," are not included in the vocabularies of most persons, they are used by writers, and are confused sometimes, owing to the similarity in spelling.

"Venal" means "ready to sell one's influence, vote or efforts for money or other consideration, entirely from sordid motives" (Standard Dictionary). Some of the judges in England in the seventeenth century were venal because they took money to influence their decisions, and the decisions themselves were called venal. If a poet wrote verses praising a patron, in return for receiving money or favor, the verses themselves were called venal.

"Venial" means excusable or forgivable; it is applied to sins or offenses which may be overlooked or pardoned. "Theft on the part of a starving man is one of the most venial offenses," says Woolsey in "Political Science."

Veracity, see *Truth*.

Verbal and Oral

These two words, "verbal" and "oral," are misused frequently. We hear dialogues such as the following: "Did you send him a letter accepting his terms?" "No, I gave him a verbal reply."

For the word "verbal," in the sentence just quoted, the word "oral" should be substituted, since "verbal" means "consisting of words," and "oral" means "by word of mouth." A verbal message may, therefore, be given either in writing or in speech, an oral message only in speech. It should be said, however, that while grammarians generally make this distinction, and express a desire for its general adoption, they say also that the word "verbal" has been employed so long and so generally as a synonym for "oral" that it is probably hopeless to try to establish the distinction in common usage.

Very

The phrase, often used in letter writing, "I am very pleased," is objectionable.

The Century Dictionary gives the meaning of the adverb "very," and comments on its use, as follows: "'Very,' in a high degree; to a great extent; extremely; exceedingly. 'Very' does not qualify a verb directly, and hence also, properly and usually, not a past participle; thus, 'very much frightened,' because 'it frightened him very much'; and so in other cases. This rule, however, is not seldom violated, especially in England; thus, 'very pleased' instead of 'very much pleased.' "

It may be said, therefore, that while this use of "very" is not approved by grammarians, common usage, especially in England, has made it a part of the language. Many authorities hold that usage makes grammar, in the long run, despite the opinions of grammarians.

Vice, see *Crime*.

Victuals

"He does not enjoy his victuals as he used to," said an old woman, referring to her husband.

Whereupon the criticism was made that she should not have used the word "victuals," but should have said "food," instead.

But "victuals" is strong English, and has been a member of the family for many, many years. It would be a pity, on historical grounds—if on no other—to lose it. It must be said, however, that some authorities object to it, saying that it is no longer recognized as the best English, but is "colloquial" or "dialectic."

It was good English when the King James version of the Bible was written. "Then we had plenty of victuals," says Jeremiah 44, 17.

Virtually, see *Practically*.

Vocation and Avocation

The use of "avocation" for "vocation" is seen frequently, especially in newspapers, and some writers on good English defend it. But others, who base their arguments on the derivation, or beginning, of the two words, hold that we should say "vocation" when we mean the regular occupation of a person, and should not say "avocation." The latter word, strictly speaking, means some-

follow, and not the individual member of the Council."

In England the pronoun "who" is used frequently in referring to the Government, which is then regarded as a body of individuals, rather than as an impersonal body. But this use of "who" is seen seldom if ever in the United States.

Whom

The word "whom" is frequently used incorrectly instead of "who," as in the following sentence, taken from a newspaper article: "Forced to face this fact at last, she decided to keep Martin who, being older, was less trouble than Margaret and whom she knew would be cared for by friends." The word "whom" in this sentence should be "who."

"Who" is the subject of the verb "would be cared for," and therefore must be in the nominative case of the pronoun—that is, "who"—and not in the objective case, which is "whom." The words "she knew" are a separate grammatical clause, and have no influence on the rest of the sentence.

Some of the best known authors have been guilty of this error of the misuse of "whom" for "who."

Widow Woman

Although a great deal of fun has been made of this expression, "widow woman," and its use is probably not so common as it was in former years, it is still heard, especially among unlettered persons.

"Since widows are always women, why say 'a widow woman'?" asks Ayres, in "The Verbalist," and he goes on to say that it would be perfectly correct to say "a widowed woman." Ayres says also that there is good authority for using the

213

word "widowhood" in speaking of men as well as of women, but there are dictionaries which do not agree with him, and tell us that we should use "widowhood" only of a woman, and "widower-hood" when we refer to a man.

Will, see *Could;* see *Shall;* see *Would.*

Willing That

"I am not willing, however, that he should say that I refused to pay the money."

While not altogether incorrect, this sentence is couched in English that is awkward. Instead of saying, "willing that he should say," it would be better to express it thus: "I am not willing, however, to have him say that I refused to pay the money." In some parts of the United States one may hear, "I am not willing for to have him say," etc., but that is clearly poor English.

Witch, Not Wizard

Several times, in referring to Mlle. Suzanne Lenglen, the famous French lawn tennis player, newspapers referred to her as "the feminine wizard of the courts." One sporting writer in New York said: "Mlle. Lenglen stood out as the wizard of the tennis courts."

This use of "wizard" in referring to a woman is incorrect. The proper term is "witch," of which the Standard Dictionary says: "The term was formerly applied to both men and women, but it is now generally restricted to women, as opposed to 'wizard.'" And of "wizard" the same authority writes: "One supposed to be in league with the devil; a male witch; sorcerer."

It will be seen that one refers to a woman as a "witch," and to a man as a "wizard."

Without Instead of Unless

The word "without" is often used incorrectly,

when it is made to do duty for "unless," as in the following cases:

"You will never live to my age without you place a check on your habits of eating and drinking, and exercise more." "I shall not go to Europe without my wife consents." In the first instance, use "unless," instead of "without." In the second sentence, you may use the word "without," but only if you change the form of the sentence as follows: "I shall not go to Europe without the consent of my wife." If you prefer the form first quoted, you must say: "I shall not go to Europe unless my wife consents."

Wizard, see *Witch*.

Woman or Lady (see also Saleslady)

There has been much discussion concerning the proper use of the words "woman" and "lady." Writers on good English are, generally, in agreement that the term "lady" is used far too often, and that "woman" should be substituted for it in many cases. "Such expressions as 'She is a fine lady, a clever lady, a well dressed lady, a good lady, a modest lady, a charitable lady, an amiable lady, a handsome lady, fascinating lady' and the like, are studiously avoided by persons of refinement," says Alfred Ayres, in "The Verbalist." In each of the cases which he cites, put the word "woman" in place of "lady," and note how much better the expression sounds. Is it not better to say, "She is a charitable woman," for example, than "She is a charitable lady"?

The old-time expression, "John Jones and lady," meaning "John Jones and Mrs. Jones," or "John Jones and his wife," is passing out of use, or has passed entirely in most places. Some old-fashioned folks still say, "I met my friend and his lady" when they mean "I met my friend and his wife."

Would and Should (see also Shall and Will)

"I would like," "I would prefer," etc., are poor English. They ignore the well recognized shade of difference between "will" and "shall." It is better to say "I should like," "I should prefer," etc.

Would Rather, see *Had Rather*.
Yet, see *Still*.

You-all

This is an expression in colloquial use in the Southern states to mean "all of you" or, simply, "you" in the plural. It meets the test of usage, since it expresses the meaning of the speaker, and is understood perfectly by the hearer.

Some writers of stories in Southern dialect—or so-called Southern dialect—place in the mouths of the Southern speakers the expression "you all" in reference to a single person. This is incorrect. Even educated Southerners use the expression "you all" habitually, but they do so only in the plural; that is, as applying to two or more persons. They do not say "you all" when speaking to or referring to only one. "It is possible that the expression (in the singular number) may be used somewhere in the mountain districts in the South, but it is certain that educated Southerners always have more than one person in mind," says the "Literary Digest."

You Said It!

The phrase "you said it!" is certainly slang. Besides, it is overworked; it is used very many times when one word such as "yes," or "certainly," or when a short phrase, such as "of course," would answer the purpose.

Any person who wishes to be known as a user

of good English is well advised to avoid such phrases as "You said it!"

Yourn, see Hisn.

ADJECTIVES AND ADVERBS

Adjective and Adverb

It is not uncommon for a person who is not well versed in English grammar to use an adjective when an adverb is required. (An adjective is a word that modifies a noun, or name word, and an adverb is a word that modifies a verb, or action word.) An example of this kind of error was noted in a newspaper article. It read as follows:

"The manager did not appear, but the team played none the poorer for his absence." Corrected, the sentence reads: "The manager did not appear, but the team played none the more poorly (or none the worse) for his absence." The adjective is "poor"; the adverb is "poorly," comparative form of the adjective is "poorer," and of the adverb, "more poorly." Therefore, as we cannot say, in correct English, "The team played poor," we cannot say, also, "The team played poorer," but must say, as noted, "The team played more poorly."

Sometimes poets, by what is known as "poetical license," which permits them to violate the rules of grammar on occasion, employ the adjective for the adverb.

Comparison of Adjectives

It is an oft-repeated rule in English, and one that is, perhaps, familiar to most readers, that one should use "more" in reference to two persons or objects, and "most" in reference to more than two. But the rule is violated so often in speech, and examples of its violation occur so frequently in writing, that it is well to emphasize it, even at the risk of too frequent repetition.

An example of the error was noted in an account of a lawn tennis match. It was said that a certain British player "will probably encounter Robert Kinsey, the most formidable of the two brothers." This should read, "will probably encounter Robert Kinsey, the more formidable of the two brothers."

"Most" is, in the language of the grammarians, the mark of the superlative, or highest; and there can be no highest when two are concerned, only a higher.

Misplaced Adverbs

An adverb is a verb used to modify a verb, a participle, an adjective or another adverb, and generally expresses time, place, degree or manner. Most adverbs end in "ly," but there are many which do not have that ending.

Frequently persons who are not very careful in writing or speaking misplace the adverb in a sentence. Examples of incorrect usages, with corrections, are given here:

Incorrect: "I shall do what you request readily." Corrected: "I shall readily do what you request."

Incorrect: "I have only seen him once." Corrected: "I have seen him once only."

Incorrect: "We not only found him engaged in his work, but happy in it." Corrected: "We found him not only engaged in his work, but happy in it."

Position of the Adverb

"May we be never hasty," or "May we never be hasty," which is correct?

The word "never" is an adverb, belonging to the class of adverbs of time, and it may be placed before or after the verb "be" which it modifies, in the sentence quoted. In "English Grammar," by Prof. George R. Carpenter, it is stated that "The adverb usually immediately precedes or follows the word which it modifies." Therefore, it will be seen that either of the sentences quoted is correct. However, in ordinary usage, probably most persons would prefer the form, "May we never be hasty."

Bad or Badly

It seems to be natural to say or write, "to feel badly," but it is incorrect. Say, "I feel bad." The verbs "be," "seem," "look," "taste," "smell" and "feel" should be followed not by adverbs (words ending in "ly") but by adjectives, which have no such ending. Thus, do not say, "The rose smells sweetly," but say, "The rose smells sweet." Do not say, "The bread tastes bitterly," but, "The bread tastes bitter."

Of course, there are cases in which judgment must be used. For example, it is proper to say, "The child looks cold," but "He looks coldly upon my proposal." Do not say, "Did you sleep good last night?" Say, "Did you sleep well last night?"

Chiefest

If "chief" means "highest in rank or position. most important, most distinguished," etc., as the dictionaries say it does, how can one use the term "chiefest?" It seems to be contradictory of the rules of grammar, yet it is used by some good writers. For example, the London "Times" said not long ago:

"In lands where peace is cherished as the chiefest of blessings, it will be welcomed with profound satisfaction."

Webster's Dictionary says of "chiefest" that

it is now "literary or archaic," which means that while it was good English long ago, it is no longer in common use. Shakespeare uses it, in the expression, "our chiefest among ten thousand."

We may conclude, that while "chiefest" was formerly good in literary use, it is better in common language nowadays to use "chief," without the addition of "est."

Easier

"We are both studying French, but he is making better progress than I. He seems to learn it easier than I do."

The speaker should have said, "He learns it more easily than I do." In the language of the grammarians, the error here consists of using an adjective, "easier" (the comparative form of "easy") instead of an adverb, "more easily" (the comparative form of the adverb "easily") to modify a verb.

Illy

Although some dictionaries recognize the word "illy" and give it a place in their pages (the Standard Dictionary says that it is used but is "rare"), many authorities agree in condemning the word, and some of them deny that there is such a word. They assert that the proper form is "ill" for both the adverb and the adjective. That is, we must say, "The man is ill," and also, a thing is ill formed, or ill done, or ill made, or ill constructed, or ill put together, but not illy formed, illy made, etc.

Louder

"Talk louder" or "talk more loudly." Which is correct?"

Speaking strictly "by the book," perhaps, the

majority of authorities on correct English would say that "more loudly" is correct. But there is good authority for saying that "louder" is equally correct. For example, the Standard Dictionary gives "loud" as an adverb, and defines it thus: "with loudness; loudly." Of course, if one may say, "He speaks loud," one may say "He speaks louder," etc.

In a newspaper account of a trial it was said that "the lawyer, shouting louder still, shook his finger in the face of the witness."

Regular

We often hear people say, "He eats his meals regular." In a newspaper account of the training of one of the principals in a prize fight, it was said that he "is feeling better than ever in his ring career, is eating regular and heartily, and is getting plenty of sleep."

Do not say, "eating regular"; say, instead, "eating regularly." The newspaper man was not consistent. If he had said, "eating regular" and "hearty," he would have been guilty of two errors; but he used "regular," which was incorrect, and "heartily," which was correct. "Regular" is an adjective, and should be used only in connection with nouns, while "regularly" is an adverb and should be used with verbs. Of course, you may say, "He eats regular meals."

Safely or Safe

Should one say, "The traveler arrived safely at his destination," or "The traveler arrived safe at his destination"?

The latter is the correct form. We should use the adjective "safe," not the adverb "safely," because in the sentence quoted the reference is made not to the action of the verb "arrived," but to the condition of the subject of the sentence, which is the noun "traveler"; that is, the traveler was safe when he arrived at his destination.

Slow or Slowly

"There is only one excuse," said a recent writer, "for the use of the words 'Drive Slow' on a signboard instead of 'Drive Slowly.' That excuse is found when the board is so narrow that there is no room for the two letters 'ly.'"

But the dictionaries do not uphold his contention. They give "slow" as a synonym for "slowly"; that is, "slow" is used as an adverb as well as an adjective.

It is quite probable, of course, that the coming of the automobile, which has introduced so many words into the English language and others, has made "Drive Slow" good English. The phrase, or command, is seen in many places on signboards.

Two Best

In a paragraph published in a newspaper which is well edited and is ordinarily accurate in its choice of words, the following sentence was noted:

"Carefully selecting the two best oranges from her basket, she laid them beside the sleeping child, and departed."

Now, there could not have been two best oranges in the basket. There could have been only one best, since "best" means better than any of the others. But, just as there could be only one best, there could be two that were better than the others, three that were better, etc. And the proper way in which to express this is to place the word "best" before the numeral adjective, thus: "Carefully selecting the best two oranges from her basket," etc. "The captain was instructed to select for the dangerous duty the best three men in his company," not "the three best men."

ARTICLES

The

The little word, "the," which is called by grammarians the definite article, is often misused, being placed in sentences where it does not belong, and being left out where it should be used. Often such misuse causes misunderstanding of the meaning of the writer or speaker. For example, suppose you say, "The president and secretary of the lodge attended the meeting." This is correct if the offices of president and secretary are united in one person; that is, if there is one man who is both president and secretary. But if there are two men, one of whom is the president and the other is the secretary, the sentence should read, "The president and the secretary of the lodge attended the meeting." The article should be repeated; then there is no room for misunderstanding the speaker or the writer.

When we say, "the black and white horse" we mean one horse which is marked with the two colors; but when we say, "The black horse and the white horse," we mean two horses, one black and one white.

A Historian or An Historian

"Shall we say, 'a historian' or 'an historian,' 'a historical romance' or 'an historical romance'?"

This is a question that is often raised, and the matter is in dispute. Probably in the United States the general usage and the opinions of the authorities favor the use of "a" rather than "an" before such words as "historian" and "historical," on the ground that the "h" is pronounced. Some authorities, especially in England, hold, however, that when the syllable beginning with "h" is unaccented, as in the examples quoted, it is better to use "an" as better sounding. In "The

Queen's English," by Dean Alford, an English writer, we are told:

"We cannot aspirate with the same strength the first syllables in the word 'history' (first syllable accented) and 'historian' (first syllable unaccented) and, in consequence, we commonly say 'a history' but 'an historian.'"

An Hotel or A Hotel

The question is asked sometimes, Should one say "an hotel" or "a hotel," etc.? It is correct to say "a hotel," because the "h" in "hotel" is sounded. Before words that begin with "h," but in which the "h" is not sounded—such words as "heir, honor, and hour"—the proper article to use is "an."

There are words that begin with an opening vowel, but which are sounded as if beginning with a consonant. Examples of such words are "one," "unit," "university." Before such words it is necessary to use the article "a," not the article "an." We say "a university," not "an university."

The same rule governs when an adjective comes between the article and the noun. Thus, we say "an apple," but, "a ripe apple."

CONSTRUCTION OF SENTENCES

Misplaced Phrases

Of all errors to which writers are prone, probably the most common is that of the misplaced phrase; that is, the placing of a phrase in such position that it does not refer to the subject to which the writer intends it to refer, but to something else. An example is found in the "Life of Queen Victoria," by Lytton Strachey:

"Under Disraeli's tutelage, the British dominions over the seas had come to mean much more to her than ever before."

As this is written, it seems to say that the British dominions were under the tutelage, or care, of Disraeli. But the writer meant that Victoria was under Disraeli's tutelage, and he should have worded the sentence differently, perhaps as follows:

"To Victoria, under Disraeli's tutelage, the British dominions over the seas had come to mean much more than ever before."

"Having fallen asleep while reading, the flimsy hangings of her bed caught fire from the lamp standing by her bedside, and she was entirely consumed in the flames."

As it reads, the phrase, "Having fallen asleep while reading," refers to "hangings," according to the rules of grammar. But that is, of course, absurd. The hangings did not fall asleep, but the woman. Therefore the sentence should read:

"Having fallen asleep while reading, she was entirely consumed in the flames when the flimsy hangings of her bed caught fire from the lamp standing by her bedside."

Writing in the "New York Sun" on "What We Do to Words," Rossiter Johnson, author of "The Alphabet of Rhetoric," "The Art of Elocution," etc., said:

"It is common for obituary sketches to begin with this formula: 'Born in Boston, he emigrated at an early age to the far West.' That may be good Latin construction, but it is not good English. Being born in Boston does not oblige one, either as a necessity or as a custom, to emigrate to the far West. But that must be implied, if we hold the sentence to be good English.

"Strike it out, and in place of it write, in straightforward, simple style: 'He was born in Boston, and (or but) at an early age he emigrated to the far West.'"

225

Misplaced Clauses

"The sandwiching of a clause between a subject and a second verb often gives amusing results," says "Handbook for Newspaper Workers," by G. M. Hyde. The book gives the following examples:

Faulty:—"Bud dropped into the trench where the wounded German lay and kicked open the dugout barrier."

Better:—"After dropping into the trench where the wounded German lay, Bud kicked open the dugout barrier."

Faulty:—"William Reeder, a farmer, was fatally injured when his house collapsed and died a few hours later."

Better—"William Reeder, a farmer, died a few hours after receiving fatal injuries in the fall of his house."

Incorrect Phrasing

"As a boy in the country, my father had to drive with me ten miles to the nearest town, in order that I might attend school daily." Now, the meaning of the writer of this sentence is clear. He means to say that when he was a boy in the country his father had to drive with him ten miles daily, etc. But from the point of view of the grammarian and the person who wishes to speak and write English correctly, the sentence is absurd. As it stands, it means, grammatically, that when the father was a boy in the country, etc. Corrected, the sentence should read, "When I was a boy in the country," etc.

Another example of the same error in sentence construction is found in the following: "When a few years old, the family moved to Chatham, and Dickens always remembered this time as the happiest days of his life." This should be corrected to read, "When Dickens was a few years old, his family moved to Chatham; he always remembered this period as the happiest of his life."

The following extract is made from a recent sporting article:

"Tad Jones has made a proposition to the big Eastern schools which should be adopted. Failing to agree with him on the proposition to place an absolute bar against all athletes, he suggests a two-year residence rule."

Examine the last sentence, beginning with the word "failing." To what does the word "failing," which belongs to the class of words known in grammar as participles, refer? To nothing discoverable in the sentence, unless it be the word "he," but that is, of course, impossible. The sentence should read:

"If the authorities should fail to agree with him on the proposition to place an absolute bar against all athletes, he would suggest a two-year residence rule."

"After having been incapacitated from business for a full year, it was announced that the ablest doctors in America had been called into consultation as to the advisability of performing a very critical operation."

Attention is called to the phrase beginning with "after" and closing with "year." Evidently, the writer intends to refer to the patient, but the name appears nowhere in the sentence. It is incorrect, from the point of view of the grammarian. The sentence should be recast to read: "After he had been incapacitated from business," etc., or, "The patient having been incapacitated from business."

Not long ago there died a man who had written a useful text book on science. Wishing to pay a tribute to him, a man who had assisted in editing the book wrote:

227

"A born teacher, every letter to me contained helpful suggestions. He counted on one grasping his points without wide discussion."

The sentence beginning "A born teacher" will not bear analysis by a grammarian. To what does "a born teacher" refer? Surely not to "every letter" and also not to "me." The sentence should be recast to read as follows:

"He was a born teacher, and every letter to me contained helpful suggestions." Or the writer might have said:

"A born teacher, he wrote letters to me, every one of which contained helpful suggestions."

Poorly Constructed Sentences

From a newspaper article the following was taken as an example of faulty construction:

"Henry Thompson was twice divorced before he married the wife who is seeking a separation in 1906."

From the context it is clear that what the writer meant to say was:

"Henry Thompson was twice divorced before he married, in 1906, the wife who is seeking a separation"—that is, who is seeking a separation now.

A newspaper printed a picture of a man addressing a crowd, but the greater part of the crowd, or all of it, was shown with backs turned toward the speaker. Under the picture was printed the following description:

"The German delegate Sax, making his speech at Moscow, while the Third Internationale was sitting, in which he attacked Lenin. After making his statements against the head power, nobody paid any attention to what he had to say and turned their backs on the speaker."

There are two errors in the second sentence quoted. It should read:

"After he had made his statements against the head power, nobody paid any attention to what he had to say, and all turned their backs on the speaker."

Some Awkward Sentences

The following sentences are given in "Standards of English," by John J. Mahoney, as examples of "awkwardness" that are encountered, frequently:

"My parents, after hearing the story of the wreck, they were very glad to see us." (Omit the word 'they')

"The sleigh was very large, composed of twenty-five boys and girls." (Say, "The sleigh, which was very large, contained twenty-five boys and girls.")

"Once in a while they take the mules that can see out of the mines." (Say, "Once in a while the mules that can see are taken out of the mines.")

"On the train looking out of the windows could be seen vast forests and cows feeding in the pastures." (Say, "Looking from the windows of the train, we could see vast forests, and cows feeding in the pastures.")

There is a class of error, frequently encountered, which consists of using incorrectly the passive voice of the verb—that is, that form of the verb which indicates that the subject of the sentence is acted upon. For example, "Bills are requested to be paid monthly." This should be changed to, "It is requested that bills be paid monthly."

Another example is, "But as soon as the whole body is attempted to be modeled, a disproportion among its various parts results." This may be expressed much better thus: "But as soon as an attempt is made to model the whole body," etc.

"The offense which is attempted to be charged should be alleged under another section of the statute." Change this to, "The offense which it is attempted to charge should be alleged," etc.

One authority on English grammar criticizes such errors severely, and calls them examples of "slipshod construction."

Incorrect Use of the Participle

A participle is a word derived from a verb, and is so called because it "participates" in the properties of a verb. It has the uses or properties of a verb, and of an adjective or a noun, and is generally formed by adding "ing," "ed" or "d" to a verb. Thus, the participles formed from the verb "love" are "loved" and "loving."

A participle should refer grammatically to the noun to which it refers in sense. This rule is violated frequently, even in some cases by writers who are ordinarily careful. Here is an example: "Partly buried in the sand, he saw a large sea shell." While the sense of this is clear, grammatically it is nonsense. It says that the observer was partly buried in the sand, and not the shell. The sentence should be recast as follows: "He saw a large sea shell partly buried in the sand."

Dislocation of Words

"Dislocation" is the name that is given by some writers on grammar and rhetoric to the error of arranging words in a sentence in such order that the sense is obscured or hidden, or the sentence is made ridiculous. Following are examples of such "dislocation"; the errors are seen easily: "Milton's 'Paradise Lost' is a poem about Satan divided into twelve parts."

"I heard of the sale of Ford's Theater where

President Lincoln was assassinated for Government purposes."

"She wore earrings in her ears that had been her grandmother's."

"Wanted, a room for a gentleman with two front windows looking out on the street."

Getting the Time Mixed

The following is taken from a newspaper article:

"Princeton's football squad began intensive preparation for the Harvard game this afternoon, although the battle with the Crimson will not be staged until Nov. 5."

The meaning of the writer is not expressed well. He means, evidently, that the game is to take place Nov. 5, and not "this afternoon." If he had closed the sentence with the word "afternoon" the meaning would not have been clear. The sentence should be recast as follows:

"Princeton's football squad this afternoon began intensive preparation for the Harvard game, although the battle with the Crimson will not be staged until Nov. 5."

The Use of "Only"

In speaking, the proper placing of the word "only" in a sentence, in order to convey the meaning intended to be conveyed, is not so important as it is in writing. That is because the mind grasps the meaning of the speaker quickly, and the impression passes quickly. But in writing the improper placing of "only" causes, or should cause, adverse criticism.

For example, do not say or write, "He only lent me a dollar," when you mean to say, "He lent me a dollar only." In the first case the meaning is that the dollar was lent only, not given. But if you mean that the sum lent was one dollar, and no more, say "He lent me a dollar only." The difference in meaning, it will be seen readily, is expressed by the placing of the word "only."

A Crab With Eyebrows

Writing to the "New York Evening Post," a correspondent poked fun at the English used by a popular novelist. The correspondent said:

"You may be interested in the following data on the anatomy of crabs. On page 1 of a story I read:

"'Columbus wagged a cheery tail and expressed complete agreement. He was watching a small crab hurrying among the stones with a funny frown between his brows.'

"Now, I never knew that crabs had brows."

You have to read the sentence carefully to get the meaning of the author. She (it is a woman writer) would have made her meaning perfectly clear if she had recast her sentence thus:

"With a funny frown between his eyes, he was watching a small crab scurrying among the stones."

Making a Home Run on His Mind

One does not expect perfect English from baseball writers and experts in other sports, and perhaps it is just as well that they do not stick closely to the rules of grammar, for if they did American readers would lose much interest and amusement. But—also perhaps—they should avoid such sentences as the following, which is quoted from a newspaper article:

"It is a fact that he has something other than an idea of making a home run on his mind every time he steps to the plate."

Now, the player makes home runs, but he does not make them on his mind, as this sentence expresses it. He makes them on the diamond. The sentence, to be grammatical, should read:

"It is a fact that he has on his mind something other than a home run every time he steps to the plate."

Was the Train "Traveling"?

Some grammatical errors are amusing to the person who reads carefully, or whose ear and mind are trained to detect such errors when they occur in speech. One such error was noted recently in a letter received from Europe. It read:

"While traveling in Norway last month, my train halted at a small wayside station in an isolated district."

Now, if this sentence is analyzed, the reader will see that, according to the rules of grammar, the phrase, "While traveling in Norway last month," seems to refer to the train. But it was not the train that was traveling in Norway, but the passenger. Therefore, he should have written:

"While I was traveling in Norway last month, my train halted," etc. Of course, in the uncorrected sentence, his meaning is clear, and therefore the sentence might be defended, but from the viewpoint of the grammarian it is incorrect.

CONTRACTIONS

"Don't," "Doesn't," Etc.

Such contractions as "don't," "doesn't," and the like have made places for themselves in colloquial English. "Whatever may be said against employing contractions in dignified discourse, their use in colloquial speech is too firmly established to justify our censure," says John H. Bechtel in "Slips of Speech."

DOUBLE NEGATIVES

Never But

"Mr. Barnes said in all his experience he had never seen but occasionally the euphorbia."

The foregoing sentence occurred in an article describing explorations in Africa. (The euphorbia is an African plant.)

The sentence is incorrect. The word "never" should be omitted, making the sentence read, "he had seen but occasionally the euphorbia." As it reads, uncorrected, it means: "Mr. Barnes said in all his experience he had never seen the euphorbia, but occasionally he had seen it," which is, of course, incorrect and contradictory.

The error lies in the use of "never" and "but" each of which is a negative, together in one sentence, violating the rule against the use of a double negative.

No Unmistakable Language

From a magazine story the following was taken:

"She was greatly excited; in no unmistakable language she announced her determination to recover the ring, if she had to follow him to the end of the earth."

In using the term, "no unmistakable," the author was guilty of what is known in grammar as a "double negative" that is, one negative is expressed by the use of the word "no" and another by the prefix "un" in "unmistakable."

"No unmistakable language" is, therefore, the same as "mistakable language," language about which there could be a mistake. This was, of course, the exact reverse of what the writer intended to say. He should have written, "In unmistakable language she announced her determination," etc.

This error is not an uncommon one, and should be guarded against carefully.

Nobody Hardly

"Although the outside world was talking about his exploit, nobody hardly paid any attention to him as he walked down the village street."

Such use as the above of the word "hardly" with the word "nobody" is not uncommon, but is incorrect. Each of these two words is a negative, and the rule declares that in English two negatives contradict each other, and make an affirmative. Therefore, the sentence quoted should be corrected to read, "hardly anybody paid any attention to him."

"The use of two negatives in a sentence is much more common than is generally supposed," says Bechtel, in "Slips of Speech." "To assume that only those who are grossly ignorant of grammatical rules and constructions employ them is an error. Writers whose names are as bright stars in the constellation of literature have slipped on this treacherous ground."

NOMINATIVE AND OBJECTIVE

As Much As Me

Writing about certain words which are frequently used incorrectly, a critic said:

"I hope you dislike these words as much as me."

Whereupon a keen observer wrote:

"But except for his carelessness there is no reason to dislike the critic."

The sentence should have read:

"I hope you dislike these words as much as I," or, "as much as I do." When you say "I hope you dislike these words as much as me" you are saying, "I hope you dislike these words as much as you dislike me," is not meant.

Better Than Me

"Yes, John's a good workman; he does some things better than me, but I can do repair work better than him."

In this sentence, the words "me" and "him" are used incorrectly. The sentence should read, "Yes, John's a good workman; he does some things better than I, but I can do repair work better than he." The grammatical reason for this correction is found in the fact that the pronouns "I" and "he" are subjects of verbs which are not expressed, but only understood.

A little thought will make this clear to the reader. He would not say or write, "He does some things better than me do them, but I can do repair work better than him can do it." That sounds absurd to any user of English. But substitute "I" for "me," and "he" for "him," and the sentence reads smoothly enough: "He does some things better than I can do them, but I can do repair work better than he can do it."

Between You and I

"Between you and I," says the careless speaker, "I do not like that fellow." Probably the speaker has been taught, in school, the rule of grammar which says that in English all prepositions govern the objective case; that is, the word which follows a preposition must be in the objective case, but he has forgotten the rule.

Now, "between" is a preposition—a word used before a noun or pronoun to show the relation between the person or thing named and the idea expressed by some other word or phrase in a sentence. And "I" (used incorrectly in the phrase "between you and I") is a pronoun and should not be "I" at all, but "me," since "me" is the objective form of the personal pronoun, first person singular.

All of the above, expressed in simple English, means simply this: Never say "between you and I"; say "between you and me."

He Used Wrongly for Him

"Should not a Christian community receive with open arms he who comes out into the world with clean hands and a clean heart?"

In the foregoing sentence the word "he" should be "him." It is, speaking in the language of the grammarian, in the objective case, the object of the verb "receive," and as such should be put in the objective form of the personal pronoun "he," which is "him," not "he." If the clause, "who comes out into the world," etc., is omitted, the error becomes apparent at once. You would not say, "A Christian community should receive he."

Similar errors are the following:

"He would not believe we boys," instead of "He would not believe us boys."

"The spoils belong to he who has gained the victory," instead of "to him."

It's Me, Etc.

"Who is there?"

"It's me," answers the ungrammatical or unthinking person, thereby helping to keep alive an error which is condemned by all grammarians. The proper reply to such a question as the one printed above is, "It is I," "it is he," "it is she," etc., and not "It is me," "it is him," "it is her," etc. Unfortunately for the purity of English speech, this error is very common; even well educated persons seem to fall into it easily. It has been defended by some educators.

The grammatical rule governing such cases is that after "am," "are," "is," "was," and other forms of the verb "to be," the pronoun must be in the nominative case. "I saw a man walking down the street, and I think you were him." Substitute "he" for "him." "Who did you say it was?" "It was her." Change "her" to "she."

In commenting on a controversy over the expression, "It is me," which was called allowable by the superintendent of schools of Chicago, the occupant of "The Lexicographer's Easy Chair," in the "Literary Digest," wrote:

"The form 'It is me,' or 'It's me' is condemned as illiterate by grammarians, and there is no need of it. Admit it as colloquial usage or idiomatic English, and where are you going to draw the line between the literate and the illiterate?

"If you do admit it, then you must admit its congeners, 'How come?'; 'Between you and I'; 'he done it'; 'I seen him do it'; and a thousand more. Unquestionably, English both in form and in combination is the greatest hodgepodge of modern times, but that is no reason for allowing 'jazz' English to run riot over the land."

Let You and I Do It

"Let you and I go to the theater to-night," we hear. It is incorrect. The correct form is "Let you and me go to the theater to-night," although this may sound queer. The explanation is simple. "Let" is a transitive verb; that is, it must have an object or objects. And the objects in the sentence quoted are "you" and "me" (not "I"). They must, therefore, be in the objective case.

None Cared But Her

Should one say, "None cared for him but her?" or "None cared for him but she?"

According to the older grammarians, notably Goold Brown, who wrote the monumental "Grammar of English Grammars," we should say "None cared for him but she." But some more recent writers assert that "None cared for him but her" is a perfectly correct English idiom.

The argument advanced by Goold Brown and those who agree with him is that the words "cared for him" are to be "understood" in the sentence quoted. We cannot say, of course, "None cared for him but her cared," but must say, "None cared for him but she cared." Those who support the "her" theory say that the word "but," meaning "excepting," is a preposition, and should therefore be followed by the objective case, which is "her," not "she."

Who and Whom

"Who do you refer to?" says the careless speaker, ignorant of, or ignoring, the difference between "who" and "whom." The question should be worded, "Whom do you refer to?" or, better, "To whom do you refer?" since it is well to avoid closing a sentence with a preposition when possible to do so. The pronoun "who" is in the nominative case; "whom" is in the objective case; in this instance it is the object of the preposition "to."

"Who do you take that man to be?" asks a speaker. The wording is incorrect. He should say, "Whom do you take that man to be?" since in this case the pronoun "whom" is in the objective case, to agree with the noun "man," to which it refers.

"Who should I see coming but my friend?" In this case "who" should be "whom," because the pronoun is the object of the verb "see."

POSSESSIVES

The Use of " 's "

Let us consider the two phrases, "An anecdote of George Washington," and "An anecdote of George Washington's." Is not the difference in meaning of the phrases easily apparent, without much reflection? In the first case, we mean "an anecdote referring to or relating to George Washington"; in the second, we mean "an anecdote told by Washington." Another example: "A portrait of Brown" and "A portrait of Brown's."

"No precise rule has ever been given to guide us in our choice between these two forms of the possessive case," says Alfred Ayres in "The Verbalist." "Sometimes it is not material which form is employed; where, however, it is material —and it generally is—we must consider the thought we wish to express, and rely on our discrimination."

Some writers call such expressions as "A story of Washington's" a peculiarity of idiom; but it will be seen from the foregoing that sometimes a real difference in meaning is shown by such usage.

"Some One Else's"

An old controversy is the one over "some one else's" and "someone's else."

While supporters of the latter form are not wanting, and it is upheld by some authorities, the general opinion is favorable to the form "some-one else's." One writer argues as follows:

"When we were youngsters it was explained to us that the apostrophes used in forming the possessive of nouns and pronouns represented the word 'his'—as 'John's book,' an abbreviation of 'John, his book.'

240

"This being the case, we must perforce say, 'Some one, his book,' and 'some one else, his book'; whence, of course, 'Some one else's book.'"

PREPOSITIONS

Perhaps in no other way does the carelessness of a writer or speaker betray itself so much as in the misuse of the little words that are known as prepositions ("in," "on," "at," "among," "with," etc.)

According to usage, certain verbs must be followed by certain prepositions. There is no rule to tell the student which preposition is to be employed after a verb; this must be learned through familiarity with the language. A standard work on English gives a list of phrases showing the idiomatic use of prepositions; the list contains about 125 entries.

Very often these little words are omitted when they should be used, and very often they are used incorrectly. An example of such omission is taken from a newspaper report of a robbery:

"Burglars who left no fingerprints pried open the front door of the home of John Smith, manufacturer and dealer of sporting goods, ransacked the house and escaped with jewelry and clothing."

It is correct to say, "manufacturer of sporting goods," but it is not good English to say "dealer of sporting goods." Therefore the sentence should be changed to read: "The home of John Smith, manufacturer of and dealer in sporting goods," etc.

"Nothing but study of the best writers and practice in composition will enable us to decide what are the prepositions and conjunctions that ought to go with certain verbs," says Alfred

Ayres in "The Verbalist." The following examples illustrate some common blunders:

"It was characterized with eloquence." Instead of "with," use "by."

"A testimonial of the merits of his grammar." Instead of the first "of," use "to."

"It was an example of the love to form comparisons." Instead of "to form," use "of forming."

"Repetition is always to be preferred before obscurity." Say "to" instead of "before."

"He made an effort for meeting them." Use "to meet."

"He believes that the preparation will prove useful as a preventive against paralysis."

The use of "against" after "preventive" is incorrect. Use "of" instead; say "a preventive of paralysis."

"A mass meeting of the citizens of the town was held, and it was decided to protest at the plan to remove the hospital."

The foregoing quotation was taken from a newspaper article. The word "at" is used incorrectly in the sentence. It should be "against." You protest "against" something, not "at" something.

In or At

Should we say, a man lives "in" or "at" a certain place? This is one of the questions concerning grammar that is frequently asked, and perhaps it is the most common. Possibly the best explanation of the matter is to say, Use "at" if the place is regarded as a point, and use "in" if it may be considered as inclusive, or containing, a person or thing.

Thus, say, "We arrived at New York, and went to a hotel in Brooklyn." "Our vessel touched at Southampton." "There are several churches in this town." "'At' is the preposition of the point, denoting occupancy of, or nearness to, a point in space or time; as 'at the table at the instant.' 'In' is the preposition of inclusion, as 'Fish live in water,'" says Fernald's "Working Grammar of the English Language."

In and Into

The distinction between the uses of these two words, "in" and "into," can be expressed best by giving examples of proper and improper usage. Therefore, compare the two sentences which follow: "The man walked in the house" and "The man walked into the house." In the first case, the action was confined entirely to the house; that is, the man was in the house, and he walked therein. But in the second case, the man was outside the house, and he entered it. "In" shows state of being, or position; "into" denotes action, movement, tendency or direction.

Absorption In and Of

Complete absorption "in" a subject means that it takes up the entire attention of a person, to the exclusion of everything else. On the other hand, complete absorption "of" a subject means complete mastery of it, so that nothing further is to be learned concerning it.

Of or To the Hour

Should we say, "twenty minutes 'of' ten," or "twenty minutes 'to' ten"?

There is good dictionary authority for both of these forms. Concerning the use of "of," the Standard Dictionary says:

"'Of' is used as regards nearness, distance or direction, as, within an inch of his life; north of Cape Hatteras; it lacks five minutes of the

243

time." Regarding "to," the same authority gives as one of the meanings of the word: "Until, denoting a time not reached; as, it is ten minutes to twelve; or an hour to noon." However, in England the only form that is used is the one with "to"; in America the form with "of" has made its way into common usage, and both forms are used in the United States.

Decline Over

From a newspaper article the following sentence is taken:

"Although the business of the port showed a decline over the previous month, it reached three-fourths of the peacetime commerce."

Now, at first reading, this seems to say that the business of the port showed a decline from that of the previous month, and therefore the use of the word "over" seems incorrect, and "from" should be substituted for it. But the meaning of the writer, as shown by the context, is that the decline in the business of the port for the month in question was greater than the decline for the preceding month.

The writer should have said so, in plain language. He should have written:

"Although the business of the port showed a decline greater than that of the previous month," etc.

Contrast To

Do not say, "I contrasted that piece of goods to the other." Say, instead, "I contrasted that piece of goods with the other." The proper preposition to use after the verb "contrast" is "with," and not "to."

This error occurred recently in an editorial in a leading American paper, which said:

"This dispatch from an impartial American

source may be contrasted to the statements of Sir Philip Gibbs."

Correspond To or With

After the verb "correspond" we may use either "with" or "to," according to the sense. That is because "correspond" has several meanings, some of which differ widely from others.

We correspond "with" a person when we exchange letters or other communications with him. We correspond "to" him when we are similar to him in height or weight or appearance, or in some other detail or details. Sometimes "correspond" is used without a preposition. Thus we say, "The two men correspond in general appearance, but they differ materially in particulars."

Dissent To

In one of the most widely read newspapers of America, the following sentence was noted recently:

"We do not state the language of the decision, to which three judges dissented, but only its effect."

This sentence affords another example of a very common kind of grammatical error, the misuse of prepositions. The sentence should read, "We do not state the language of the decision, from which three judges dissented." The proper preposition to use after the verb "dissent" is "from," not "to." We do not dissent "to" anything; we dissent "from" it. After the verb "assent" meaning to agree with, it is proper to use "to."

Immune To or From

The use of the word "to" after the word "immune" is criticized by some writers on English, by whom we are told that the proper preposition to use after the word "immune" is "from," not "to." The Standard Dictionary defines "immune" as "exempt, as from disease; especially protected by inoculation." It is interesting to note that in an edition of the dictionary published about twenty years ago the word "immune" is marked "rare," but it has made its way into the common use of the people and is no longer rare. "Immune to" is also coming into common use.

Subscribe To

"I see that you are reading 'Somebody's Magazine.'"

"Yes, I subscribe to it, and get it every month."

It is quite common, but incorrect, to say that one subscribes "to" a magazine. The proper word to use is "for." You subscribe "for" a magazine, not "to" a magazine.

There is one use of the word "subscribe" after which it is proper to use the preposition "to." That is when one agrees to, or gives one's assent to a creed, statement, proposition, etc., as in the sentence: "He asked whether I agreed with him in the matter of the League of Nations, and I subscribed to some of his statements."

Then there is the use of the verb "subscribe" with a direct object, as in the sentence: "He was asked to contribute to the building fund of the church, and he subscribed five hundred dollars."

Under or In the Circumstances?

We are told by some purists that we should not say "under the circumstances," but should say, instead, "in the circumstances."

The question is often discussed in newspapers and magazines. It seems to be settled, however, that the phrase, "under the circumstances," has found a place in good English, by general consent.

It occurs so frequently that it is generally understood, and the phrase, "in the circumstances" has an unfamiliar look to many eyes.

In Murray's "New English Dictionary," the following distinction is made: "Mere situation is expressed by 'in the circumstances,' action affected is performed 'under the circumstances.'"

"Rise Up," "Fall Down," "End Up"

A moment's reflection will show the reader the absurdity of the first two of the phrases printed above. Of course, when a person rises there is only one direction in which he can go, and that direction is up or upward. Therefore, do not "rise up," in the morning or in the world— simply rise.

Likewise, when you fall do not "fall down"— simply fall. There can be no such thing as "falling up."

A somewhat similar error is the use of the preposition "up" after the verb "end," as in "This ends up the affair." Omit the "up"; the sense is expressed by saying, "This ends the affair."

Die With

We frequently hear a person say of another who has passed away, "He died with pneumonia." This is incorrect; say, instead, "He died of pneumonia." "Man and brute die of and not with fevers, consumption, the plague, pneumonia, old age, and so on,' says one authority.

The verb "die" may, however, take any one of the several prepositions after it, according to the word which follows. For example, one may die of fever, from hunger or thirst, by violence, for another person or for one's country, in agony, at sea, etc. Sometimes the word "die" is used in a figurative sense; that is, the word is not to be taken literally, as in the sentence, "When the emperor was sent into exile, he died to his country."

Accuse With

"Jeremiah Jenks, having sold butter for more than the market price, was accused with being a profiteer."

This sentence, taken from a newspaper article, illustrates an incorrect use of a preposition. We must not say that a man is accused "with" something, but that he is accused "of" something. It is correct to use "with" after the word "charge"; thus, the sentence quoted may be altered to read, "Jeremiah Jenks, having sold butter for more than the market price, was charged with being a profiteer."

"Accused" is regarded, sometimes, as a more formal word than "charged." Thus, we may charge a friend with forgetfulness, or indifference, or some other minor fault, but we accuse a man of theft or murder. However, the two words are frequently used interchangeably, since a person may be charged with a fault that is grave as well as with one that is trifling.

PRONOUNS

Incorrect Use of Pronouns

In "Expressive English," by Dr. James C. Fernald, are to be found examples of the incorrect use of pronouns by careless speakers or writers. He cites the following: "Lisias promised his father never to abandon his friends." He says that it makes us ask, "Whose friends? His own or his father's?"

To avoid the difficulty, we may say, Dr. Fernald declares, "Lisias promised his father, 'I will never abandon your friends,'" if that is the meaning; or, "my friends," if that is the intent. Of course, we may repeat the noun, as in "Lisias promised his father never to abandon his father's

248

friends," but the expression, "Lisias promised his father never to abandon his, Lisias', friends," is awkward. "For the lad cannot leave his father; for if he should leave him, he would die." Who would die, the lad or his father? But if we use the language of Gen. xliv., 22, the meaning is perfectly clear: "For the lad cannot leave his father; for if he should leave his father, his father would die."

He Instead of Him

The following violation of a rule of grammar relating to the use of "he" and "him" was taken from a headline in a New York newspaper:

"Convince Both He and Her Mother He Is an Honest Suitor." It should have read, "Convince Both Him and Her Mother," etc. The pronoun is in the objective case—object of the verb "convince"—and should therefore be "him," not "he," which is the nominative case form of the pronoun.

To Defy Either He or She

In a street-corner speech, a political orator said:

"And if any man or woman here doubts the truth of what I say, I defy either he or she to bring forward proofs to the contrary." His grammar was faulty. What he should have said, is: "I defy either him or her to bring forward proofs to the contrary."

The verb "defy" belongs in the class of verbs that are known as "transitive"; that is, verbs that take a direct object. These objects must be in the objective form of the noun or pronoun. In the case quoted, "he or she" is not in the objective case, but in the nominative case, and must therefore be altered to the objective case, which is expressed by the form "him" and "her," and not by "he" or "she."

"Which," "What," "That," and "Who"

The following explanation of the proper use of "which," "what" and "that" is taken from Longman's "English Grammar":

"Formerly 'what' was used just as we now use 'which,' Thus, Shakespeare wrote, 'That what we have we prize not to the worth.' But in modern English, though 'what' is frequently a relative pronoun, its antecedent is never expressed; thus, 'Give me what I have earned.' Here the antecedent of 'what' is some such noun as 'pay,' understood; but if we supply this noun we must then use 'which' or 'that' instead of 'what,' as, 'Give me the pay which I have earned.'"

The difference between "that" and "which" may be shown best, probably, by giving an example. "The members who were present voted for Jones." This means that the members were present and voted for Jones. But when we say, "The members that were present voted for Jones," we mean that some of them were present, etc.

Him or His

Such expressions as the following are often heard:

"What do you think of him studying Latin?" "The boy's advancement in business will depend upon him attending to his duties." "Her mother was opposed to the girl entering the school for nurses."

In each of these cases, and in other similar cases, the possessive should be used, and the sentences should be changed to read: "What do you think of his studying Latin?" "The boy's advancement in business will depend upon his attending to his duties," and "Her mother was opposed to the girl's entering the school for nurses."

The rule of grammar which governs such cases is given in Lockwood's "Lessons in English," as follows: "The possessive case of the pronoun should be used before the verbal noun, sometimes called the infinitive in 'ing.'"

His or Her or Their?

If you found a purse, and, not knowing whether it belong to a man or a woman, wished to return it to the owner, would you say:

"If any lady or gentleman has lost her or his purse, and if she or he will call at my office, and identify the same as her or his property, it will be returned to her or him?"

That would be correct grammatically, but no one would say or write it. However, it is incorrect to use "they" and "their" in this connection, as so many persons do. Never say "If any lady or gentleman has lost their purse, and if they will call at my office, it will be returned to them."

What shall we say, then? "Steer around the difficulty," says Dr. Fernald, in "Expressive English." Say, "Any lady or gentleman who has lost a purse may obtain it at the office by proving property," or, "A purse has been found, which the owner may obtain at the office by proving property."

I Instead of Me, Etc.

"It was our bond of sorrow that brought Mary and I together." "I" is in the nominative case. But the objective is required here, following the verb "brought," and the sentence should read: "It was our bond of sorrow that brought Mary and me together."

Another example: "You never think of giving her or I any pleasure." Again, "I" should be "me."

"Most of the property was held jointly by he and his wife." In this case "he" should be "him."

Me Instead of I

An example of the use—or, rather, the misuse—of "me" for "I" was remarked not long ago in a letter to a newspaper criticizing a recent book. The letter writer said that "The soldiers who died in the great war gave their lives so that you and yours, and me and mine, and the author of this book and his, could continue to live and enjoy in peace the pursuit of happiness."

For the word "me" in this sentence, the word "I" should be substituted. The subject of the clause is the compound noun, "You and yours, I and mine, and the author of this book and his," and the first person pronoun must therefore be in the nominative case, which is "I." The form "me" is the objective case.

Myself

"Who is going to the ball game to-day?"

"Bob and myself are going."

This use of "myself" is incorrect. The proper form is, "Bob and I are going." Often the answer to the question printed above would be, "Bob and me," but such answer would be grammatically absurd. Another example of the incorrect use of "myself" is found in the following: "She told the news to Jane and myself." This should be, "She told the news to Jane and me."

The words "myself," "yourself," "himself," "ourselves," etc., have two uses which are correct. One is when they are used for emphasis, as in the sentences, "I shall go myself and break the news to him"; "we ourselves are at fault in the matter." The second proper use is when the word is employed reflexively; that is, when the action is "turned back" upon the speaker or writer; as in the sentence, "I dressed myself quickly."

252

That and Which

In considering the proper uses of "that" and "which," take, for example, the sentence: "The cat, which you despise so much, is a very useful animal." The writer or speaker means to convey the meaning that all cats are useful animals. But if he says. "The cat that you despise so much is a very useful animal," the idea conveyed is that one individual cat, which is despised, is a very useful animal.

The two words are often used interchangeably, even by careful writers and speakers. Oliver Goldsmith is criticized for writing: "Age, that lessens the enjoyment of life, increases our desire of living." Many grammarians hold that he should have said "which" instead of "that." "Thackeray also was fond of this usage, but it is not very common," says Alfred Ayres in "The Verbalist." He quotes the following: "All words, which are the signs of complex ideas, furnish matter of mistakes." This gives an erroneous impression, and should be, "All words that are the signs of complex ideas," etc.

They

The use of the word "they" in such sentences as, "They make many automobiles in Detroit," is criticized by grammarians. It is better to say, "Many automobiles are made in Detroit."

Other examples of this error are found in the following sentences:

"They had a serious accident downtown to-day." Say instead, "There was a serious accident downtown to-day," or "A serious accident occurred downtown to-day."

"They don't teach French in that school, do they?" Better, "French is not taught in that school, is it?"

Sometimes, "they" is employed in the sense of

"everyone," as in the expression, "In a large city they are always in a hurry." It is better English to say, "In a large city everyone is always in a hurry."

"The use of 'they' as an indefinite pronoun should be avoided," writes one grammarian.

Too Many Pronouns

Frequently we hear such expressions as "The man he did something," or "The girl she wore a blue dress," or "The people they were dissatisfied." In these examples the pronouns "he," "she" and "they" are unnecessary to express the meanings desired, and should be omitted.

This error is one form of the rhetorical fault called "redundancy"—that is, the use of too many words to express an idea. There are several forms of redundancy.

Who, Whom, and Which

The relative pronouns "who," "whom" and "whose" should be used only in speaking or writing of persons. When reference is made to animals or inanimate objects, the proper usage requires the use of "which" and "of which." (But "whose" may be used instead of "of which" when the use of the latter expression makes the phrase or sentence awkward.)

Do not say, "Those which say so are mistaken." Say, "Those who say so are mistaken." Do not say, "He has some friends which I know." Say, "He has some friends whom I know."

Do not say, "The girl which was here this morning has gone home"; "the dog who was bought last week has run away."

However, formerly the pronoun "which" was used for persons also, and even in referring to the Deity. In the Authorized Version of the Bible we read, in the Lord's Prayer, "Our Father, which

254

art in Heaven." Such use is now considered incorrect.

It should be observed, also, that "which," when used as an interrogative pronoun—that is, for asking a question—is applied correctly to persons, animals or things. "Which of the men did this?" and "which of the dogs did you buy?" are grammatically correct.

Whom May Be

"Southpaws," writes an authority on sports, referring to left-handed boxers, "are far below par. They seem to lack boxing skill and general smartness. They have one set style and never vary from it, no matter whom their opponents may be."

In the concluding sentence of the foregoing quotation, the word "whom" should be "who," the nominative case form of the pronoun, and not "whom," which is the objective case form. It should agree in case with the subject of the sentence, which is "opponents."

Whom Were There

There is an error in the use of "who" and "whom" which is very easy to make, and which one hears often in spoken English, and reads frequently. That is the use of "whom" as the subject of a verb, instead of "who." An instance of this occurred recently in the "society" column of a newspaper. The writer said:

"The majority of the social celebrities whom I imagined were basking in the sunshine at Newport or enjoying the cooling breezes at Southampton were very much in evidence in the Japanese gardens and the palm court."

For "whom" in the foregoing sentence read "who." The pronoun is the subject of the verb "were basking," and as such should be in the nominative case, which is "who." "Whom" is the form of the objective case. In other words, one must say "who were basking in the sunshine," and not "whom were basking in the sunshine."

Whomever or Whoever

The sentence, "He is picked up by whomever happens to be near," should read, "He is picked up by whoever happens to be near." The preposition "by" does not govern the pronoun "whoever," as might be thought, but another word which is not expressed but is "understood," as the grammarians say. In other words, there is a word missing in the sentence, between "by" and "whoever." That word is "him," or "her," or "anyone," for example, and that word is the object of the preposition "by."

The pronoun "whoever" (correctly thus, not "whomever") is the subject or nominative of the verb "happens," and must therefore, according to the rules of grammar, be expressed in the nominative form "whoever," and not in the objective form "whomever."

REDUNDANCY

Among the most common of the errors committed by careless or inexact writers and speakers is the use of words that are not needed. Some good examples of this error are given by Alfred Ayres, in "The Verbalist." The words that should be omitted are given here in quotation marks.

Whenever I try to write well, I "always" find that I can do it. I shall have finished by the "latter" end of the week. Iron sinks "down" in water. He combined "together" all the facts. My brother called on me, and we "both" took a walk. I can do it "equally" as well as he. We could not forbear "from" doing it. Before I go, I must "first" be paid. We were compelled to return "back." We forced them to retreat "back" fully a mile. His conduct was approved "of" by everybody. They conversed "together" for a long while. The balloon rose "up" very rapidly. Give me another "one." Come home as soon as "ever" you can.

"Redundancy," says Webster's Dictionary, "is the generic term for the use of more words than are needed to express one's meaning; tautology is needless or useless repetition of the same idea in different words; pleonasm (which may sometimes be a means of proper emphasis) denotes the use of words whose omission would leave one's meaning intact; as 'Boldly dare' is a pleonasm."

The rule which tells us that it is not desirable to repeat a word in a sentence, or to use a word too often, applies with greater force to writing than to speaking, of course. Sometimes a writer of good English repeats words for the sake of emphasis, or driving home an idea; but as a rule he avoids repetition. Meiklejohn, in "The Art of Writing English," gives the following examples of the repetition of words:

"The very things which I needed for the journey which I was going to make were not to be procured in the little village which was then my home." Too many "whiches," The first two might be left out.

"No learning is generally so dearly bought, or so valuable when it is bought, as the learning that we learn in the school of experience." The word "learn" is too frequently repeated. It would be better to say, "that we gain" or "that we acquire."

"The public library will be of special value, especially to the young men." "Special" followed by "especially" is unpleasant to the ear. Say, "particularly to the young men."

Beyond a Question of Doubt

The phrase, "beyond a question of doubt," is incorrect. It affords an instance of what grammarians and rhetoricians call "redundancy," which means the use of too many words to express an idea. You may say "beyond a question" or "beyond question," or "beyond a doubt" or "beyond doubt," but do not say "beyond a question of doubt."

Equally As Good

"Have you So and So's cough medicine?" asked the man in the drug store.

"No," said the clerk, "but I have something equally as good."

He should not have said, "I have something equally as good," but should have said, "I have something equally good," or, "something as good," or, "something just as good." But not, "equally as good."

The same observation applies when the adverb "well" is used. "Clara plays the piano well, but Jane plays it equally as well." "As well" or "equally well" or "just as well" should be used instead of "equally as well."

Favorable Commendation

"When the regiment marched down the avenue, there was much favorable commendation."

This sentence, quoted from a newspaper article, contains an example of the rhetorical error known as redundancy. The word "favorable" is not needed, since commendation (which is praise) can be only favorable. The word the writer had in mind, no doubt, was "comment." Comment may be either favorable or unfavorable.

Examples of redundancy are found in sentences such as the following:

"Throughout his whole career." (The word "whole" is not needed.)

"Being content with deserving a triumph, he refused to receive the honor that was offered him." (The words "being," "to receive," and "that was" are not needed.) The sentence is much more forcible when it reads: "Content with deserving a triumph, he refused the honor offered him."

Final Completion

"With great effort of mind and body, the engineer in charge of the work carried it to its final completion."

The sentence is incorrect. The word "final" should be omitted. "Completion" means the act or process or result of bringing something to a final, desired state; therefore, to say "final completion" is about the same as saying "complete completion" or "final finality," which is, of course, absurd. Ayres says, "If there were such a thing as a plurality or series of completions, there would be, of course, such a thing as the 'final' completion; but, as every completion is final, to talk about a 'final completion' is as absurd as it would be to talk about a 'final finality.'"

Final Upshot

"What will be the final upshot of the colossal industrial and mining consolidations now under consideration?" asks a writer on financial subjects.

He should have omitted the word "final." The word "upshot" means, according to Webster, "final issue; conclusion; the sum and substance; the end, result or consummation; as, the upshot of the matter."

To use the term, "final upshot" is, therefore, to use too many words to express an idea.

Nodding the Head

More often than otherwise, perhaps, we read and hear. "She nodded her head," instead of the simpler, correct expression, "She nodded."

Now, if you nod at all, you must nod your head. You cannot nod anything else. The dictionary defines "nod" as follows: "To incline or bend downward or forward, as the head or top; specifically, to make a quick downward motion of the head as a sign of assent, salutation, or command, or involuntarily because of drowsiness or sleep."

Other

In describing a meeting of the French Academy, a newspaper dispatch from Paris read:

"Except for Marshal·Lyautey, who is detained in Morocco, the other marshals, including Joffre and Foch, were present, as well as Premier Poincaré, Minister of Justice Barthou and Alexandre Ribot."

The word "other" is used in this sentence without need for it, since its meaning is conveyed by the use of "except." The writer might have said:

"Marshal Lyautey, who is detained in Morocco, was absent, but the other marshals who are members of the Academy, including Joffre and Foch, were present."

Possible . . . May Be

"The Governor has overtaxed his strength, and has been compelled to give up for a time the duties of his office. It is possible that his retirement may be permanent."

The foregoing sentences are quoted from a newspaper article. The second sentence is incor-

Now, unless Dr. Wright had died, Mrs. Wright could not be his widow. It is therefore unnecessary to use the words "the late," which indicate his decease, with the word "widow." The writer should have said, instead: "Mrs. Wright, widow of Dr. Clark Wright, celebrated her birthday."

On good authority, it may be stated that the word "late" should be used only in speaking of persons who died recently. This rule is violated frequently, however. We see sometimes reference to "the late President Washington," "the late Abraham Lincoln," etc.

SINGULAR AND PLURAL

Wrong Use of the Plural

In speaking and in writing there is a tendency —which is natural, perhaps—to make the verb in a sentence agree in number with the noun that is near it, without regard to grammatical accuracy. An instance of this was noted in a newspaper account of a reception given to a soldier returning from abroad. It ran thus:

"The mayor of the city, flanked by his official aids, were waiting at the railroad station to receive the city's guest." Of course, the word "were" in this sentence should be "was," since it refers to "mayor" and not to "aids." It was the latter word, preceding the verb, that the writer had in mind, incorrectly, when he framed the sentence. The subject of the sentence, sometimes called the nominative, governs the verb; that is, a verb must agree with its subject in person and number. The subject in this sentence is "mayor," a singular noun, therefore the verb must be singular.

Agreement of Noun and Verb

In a letter to a newspaper the following question was asked:

"Is the following sentence correct grammatically: 'Each of you gentlemen was furnished with a copy of my weekly report'? Also, is there a rule which says that a verb must agree in number with the noun immediately preceding it, whether or not that noun acts as subject of the sentence?"

To these queries the editor of the newspaper replied that the sentence as quoted was grammatically correct, and that the answer to the second query was "no."

In the sentence quoted the subject of the verb "was furnished" is not "gentlemen," but "each." The phrase "of you gentlemen" is only a modifier of "each." As that word is in the singular, it must take a verb in the singular: in this case, "was furnished." Therefore, it would be incorrect to write or say, "Each of you gentlemen were furnished with a copy of my weekly report." The error of using a plural verb in such sentences is very common.

Collective Nouns and the Verb

The collective noun has always been troublesome to writers and others who wish to speak and write correctly. Should it take a singular verb or a plural verb? For example, should one say, "The committee held its meeting yesterday," or "The committee held their meeting yesterday?" One authority says, "Collective nouns take singular or plural predicates, according to the meaning intended; thus, 'The crowd is densely packed in the public square,' and 'the crowd are not all of the same mind.'" In the first case we think of the crowd as a whole; in the second we think of the individuals who compose the crowd.

In a newspaper article it was said that "the Navy should be the favorite in to-morrow's game, because the team has fine material, and are well coached." The sentence is very awkward, with its singular verb "has" and its plural verb "are," although it conveys the writer's meaning. It would have been better thus: "The team has fine material, and the members are well coached."

Plural Noun, Singular Verb

Some writers and speakers use correct English and speak and write well enough when they arrange their sentences in the usual form—that is, with the subject or noun first, and then the verb —but are guilty of errors in grammar when they reverse the order, putting the verb first and then the noun. This method of forming a sentence is called by grammarians the "inverted construction."

A case in point read:

"To this strange union (the marriage of a dwarf and a person of normal size) was born three daughters, who attained normal stature."

This should read: "To this strange union were born three daughters," etc.

The subject of the verb is "daughters," not "union," and as "daughters" is in the plural, the verb should also be plural, "were," not "was," which is singular.

"Another heavy attack on his lines, and even the threatened shortage of his ammunition, finds the general still confident of victory."

The sentence may have been written incorrectly, or putting the "s" on the verb "find" may have been a printer's error. In either case, it is incorrect. The verb should be "find." The sentence has two subjects or nominatives, "attack" and "shortage," and therefore the verb should be in the plural form, "find," and not in the singular form, "finds." The rule is, "When a verb has two or more nominatives connected with 'and,' it must agree with them in the plural number."

Singular Subject, Plural Verb

"The co-operative societies are also given the right to organize enterprises for production or working over raw products. To the co-operative societies are assigned the sole right to organize distribution and exchange of products throughout the country."

The two sentences contain two examples of a very common error. It is the use of a plural verb with a singular noun. In the first sentence, the subject noun is "right," not "societies"; it is the right that is given, not the societies. The sentence should read, "To the societies is also given the right," etc.

In the second sentence the subject noun is also the word "right," and the sentence should read, "To the co-operative societies is assigned the sole right," etc.

These two sentences afford examples of what is known as the "inverted sentence," in which the noun is placed after the verb, instead of before the verb, as is far more common.

Singular Noun, Plural Pronoun

Describing a championship baseball team, a sporting writer said that "the team has the gameness to make them dangerous."

The grammatical error in this sentence lies in the use of the singular verb "has" with the plural pronoun "them." Corrected, the sentence reads, "The team has the gameness to make it dangerous," or, "The team have the gameness to make them dangerous." Some authorities on grammar would criticize the latter form. They would hold that the team is taken, in this case, as a whole, that is, as one body, and therefore is singular in number and should have only the singular form of the verb, "has."

But others would look at the team as composed of individual players, and therefore would argue that the plural form is correct. The question is known as that of the "collective noun," and is one of the most disputed in grammar. Probably it will never be settled to the satisfaction of all grammarians and rhetoricians.

Confusion in Numbers

Commenting on a charge that railway executives were paid too highly for their services, a leading American railway president said recently:

"Good men now in the business will leave, and good men who might have come into it will keep out when they see that in it they cannot make as much money as they could in other lines of work where their ability as an executive would be appreciated and paid for."

Note the expression, "where their ability as an executive would be appreciated and paid for."

It contains an error which a grammarian would call a confusion in numbers. "Their ability" refers to "good men," and is plural in form. "As an executive" refers also to "good men," but is singular in form.

It should be changed to the plural, making the sentence read: "Where their ability as executives would be appreciated and paid for."

The Plural with Is

From one of the most carefully written and edited of American newspapers the following was taken:

"Bulgaria and her government, more sensitive to public opinion in the United States and elsewhere than is the former senator, his senatorial friends and his lawyers, have taken the trouble to repudiate the divorce from his American wife which he obtained in that far-off land."

The error in the sentence quoted lies in the use of the singular verb "is." It should be "are." The subject of the sentence is "The former senator, his senatorial friends and his lawyers," which is, clearly, plural. The fact that the verb is placed before the subject, instead of after it as is usually the case, does not affect or alter the rule that a plural verb must be used with a plural noun.

Any Person and They

Such expressions as "someone," "anyone," "anybody," "somebody," "any person" are singular in form, and the pronoun which refers to them should also be singular.

Violation of this rule is one of the commonest forms of transgression against good form in grammar. One does not have to be a stickler for the best English to be offended by such expressions as the following, taken from a newspaper:

"As for Mrs. Jameson, it is a wonderful thing for any person to be so imaginative that they think they are still attractive."

This should read:

"As for Mrs. Jameson, it is a wonderful thing for any person to be so imaginative that she thinks she is still attractive."

"They" is always plural and should never be employed with an expression or a word that is singular. And "any person" is clearly and unmistakably singular.

Each and Every with Their

One of the most common of grammatical errors, in writing and speaking—even among persons who usually speak and write correctly—is the use of "their" with "each" and "every."

268

For example, we hear: "If each one did their duty"; "if every one had their rights."

Two recent examples of this error, taken from newspapers, are as follows: "Each would pay 1 per cent on their commodity expenditures." "Possibly if every person of similar thought were so to address their political representatives, something could be done to clear the general atmosphere." In every one of these cases, use "his" instead of "their." Say, "If each one did his duty"; "if every one had his rights"; "if every person were to address his political representatives."

This error is called, in the language of the grammarians, the use of a pronoun that differs in number from its antecedent. That is, the antecedent, the word that goes before, is singular in number, while the pronoun that relates to it (in this case, "their") is plural in number. They should agree.

Each and the Plural

The following sentence is taken from a newspaper article describing a famous French castle or chateau:

"Sceaux has belonged in turn to the Duke de Tresmes, then to the famous statesman Colbert, who, with his three daughters each of them duchesses, entertained there King Louis XIV."

Attention is called to the phrase, "each of them duchesses." It is incorrect. It should be altered to the following form: "each of them a duchess."

The word "each" is singular, meaning one, and therefore the word which follows it should be in the singular also. In this case the word "each" is used "distributively," as the grammarians say; that is, refers to "every one of a number of individual persons or objects taken individually or possessing character and relations in common with the others with which it is named or connected, and yet having a position or characteristics of its own."

Every One Are

There is always a strong tendency among writers or speakers to make a verb agree in number with the noun that is nearest to the verb in position in the sentence. For example, many persons use such sentences as the following, "Every one of these letters were signed by me," without recognizing the grammatical error involved.

The subject (nominative) of the sentence is not "letters" but "one," modified by "every." One is in the singular number and requires, therefore, a singular verb. "Letters" is in the objective case, governed by the preposition "of." You cannot say, "Every one were signed," and the use of the phrase "of the letters" does not change the rule of grammar involved. Therefore, instead of saying "Every one of these letters were signed by me," say "Every one of these letters was signed by me."

The same rule applies to "each." Do not say, "Each of these letters are mine"; say, "Each of these letters is mine."

An officer of the United States Navy was quoted as saying, in a recent interview:

"Basketball requires quick thought and quick action, and these are the qualities needed by officers. Every one of our team will make good officers. We want these qualities in the man on the bridge."

If the admiral was correctly quoted by the newspaper reporters, his grammar was faulty in one of the sentences quoted. He should not have said, "Every one of our team will make good officers," but should have said, "Every one of our team will make a good officer."

The expression, "every one," is singular in form and sense, and should therefore be followed by the singular, "a good officer," and not by the plural, "good officers."

Two instances of the incorrect use of the plural verb in connection with the word "every" are the following:

"Nearly every one of the soldiers present were veterans of the great war."

"Nearly every celebrated crime in the latter half of the eighteenth, and all of the nineteenth and the twentieth centuries, have figured on the records of this court."

The first should read: "Nearly every one of the soldiers present was a veteran of the great war."

In the second case the proper form is: "Nearly every celebrated crime in the latter half of the eighteenth, and all of the nineteenth and the twentieth centuries, has figured on the records of this court."

Has Come and the Plural

"To the farmer has come the earlier and the heavier burdens of readjustment."

This should read, "To the farmer have come the earlier and the heavier burdens." The subject of the sentence is not "farmer," although it is placed nearer to the verb than "burdens," which is the subject. If the sentence is inverted, or "turned around," it will be seen that one could not say, "The earlier and the heavier burdens has come to the farmer."

Is and Their

A sentence that offened the eye was noted in a newspaper that is usually edited with great care. It read:

"The Baltimore baseball club is planning to introduce the game of soccer as part of their training program when the players go South in the Spring."

The error lies in the use of "is" with "their." The sentence may be corrected in either of the following ways:

"The Baltimore baseball club is planning to introduce the game of soccer as part of its training program," or, "The members of the Baltimore baseball club are planning to introduce the game of soccer as part of their training program."

Is or Are

Should one use "is" or "are" in the following sentence, after the word "who"? "John is one of the boys who is (or are) going to the ball game next week."

It is proper to use, in such cases, the plural verb "are," not the singular verb "is." The rule that governs such cases reads thus: "When the nominative is a relative pronoun, the verb must agree with it in person and number, according to the pronoun's agreement with its true antecedent."

Since the antecedent of the pronoun in this case is the plural noun "boys," and not the singular noun "one," the rule requires that the verb take the plural form "are," instead of the singular form "is."

"A copy of the document and of the envelope in which it was mailed is attached, for your information." Should one use "is" or "are" in the foregoing sentence?

The verb should be in the plural, ("are") for the following reason:

The words "a copy" are understood after the word "and." This makes the subject plural, and the verb should agree with it in number, of course.

It Followed by They

From one of the most carefully edited of

American newspapers, the following is taken:

"The box turtle is one animal which seems to have an abundance of leisure through life. In Long Island, where the naturalist is most familiar with it, they are not commonly found moving about until early summer."

The second sentence should have been written, "In Long Island, where the naturalist is most familiar with it, it is not commonly found," etc. Possibly the writer thought that the repetition of the word "it" would make the sentence awkward. If he did, he might have written, "where the naturalist is most familiar with the turtle, it is not commonly found," etc. Following the word "it" with the word "they," as in the sentence quoted, is objectionable from the point of view of the grammarian. Both "it" and "they" refer to "turtle," which is singular in number, while "they" is plural.

Means Are or Is

"Better than any protestations of a desire for peace are some definite and practicable means of averting war and compelling nations to settle their quarrels out of the court of Mars," said an editorial writer.

Should the writer have said, "Are some definite and practicable means," or "Is some definite and practicable means?" This is a question that has evoked much discussion among grammarians, without, however, bringing forth any very definite decision. Dr. James C. Fernald, a well known authority on word usage and similar questions, wrote:

"'Means' may be either singular or plural, according as we think of one thing or of more than one as intervening between purpose and execution. We may say: 'Various means were tried,' or 'This is a means to an end.'" According to this opinion, the sentence quoted should contain the singular verb "is."

Money, Singular or Plural

In a newspaper account of a suicide, it was said that "near the body were found a purse, a hat and a pair of eyeglasses. In the purse was 75 cents."

"Should the last sentence not have read, 'In the purse were 75 cents?'"

The answer it, No. We do not regard the amount named—in this case 75 cents—as made up of a number of individual cents or units, but as a whole sum or amount; that is, as one thing. It is therefore proper to use with it the singular verb "was" and not the plural verb "were."

According to some grammarians, in sentences such as the one quoted the words "the sum of" are "understood"; that is, they are to be supplied by the mind of the reader or hearer, without being expressed by the writer or speaker. The full sentence would read, "In the purse was the sum of 75 cents."

Neither, Verb After

"Neither Mr. Smith nor myself are acquainted with Miss Jones."

The sentence should read, "Neither Mr. Smith nor I am acquainted with Miss Jones." The rule governing such cases requires the verb to agree in person and number with the noun or pronoun that is nearer to it in the sentence. One grammarian says, "When the members of a compound subject connected by 'either,' 'nor,' differ as regards person and number, the verb agrees with the nearer of the two."

"Myself" may not be used in place of "I" in the sentence quoted, since "myself" is used in the nominative case only when increased emphasis is desired, as in the sentence, "I myself have done it."

Neither Were

In a newspaper report of a trial which attracted wide attention, a lawyer was quoted as saying to the jury:

"And were you not surprised that neither the complainant's brother nor her husband, both of whom must have known of this alleged arrangement between the plaintiff and the defendant, were called to testify?"

The lawyer, being presumably, a man of education, should not have used "were" with "neither." He should have said: "Neither the complainant's brother nor her husband, both of whom must have known of this arrangement between the plaintiff and the defendant, was called to testify."

"Neither" means "not either, not the one nor the other," and is a singular word and must take a singular verb. "Were" is a plural verb.

News Are

There are certain words in English which are seemingly plural in meaning because they are plural in form, ending in "s." But they are really singular in meaning, and therefore they should take the singular verb, not the plural, although the proper use may seem incorrect. Among such words are "news," "politics," "economics." One should not say, for example, "The news concerning the war are good"; "politics, when properly conducted, are a good pursuit for a citizen"; "economics have been called the dismal science." In all these cases, use the singular verb.

There are, however, certain words ending in "s" concerning which there is doubt. Grammarians differ frequently concerning the proper verbs to be employed with such nouns as "headquarters" and "alms." "The general's headquarters were (or was) at Richmond," we may say; "the alms given to the poor family are (or is) not sufficient for its maintenance." "Means" may be either singular or plural, accordingly as the means is or are singular or plural.

No One—They

Not long ago the newspapers reported that a famous actor was bankrupt; that he had filed a voluntary petition in bankruptcy. Naturally, he was interviewed in regard to his financial affairs, and the newspapers reported that he said that no one would get any money from him except over his dead pocket-book, and that no one was really hard up as long as "they" could laugh.

Now, the second part of this remark is unquestionably good philosophy, but it is expressed in poor English. It should be, "No one was really hard up as long as he could laugh," not "as long as they could laugh."

"No one" is singular in form, and the pronoun that follows it and refers to it should also be singular in form. "They" is plural, meaning more than one.

None Are

"Sir," said a letter to the New York Tribune, "it is startling to a mere lover of good English to note that to the New York grammarian 'none are' is incorrect. I suppose the critic is of the tribe that write 'illy' and 'overly.' According to the poor old dictionaries, 'none' may be either singular or plural, according to the meaning. Sometimes it means 'not one'; sometimes it means 'not any.' The problem is complex, but it is just the sort that invites some people to rush in where others would tread warily.

"As to 'none of these move us,' an examination of Acts xx, 24, will show 'None of these things move me.' Probably Boston still follows the Bible."

To which the conductor of the "column" in the Tribune replied:

"With the dictionaries and the Bible refuting us, we are driven straightway out of logic and into truculence. Just as long as we are care-taker of this turret 'none' will be admitted only when accompanied by a singular verb. We are probably one of the world's worst grammarians, but we're awful stubborn."

Number Is or Number Are

After the word "number," it is sometimes correct to use a singular verb such as "is," and sometimes correct to use a plural verb such as "are."

"When the word 'number' is used to express a unit of some sort, it is singular, as 'The number of men was small,' 'the number of members is increasing,' says the occupant of "The Lexicographer's Easy Chair," in "The Literary Digest." (A "lexicographer" means a writer of dictionaries.) "Used in the sense of 'several,' the word 'number' is plural, as 'a large number of men speak in favor of the single tax.' In the sentence, 'As a large number of gears of your manufacture is (or are) used by our company, it would be of assistance to me,' etc., the word 'are' and not 'is' should be used. 'As a large number of gears of your manufacture are used by our company,' etc."

One After Another Have

An error that is quite common is the use of a plural verb, such as "have," with the expression "one after another," as in the following sentence:

"One person after another have passed the courthouse without noticing that the upper panel of the bronze front door is damaged."

This should be, "One person after another has passed," etc. If we transpose the words of the sentence slightly, we shall see why this is so. We should not say, "One person have passed after another," etc. Even a very elementary knowledge of grammar would teach us that in this case we should say, "One person has passed after another."

One Have

When you use the word "one," referring to one person, one object, be careful to use with it the verb in the singular number, since "one" is singular, and not plural.

An example of the error that is commonly made in connection with the use of this word "one" was noted in a report of a lawn tennis match. It read: "She was always on the move, darting from side to side, anticipating with that keen tennis sense that only one out of a thousand players have," etc. This should have read, "that only one out of a thousand players has." The subject of the verb is "one," not "players," although the latter word is placed nearer to the verb than is the former. You would not say "only one player have that keen tennis sense"; you would say, "only one player has that keen tennis sense."

One . . . They

"One should be considerate of the persons whom they meet." This is a typical example of a very common error. According to the rules of grammar "a pronoun must agree with its antecedent, or the noun or pronoun which it represents, in person, number and gender." Now, the antecedent of the pronoun "they" (used incorrectly above) is "one," which is, of course, singular in number. Therefore, the sentence should read, "One should be considerate of the persons whom one meets." The use of "they" in such a sentence should certainly be avoided. It rises from the absence from the English language of any word meaning "he or she."

278

Or Followed By Their

George Bernard Shaw, who usually writes good English, was guilty of a lapse when he wrote the sentence that is reprinted below, unless he was quoted incorrectly. The sentence containing the grammatical error read:

"The occasion was infinitely more important than the Derby, the Goodwood Cup finals, the Carpentier fights, or than any of the occasions on which the official leaders of society are photographed and cinematographed industriously shaking hands with the persons on whom Moliere's patron, Louis XIV, or Bach's patron, Frederick the Great, would not condescend to wipe their boots."

This should read, "would not condescend to wipe his boots." The pronoun (incorrectly, "their," and correctly "his") refers to Louis XIV *or* Frederick the Great (one person, not two) and must therefore be in the singular number, which is "his," not in the plural, which is "their."

Or Followed By Themselves

When two nouns or pronouns are connected by "or," the grammatical construction is singular in form, not plural. Therefore, the references to such nouns or pronouns should be put in the singular, not in the plural. To illustrate what is meant by the foregoing, the following incorrect sentence is quoted:

"The wage-earning invalid, male or female, who has a family to support and cannot, therefore, afford to cease working, may avail themselves of this unusual opportunity."

"Themselves" is incorrect. It should be "himself or herself," because the subject of the sentence quoted is "invalid," which is singular in number. "Themselves" is, of course, plural.

279

Press Is

"The press of the city is united in support of the presidential candidate of the party." Should we not say, "The press are," etc.?

The question is one over which much ink has been spilled, and cannot be answered with decision in one way or another without arousing controversy. It is the old question of the collective noun—whether it should take a singular or a plural verb. In this case, if you consider "the press" as one body of newspapers, or of newspaper opinion, it is better to say "The press is." But if you look upon "the press" as several newspapers, taken individually, it is better to say, "The press are united," etc.

"Collective nouns may be followed by either singular or plural verbs, according as the speaker thinks of the individuals or components of the collection, or of the collection itself," says one authority.

Somebody and They

"You know how it is when you are talking about somebody and, lo and behold, there they stand!"

This embodies a common error; even good writers and speakers are guilty of it sometimes. It should read:

"You know how it is when you are talking about somebody and lo and behold, there he stands!"

With "somebody," which is singular, it is not proper to use "they," which is plural. You should use "he," which is singular, and which, in grammar, embraces both sexes, in cases such as this. If you wish to be very precise you may say, "Lo and behold, there he or she stands," but very few of us are so careful.

There Is and There Are

It seems, almost, as though the use of a singular verb with a plural noun, in connection with the word "there," has made a place for itself in modern English, so common is it. An example is taken from an American newspaper which prides itself upon its correct English:

"He told the city officials that the metropolis was too dangerous for him, he was going back to the jungle, where there was quiet, security and peace of mind." No authority on grammar can be found to support the use of the word "was" in the sentence quoted, instead of "were."

In "The Principles of Rhetoric," by Professor A. S. Hill, the expression, "There's the boys" is quoted as one of a number which are heard, "some of them from ignorant persons, but some from persons who ought to know and who often do know, if they stop to think, that they are talking ungrammatically."

What Is Trumps?

A correspondent of a New York newspaper wrote:

"The writer recently asked, 'What is trumps?' and immediately received a merry 'Ha, ha!' from all those in the game, they saying that my question was incorrect grammar. Was it?"

"There is just one way to reconcile the statement with the laws of formal grammar," said the editor. "That is to contend that 'what' is a singular interrogative: That commits one to the theory that the reply would be in the singular number—diamond, heart, club or spade. Thus one might parse, but that is not the way cards are played.

" 'What are trumps?' is the accepted form, but it is not considered good gaming to have to ask the question."

With and the Plural

Although it is quite common, it is none the less

incorrect to consider the preposition "with" as meaning "and," and, therefore, to use the plural verb in a sentence where the singular verb is required.

For example, the following sentence is taken from a newspaper article:

"Of what use, asks the magazine, are a soil so generous, with precious minerals and vast natural orchards, if the dweller among them cannot profit by them?"

In the foregoing sentence, the subject or nominative is "soil." This is a singular noun. Therefore, the verb should also be singular, and the sentence should read:

"Of what use is a soil so generous, with precious minerals and vast natural orchards," etc.

VERBS

Part of a Verb Left Out

In the leading editorial in an issue of a metropolitan paper, the following sentence was noted:

"The opponents of the project haven't and apparently they can't tell the truth about it." We may omit consideration of the question whether or not the words "haven't" and "can't" should have been used in the sentence instead of the more dignified "have not" and "can not," and pass on to the error in the sentence. That error lies in the omission of the word "told" after "haven't." Without that word, the sentence is incorrect, and grates on the ear and offends the eye of the person who is well grounded in grammar. It is hardly an excuse to say that it conveys to the reader the meaning of the writer.

An example of the omission of part of a verb was noted in an editorial in a newspaper, which said:

"The ancient Spartans, the medieval Japanese and the modern American reformers have the right idea."

Now, the ancient Spartans and the medieval Japanese do not exist any longer, therefore they cannot "have" the right idea. The sentence therefore should be recast to read:

"The ancient Spartans and the medieval Japanese had, and the modern American reformers have, the right idea."

"I do not know the man and have never before heard of him; he does not now nor has he ever had any connection with this establishment, in any capacity whatever."

The second part of this statement is incorrect, from the viewpoint of the grammarian. It should read: "He does not now have nor has he ever had any connection with this establishment." Inserting the word "have" changes the incorrect sentence into one that is correct.

"The Indian wild boar is no mean opponent, and his pursuit on horseback is fraught with considerable danger unless the huntsman's heart is in the right place and his hand and eye quick and true."

In this sentence, taken from a newspaper article, there is a word left out, that should be used to make the sentence grammatical. It is the verb "are," and it should be used after "eye," making the sentence read, "unless the huntsman's heart is in the right place and his hand and eye are quick and true."

The noun "heart," being singular, governs properly the verb "is," which is also singular. But hand and eye, being two things, and consequently plural, must take a plural verb; in this case, "are."

"The archbishop could and has made suitable provision for the care of the children."

This sentence is defective because the word

283

"make" is omitted after "could." The sentence should read, "The archbishop could make and has made suitable provision for the immediate care of the children." You cannot say, "The archbishop could made."

"Richards did not play as brilliantly as he had against Walter Merrill Hall in an earlier round, but that was mainly because he was not as hard pressed as in the Hall match."

In this sentence, the word "played" should have been used, after the word "had," in order to make the sentence complete. The verb "did not play" is in the past tense and the verb "had played" is in the pluperfect tense. The best usage requires a speaker or writer to repeat the principal verb when the tense is changed as in the sentence quoted.

"Neither then nor now do either Frenchmen or Germans care how these political disputes were settled or are to be settled," said a newspaper article.

The sentence quoted is faulty. Part of the verb is omitted. The adverb "then" refers to a time past, but there is no verb to indicate time past. It should be inserted, to make the sentence correct and complete.

The sentence should be corrected to read as follows:

"Neither Frenchmen nor Germans cared then, nor do they care now, how these political disputes were settled or are to be settled."

"Any one who reads, as I have, the letters from relatives and friends describing the great work of the American Relief Administration, will have the deepest appreciation of its work."

In this sentence the verb "reads" is in the present tense, and the verb "have (read)" is in the perfect tense, known also as the present perfect tense.

Therefore, it is better to say or write, "Any one who reads, as I have read," etc.

It may be held that the word "read" is "understood," but it is better to express it.

The following is taken from a recent editorial article:

"France, one of the great nations, right in their midst, had overthrown its king, its ruling class, and appropriated their land, distributing it among the peasants who were capable of and willing to make use of it."

After the words "capable of" there should be the words "using the land," making that part of the sentence read, "the peasants who were capable of using the land and willing to make use of it." We should then have a correct, well-rounded sentence, instead of one that is incorrect and disjointed.

The Subjunctive Mood

Such sentences as "If it were clear today there would be a race," seem to puzzle many persons who are not learned in grammar. They seem to think there is something strange or unusual or foreign in the use of the word "were" in connection with the singular word "it." They have a feeling, or seem to have one, that "were" is to be used only with words indicating the plural, that is, more than one; and that the sentence quoted should read, "If it was clear today there would be a race."

But "were" is correct, and not "was," because the former is the proper word to use in expressing an event or state of things that is only thought of, and is not regarded by the speaker or writer as certain or true. There has been much dispute about the subjunctive mood, however, and some grammarians believe that it should be abolished.

Its enemies say that it is a general stumbling block; that nobody seems to understand it, or to be able to explain it, although almost everybody attempts to use it.

Although such expressions as "I wish I was there" are heard frequently, they are not correct. Say, instead, "I wish I were there," in obedience to the rule of grammar which tells us that "the subjunctive mood is that form of the verb which represents the being, action or passion as conditional, doubtful, and contingent; as 'If thou go, see that thou offend not.'" Another way of putting the rule is this: "The subjunctive mood is required in expressing prayers or wishes, as after an expressed or implied 'may' or 'wish.'"

Do not say, therefore. "She wishes she was beautiful," Say, instead, "She wishes she were beautiful." Do not say, "I wish that it was possible for me to go." Say, "I wish that it were possible for me to go."

Inverted Sentences

An inverted sentence is one in which the usual order of subject and verb is inverted or "turned around"; that is, when the verb is placed before the subject instead of after it, as in the usual sentence. This is generally done for emphasis, as in the sentences, "Greater love hath no man than this, that a man lay down his life for his friends," and, "Great is Diana of the Ephesians."

In using this mode of expression, there is danger of violation of the grammatical rule that a verb must agree with its subject in number. There seems to be a temptation to use the singular verb when the plural is required. For example, the following sentence appeared in an editorial in a newspaper which is generally well written: "Great as is the energy and the ingenuity shown

286

in the making of these machines, they do not meet the requirements of the case." The word "is" should be "are," as will be seen when the sentence is put in the usual form. "The energy and the ingenuity are great," etc., not, "The energy and the ingenuity is great," etc.

Had Broke

It is not correct to say "had broke," as in the following sentence, taken from a newspaper article:

"But the effects of the incident are just as important from a political point of view, perhaps, as if the conference had broke up to-night."

Use "broken" instead of "broke." Say "have broken," "had broken," "will be broken," etc., instead of using "broke." Centuries ago, when English was in one of its formative stages, it was correct to use "broke" in this sense, but such use is now obsolete or archaic. It is, of course, proper to say "broke" in the past tense, as in the sentence, "I broke my pencil point." But say "I have broken my pencil point," not "I have broke" it.

Some authorities defend "have broke" on historical grounds, but Professor Lounsbury says: "In regard to most of these verbs, (such as "broke") it is sufficient to say that the full forms (using the "n,") are now generally preferred."

Had Have and Had Of

The expression, "had have" (or the expression that is still more incorrect, "had of") is often used improperly for "had." It is incorrect to say, for example, "If he had have tried, he would have succeeded." Say, "If he had tried, he would have succeeded." "Had have" is also used frequently and improperly in such sentences as the following: "Had I have known that he was ill, I

287

should have visited him." The proper form is, "Had I known that he was ill," etc., or, "If I had known that he was ill," etc. "Had" or "If I had" carries the idea back into the past, and there is no need of the word "have" to express the same thing.

Of course, the expression "had of" is simply a case of mispronunciation. In the careless usage of former times, the dropping of the "h" before "have" changed the word to "ave," and from "ave" to "of" the transition was easy.

Has Not and Will Not

Do not use the auxiliary, or helping, verb, "has," or any other of the same class of verbs, without using with it the proper part of the principal verb.

An example of the violation of this rule was noted not long ago in an editorial which said:

"It is safe to assert that the French government has not and will not listen to any advice suggesting such a course."

This should have read: "It is safe to say that the French Government has not listened and will not listen to any advice suggesting such a course."

To use the word "has" alone is to leave the verb incomplete, and is therefore a grammatical error.

Have Went, Have Saw

"I should have went to the dance," said the girl, "but my mother would not let me." "I have traveled in many lands, but I have saw nothing like this," said the uneducated traveler. After the auxiliary verb "have," in any of its forms, it is proper to employ only the perfect participle of the principal verb; therefore, the girl should have said, "I should have gone to the dance," and the traveler should have said, "I have seen nothing like this."

"They have chose the wisest part" is an instance of this error cited by Goold Brown, the famous grammarian. The proper form of words to be employed is, "They have chosen the wisest part."

Have Wrote

The form "have wrote," instead of "have written" was formerly in common use, but is now considered archaic; that is, belonging to or having the characteristics of a past age. In the chapter on "The Verb" in Lounsbury's 'History of the English Language" the author says:

"'Wrote' is very common for 'written' in the literature of the eighteenth century; and at the present day these forms occasionally appear. But the language at the present time is averse to their use, and is disposed to exclude the employment of them wholly."

To-morrow "Is" or "Will Be"

Should we say, "To-morrow will be Sunday" or "To-morrow is Sunday"? The question is asked very frequently, and is answered generally if not invariably by grammarians with the reply that both forms are correct. A rule that is sometimes cited is that if the thought of the speaker or writer is fixed upon the name of the day, it is better to use "is"; if attention is paid to the future time, use "will be."

In the Bible are to be found many cases of the use of the form, "To-morrow is." "The Lord hath said, To-morrow is the rest of the holy Sabbath unto the Lord"; "And Aaron made proclamation and said, To-morrow is a feast to the Lord."

"Warn" Without An Object

An error in English that is seen frequently when the verb "warn" is used is the omission of the object after the verb. An example was noted in a dispatch from Washington which read:

"Germany's representative in the United States warned that if Germany and middle Europe are left in a desolate and defective condition, the rest of the world will suffer too."

"Warn" is what is known as a transitive verb; that is, it is a verb that expresses action which goes over to the receiver of the act. A verb that does not express such action is known as an intransitive verb. The case cited should have read: "Warned the United States, or warned the world, that if Germany," etc.

You Was

The expression "you was" instead of "you were" is heard sometimes from the lips of persons who ought to know, and who do know, if they stop to think, that they are speaking ungrammatically. Of course, there are many persons who have never studied grammar and who say "you was" without knowing that it is incorrect. They believe probably, that if "you" is employed in its singular form, it is proper to put with it the singular verb "was." But very few of them would say "you is" instead of "you are."

"You" was formerly employed only as a plural, the singular form being "thou." But "thou" has lost its place in the language, save for special uses, as in prayer, and "you" is now the pronoun for the second person, singular or plural. In grammar it has retained the plural verb—that is, "are" and "were," and the authorities on English call "you was" incorrect.

WORDS OMITTED

As Than

Sometimes, in speech or in writing, we find such expressions as the following:

"Pike's Peak is as high or higher than any mountain in Europe." To make this sentence correct, it is necessary to insert the word "as" after the word "high," or to recast the sentence. Thus, say, "Pike's Peak is as high as or higher than any mountain in Europe." Objection is made to this form, however, on the ground that it is stiff and formal, and therefore it is advisable to say, "Pike's Peak is as high as any mountain in Europe, or even higher."

One of the Greatest

"John Jones, who is one of the greatest, if not the greatest halfback that ever lived, is selected without question for this year's All-America team."

The sentence is taken from a newspaper article. It affords an example of a large number of expressions which convey the ideas of the writers or speakers, and may therefore be considered as correct, strictly speaking, but which offend the eye and ear of the person who wishes to use the language with care.

The sentence should be recast thus: "John Jones, one of the greatest halfbacks that ever lived, if not the greatest, is selected without question for this year's All-America team." The sentence that is corrected does not read as smoothly as does the one that is given as a substitute for it.

MISCELLANEOUS

The Parts of Speech in Rhyme

In former years it was believed by many educators that if you put a thing into rhyme the youthful mind could grasp it more easily. One such rhyme, aiming at instruction in the parts of speech, ran as follows:

Three little words we often see
Are articles, a, an and the.

A noun's the name of anything,
As, school or garden, hoop or swing.

Adjectives tell the kind of noun,
As, great, small, pretty, white or brown.

Instead of nouns the pronouns stand—
Her head, his face, my arm, your hand.

Verbs tell of something being done,
To read, write, count, sing, jump or run.

How things are done the adverbs tell,
As, slowly, quickly, ill or well.

A preposition stands before
A noun, as in or through a door.

Conjunctions join the nouns together
As men *and* children, wind *or* weather.

The interjection shows surprise
As, Oh, how pretty! Ah, how wise!

These, then, are the nine parts of speech
Which reading, writing, speaking teach.

Alright

The spelling of "all right" as one word (with one "l") as "alright," has crept into business usage in recent years, and is seen sometimes in the letters of some commercial houses of fair or even high standing. It never fails to shock the reader who has been taught to take his English seriously. It looks queer to him.

Beyond doubt, "alright" is incorrect at the present time. But will it remain incorrect? That is a question no one can answer. Since usage makes language—and, in time, proper language—it is quite within the bounds of possibility that the word "alright," meaning "all right," will in time take its place among the accepted words of the English language. It will almost surely do so if enough persons find it convenient to write it so.

Almost Instantly Killed

In a newspaper story it was reported that "a boy while crossing Park Avenue was almost instantly killed by an automobile." The words, "almost instantly killed" do not seem to convey any precise idea. Was the boy actually killed, after a lapse of time so brief as not to be calculable? Or did he escape unscathed, after imminent danger of immediate death?

Therefore, in view of the ambiguity, it was wrong to use the expression "almost instantly killed." If the writer meant to say that the boy was killed after a very brief lapse of time he should have said, "The boy was killed almost instantly." If he meant that the boy escaped death, he should have said so.

Change of Person in a Sentence

In grammar, the "first person" is the one speaking, the "second person" is the one spoken to, and the "third person" is the one spoken of.

Writers sometimes express their thoughts in the first person, sometimes in the third. But it is considered incorrect to change from the first person to the third, or vice versa, in one sentence. In a report of a prizefight, the writer said:

"The writer was at the ringside, and my opinion is that the Englishman never had a chance."

He should have used either of the following forms:

"The writer was at the ringside, and his opinion is," etc. Or, "I was at the ringside, and my opinion is," etc.

Commercial Slang

As Americans are, for the most part, engaged

in business, it is only natural, perhaps, that many of the words and phrases which Americans use in everyday speech have had their origin in commercial pursuits. A few examples of what is called by grammarians "commercial slang," are as follows:

The use of "balance" instead of "rest" or "remainder"; the use of "posted" instead of "informed"; the use of "calculate" instead of "believe" or "think"; the use of "reckon" for "suppose."

In spite of the critics and grammarians, however, these words, and many others of similar origin, have made or are making places for themselves in English, and they refuse to be ousted. They will remain because they do not conflict with the spirit or genius of America. Grammarians may call them "slang" or "inelegant," but the common people like them, and it is the common people who make and use the language, "in the long run."

Ending a Sentence with a Preposition

Closing a sentence with a preposition, as in, "The boy did not know what he was going for," has been citicized by some writers on good English, and occasionally one encounters a person who believes that it is quite wrong. But the weight of opinion is decidedly against considering such sentences always wrong. In fact, it is frequently the case that the sentence is stronger because the preposition is placed at the end. In the one cited, for example, it is better to say, "The boy did not know what he was going for," than to say, "The boy did not know for what he was going."

"We are told, 'Never end a sentence with a preposition,'" says Dr. Fernald, in "Expressive English," and he goes on to say: "Why not? Because it cannot be done in Latin. Very well.

That is one of the disabilities of the Latin. But English is independent in origin and idiom, and can do more and better things in many ways, than the Latin ever did or could."

How Would You Address a Mixed Firm?

A newspaper of national reputation (it was one that devoted much space to matters of perfect English, spelling, grammatical usage, punctuation, choice of words, etc.) was asked to give the proper form of address for a firm of attorneys, one member of which is a man and the other a woman.

Obviously, one cannot address the firm as "Gentlemen." To call the firm "Dear Madam and Sir," or "Dear Sir and Madam" is awkward.

"Referring to the question laid before you," says a letter to the newspaper, "why not address a firm of lawyers of which one member is a man and the other a woman as 'Dear Attorneys' or 'Dear Counselors' or plain 'Attorneys' or 'Counselors,' or, indeed, 'Doe and Roe, Attorneys and Counselors at Law' "?

This does not settle the question, of course, but can it be settled?

Poor Grammatically, But Expressive

Sometimes one encounters sentences which are poor grammatically, but which express perfectly the meaning of the speaker or writer. One such sentence drew comment from the "New York Times," as follows:

"On a card announcing a reduction of prices sent out by a New York merchant, there appears a truly interesting sentence. It reads as follows: 'This is an offer which will pay you to give me a call.' Fussy people, doubtless, will find fault with that sentence—say that there is something seriously wrong with it. Perhaps they are

295

right, but what the man meant is instantly comprehensible to everybody who reads it, which is no small merit in any sentence, and critics will not find quite easy the task of saying what and all he meant in another sentence that shall be in accord with their standards of construction and at the same time equally brief as well as equally lucid."

Sentences with Two Meanings

Careless speakers and writers often leave their hearers and readers in doubt concerning the person or thing to whom or to which they are referring, as in the following sentence: "There was a great crowd in the street; Mary could not see her mother, because she was too short." Now, of the two persons to whom reference is made, who was too short, Mary or her mother? The sentence has two meanings, and is called by grammarians, therefore, ambiguous.

If the meaning which the speaker intends to convey is that it was Mary who was too short, either of the following forms should be used: "There was a great crowd in the street; and, as Mary was too short, she could not see her mother," or, "Mary, being too short, could not see her mother." But if it was the mother who was too short, let us use either of the following forms: "Mary could not see her mother, because her mother was too short," or, "because the latter was too short."

An example of such misuse of words was seen in an advertisement which read: "If each precious stone in our collection were taken from its mounting, its finished beauty would be just as conspicuous." Now, probably the writer meant that the finished beauty of the mounting would be just as conspicuous, but as the sentence is worded

296

he may have referred to the finished beauty of either the mounting or the precious stone.

Always strive to avoid such sentences, with double meanings.

Some Preferable Forms of Words

The following examples of preferable forms of words and phrases, with the reasons given, are taken from "Principles of Rhetoric," by Professor A. S. Hill:

"By consequence" or "in consequence," in the sense of "consequently," is preferable to "of consequence," since the latter means also "important." "Admittance," as in "No admittance except on business," is preferable to "admission," since the latter also means "confession" or "acknowledgment." "Insurance," is preferable to "assurance," policy, since "assurance" means also "confidence." International "exhibition" is preferable to international "exposition," since "exposition" has long been used in another meaning, as in "an exposition of doctrine." "Afterwards," as an adverb, is preferable to "after," since the latter is also used as a preposition. "Relative," in the sense of "member of a family," is preferable to "relation."

Some Vulgarisms

In Bechtel's "Slips of Speech," it is said that "no one who has any regard for purity of diction and the proprieties of cultivated society will be guilty of the use of such expressions as the following:

"'Yaller' for yellow; 'feller' for fellow; 'kittle' for kettle; 'kivver' for cover; 'ingons' for onions; 'cowcumbers' for cucumbers; 'sparrowgrass' for asparagus; 'yarbs' for herbs; 'taters' for potatoes; 'tomats' for tomatoes; 'bile' for boil; 'het' for heated; 'kned' for kneaded; 'sot' for sat or set; 'teeny' for tiny; 'fooling you' for deceiving you;

'them' for those; 'shut up' for be quiet or be still or cease speaking; 'went back on me' for deceived me or took advantage of me; 'a power of people' for a great many people; 'a power of money' for great wealth; 'a heap of houses' for many houses; 'lots of books' for many books; 'lots of corn' for much corn, or large quantities of corn; 'gents' for gentlemen, and many others of a similar character."

Some Words That Are Misused

In the "Handbook for Newspaper Workers," by Professor G. M. Hyde, there is a useful list of "Nouns That Are Commonly Misused." From it the following examples are taken:

"Anthracite coal." The word "coal" is not necessary, as "anthracite" means hard coal.

"Autoist" or "automobilist." Prefer "motorist."

"Banquet"—except when occasion warrants; not for all dinners.

"Better half." Trite for "wife."

"Capitol"—unless you mean a building; a city is a "capital."

"Casket"—the better word is "coffin."

"Conflagration"—for "fire," unless the extent of the fire warrants.

"Individual"—when you mean simply "person."

"Name of"—Write, "a man named Smith," not "a man by the name of Smith."

Split Infinitive

One of the questions most frequently asked of writers on the correct use of English is this: "Is it proper to use the split infinitive?"

First, to define the split infinitive: It is the use of an adverb or phrase between the word "to" and a verb, as in, "He asked me to quickly go,"

298

or "That goes far to more than counterbalance the Governor's action."

Now, if the use of the split infinitive be a fault, it is one of which many writers of good English are guilty, and it is a very ancient fault. Professor Brander Matthews says that "the split infinitive has a most respectable pedigree, and it is rather the protest against it which is the novelty now establishing itself." But he also declares that careful writers are now showing a tendency to avoid the split infinitive, or at least to employ it only when there is a gain in lucidity from its use.

Therefore, do not say, "He asked me to quickly go," etc., but say, instead, "He asked me to go quickly."

INDEX

INDEX

303

304

305

308

311

RELIGION AND
POLITICS

F. W. SOLLMANN

PENDLE HILL PAMPHLET NUMBER FOURTEEN

PENDLE HILL

WALLINGFORD, PENNSYLVANIA

PENDLE HILL PAMPHLETS

———

Occasional studies or essays related to the life and work at Pendle Hill and representing a variety of individual points of view of persons competent to quicken thought on current issues. A complete list will be furnished upon request.

———

Pendle Hill is a center for religious and social study maintained by members of the Society of Friends. The year is divided into four terms. The autumn, winter, and spring terms of eleven weeks each form a unit in which each member of the resident group is engaged in some particular study, writing, research, or field work. The summer term is a four weeks session independent of the program of the rest of the year. All endeavor to live a genuine community life, sharing in the work of household and garden, in intellectual pursuits and in religious worship.

Information may be had from the Directors, PENDLE HILL, Wallingford, Pennsylvania.

INTRODUCTION

Friedrich Wilhelm Sollmann, descendant of an old Christian family, started his public career in his later teens as one of the leaders of the German youth movement about 1900. He early turned to journalism and became editor-in-chief of an important daily paper in Cologne and of a chain of ten periodicals in the Rhineland. He opposed the policy of the emperor before and during the war. Because of his efforts toward developing democracy in Germany and achieving for Europe a federation based on equal rights of all nations his papers were suppressed a dozen times by the imperial government during the first World War. In 1919 Wilhelm Sollman, as one of the founders of the German republic, became a member of the National Assembly in Weimar. He influenced the final draft of the constitution, especially the articles on education, religious freedom, and the relations between state and churches. For some time he served as commissioner of the government of the republic to the High Command of the army in cooperation with General Field Marshall von Hindenburg. He belonged to the staff of the German Peace Delegation in Versailles. In spite of his opposition to the terms of the treaty he campaigned in Weimar and in the nation for the acceptance of the peace treaty in order to end the war. He was one of the organizers of the passive resistance against the French armies in the Ruhr. He was repeatedly re-elected to the German parliament and even elected under Hitler's administration in 1933. In the hard struggle of the republic for its existence he consistently continued the work which he considers to be the task of his life: education for citizenship in a democracy. This he carried on as editor, as columnist, as director of a nationwide news service, as member of the board of directors of the National Federation for Adult Educa-

3

tion and as cabinet minister during the darkest year of Germany's post-war history, when the Reich was shaken by armed communist and national socialist revolts. As a member of the committee of Foreign Affairs and of the Inter-parliamentarian Union he was delegated to many international conferences, in which he worked for demilitarized zones between the nations and for gradual disarmament. In March, 1933, he was the first member of parliament to be attacked by Nazi stormtroopers. Though gravely wounded he succeeded in escaping to a hospital in Luxembourg. After his recovery he edited a daily newspaper in the Saar territory, then under the administration of the League of Nations, until this area came by plebiscite under Hitler's control. In the two years 1935 and 1936 he travelled over Europe contributing to numerous newspapers. Subsequently he resided at Woodbrooke, Birmingham, England, where he became acquainted with members of the Society of Friends. In the beginning of 1937 he emigrated to the United States of America. He has travelled and lectured in nearly all states of the union and has addressed almost a thousand American audiences representing all walks of life. In 1937 he became a resident staff member of Pendle Hill.

RELIGION AND POLITICS

INTRODUCTION

In a world aflame with hatred and revenge men are pondering over the relation between religion and politics. Moved by the simple truth that religion must permeate all human activities to improve and ennoble them, Mahatma Gandhi, who is both the greatest religious activist in our generation and the most active ethical and religious politician, says that

> To see the universal all pervading Spirit of Truth face to face one must be able to love the meanest creature as oneself. And a man who aspires after that cannot afford to keep out of any field of life. That is why my devotion to truth has drawn me into the field of politics; and I can say without the slightest hesitation and yet in all humility that those who say that religion has nothing to do with politics do not know what religion is.*

This passage suggests an earlier statement by the German philosopher Immanuel Kant, in his prophetic pamphlet entitled "Perpetual Peace":

> Now I can indeed imagine an ethical politician, that is, one who so conceives the principles of statecraft that they can coexist with the moral law, but not a political moralist, who so forges the moral law as to adapt it to the profit of the politician.

In commenting upon religion and politics the late Dr. Henry T. Hodgkin, one of the founders of the Fellowship of Reconciliation, expressed his own conviction in this way:

> With my conception of the Christian life I do not see that it would be possible for me to enter the world

---

*Mahatma Gandhi: *His Own Story*. Edited by C. F. Andrews. London, George Allen & Unwin Ltd.

5

of politics as it as at present run. For example anyone who wants to make his influence felt must be allied to a party and accept many compromises. He must use methods current in politics but, to say the least, highly distasteful to a moral man. If he reaches office he becomes a partner in the machinery and so forth. Time was when I felt that for anyone to embark on such a career was a comedown from the highest level of Christian living. While I am as far as ever from being able to go into politics myself, I should now hold that God may be just as truly revealed in a person who enters this field and accepts conditions which I could not accept as, let us say, a devoted evangelist.

It is difficult to conceive how anyone in the light of events today can exclude politics from the realm of religion. By politics I mean the relations among the citizens of a nation and between the nations of mankind. To ignore these relations is to be indifferent toward the integration or disintegration of society; it is to leave to irreligious people decisions about peace and war between social groups and nations; it is to waive responsibility for religious freedom or persecution.

Politics is bound to play a decisive part in the activities of the world. Whatever may be our position, the material and spiritual existence of each of us will be influenced by the prevailing conditions in our nation and by the relations between our own and other nations. Even though the religious man may abstain from political activities, he cannot escape the laws of the land in which he lives. With irresistible dynamic power politics thrusts itself even into the field of religion. Religion, on the other hand, has time and again shown itself passive toward politics. It may be doubted whether religion has ever gained from this passivity, and it is certain that politics has been the poorer for the lack of religious characters engaged in political leadership. Because of their political passivity in the past, religious people must take their share of responsibility for the oppression or persecution of religion today. The opposition to Christianity now prevalent in many countries is the result of a deep disillusionment not only with the actions of the church, but also with its complete lack of action along certain important lines.

Even oppressed or persecuted religious groups devoted to non-resistance toward evil cannot avoid political consequences. The fact that they stick to their creed and to their morality with organized solidarity makes them a political factor. They themselves may not realize this, but the dictators do. The opposition of some such groups in Germany and Russia is strictly religious and is by no means working toward a revolution against the national socialist or communist systems. Yet the one-party state rightly senses political significance in such stands. A dictatorship sets out to train the whole nation in one line of thought and action. Therefore it must consider religious independence as a political danger, especially in respect to the education of young people. Here lies the principal reason for the clash between totalitarian dictatorships and religious groups. The modern dictatorship claims by its very essence the total devotion of every citizen to the one-party state and its one-man leader. But every religious individual knows a higher loyalty; in the hour of conflict he must follow the will of God as he sees it rather than any secular command. We do only justice to the modern totalitarian dictatorships if we admit that their philosophy must exclude re-

7

ligious freedom. Yet clean separation of religion from politics is as impossible as is the attempt to separate religious influences from any other kind of human thinking, feeling and acting.

Certainly religion has a far wider range than has politics. Aiming at the hearts of all men, it can never identify itself with a single political or social creed. Religion is neither Feudalism nor Capitalism, nor Socialism, nor Fascism, nor Communism. It has existed under many systems of goverment and many social orders: monarchies, republics, oligarchies, democracies, and autocracies. These are temporary phenomena; they change in the course of decades, or at most of centuries. Religion deals with the spiritual redemption of mankind. This is an eternal task essential in all periods of history and under all systems of political administration and economic organization.

Oppression, Ancient and Modern

There is nothing new in the modern attempt to impose one religion upon all the subjects of a given regime. Caesars and Sultans, revolutionists and reactionaries, progressives and conservatives have oppressed religious minorities. We who are now shocked by the situation in Germany and Russia should remember that our own ancestors were guilty of similar persecutions. Seldom or never has a church or body politic been free from oppressive action at one time or another. The concentration camp is a new form of an old institution. Secret police, inquisitions, torture, gallows, the stake, the cross were used long before Hitler and Mussolini. Such methods are neither German nor Russian peculiarities. The Religious Society of Friends can be counted among the rare examples of reasonable tolerance through the centuries. This may explain why, in the present confusion, the Quakers refuse to participate in popular accusations and rash judgments.

In the 19th Century the world experienced a period of unusual toleration. We should not forget that this toleration was connected with the rise of capitalism and ended with its decline. In the very midst of the capitalistic system its irreconcilable enemies from Marx to Lenin developed their ideas, and were allowed to print and spread them. Millions of men and women, permitted to confess their socialist or communist ideals, organized themselves into powerful movements against capitalism. They entered parliaments and governments on equal footing with proponents of the prevailing order. Perhaps never in history did a ruling economic system accord such liberal treatment to its opponents. I admit the defects of competitive capitalism. It is true that its motive was and is egoism. I also know that its opponents experienced a long hard struggle against privileges and prejudices of the ruling economic groups. That does not alter the fact that capitalism has not shown itself oppressive in the totalitarian sense of the word, either in politics or in economy or in relation to the realm of the spirit. Under the capitalistic order freedom and tolerance were more highly developed than ever before. Here socialists, communists, anarchists, pacifists, trade unionists, cooperatives flourished side by side. Feudal relics shared equal rights with non-competitive utopian schemes. All types of religious creeds were accorded liberty, even though they exhibited anti-capitalistic tendencies. This freedom was greatest in the most capitalistic countries, Great Britain and the United States of America.

Communism, Fascism and National Socialism claim to have overcome competition and exploitation. But their systems require the ruthless persecution of all their adversaries. Never have religious groups suffered under a capitalistic regime as they suffer now in the anti-capitalistic states. No examination of the relation of Christianity to the sphere of politics can overlook this fact.

True, the shortcomings of the competitive economic system when viewed from the heights of Christian ethics loom very large. Most obvious of these defects is the increased nationalism and world-wide antagonism of our gigantic national economies. Christian statesmanship here faces one of its most complicated tasks. Yet opposition to imperialism and its wars has thrived in capitalistic democracies, while criticism of violence and conquest has been completely suppressed in countries where the governing dictators claimed to have replaced capitalistic egoism by a true community spirit. But the idea of community has in such states always been restricted to one race or to a single class.

Many Christians, especially of the younger generation, condemn the competitive system of economy. The idea of a human society without hard economic competition is indeed very close to the belief in the kingdom of God. Christian democracy cannot deny that the problem of how to develop a non-competitive society without sacrificing all individual freedom is as yet completely unsolved. Before the terrible experiences in Russia and Germany most supporters of a new social order did not even see or they greatly underrated this problem. To the few Christian documents which have combined criticism of liberal Capitalism with a warning against omnipotent power of the state belongs the Encyclical of Pope Pius XI, "Quadragesimo anno". We may disagree with its theology, but no discussion of a Christian economic and political order can exclude this contribution of the Roman Catholic Church to the social issues of our time.

Serious political thinkers inside and outside the Christian world are wrestling with the problem of how to combine organized economy with individual incentive without the motive of profit. How to plan, control, and dominate the economic life of a country without controlling and dominating its spiritual activities is the very difficult problem which confronts them. Is democracy of the masses possible without dictatorship by the masses? Many believers in a radical democracy underrate this danger in spite of the alarming example of Russia. Political thinkers have known ever since Aristotle that extreme democracy is inclined to slip into extreme dictatorship. At present too many people seem to forget this age-old truth. Belief in democracy does not mean belief in the infallibility of the masses. To flatter and to adore the masses is only a step to the flattering and adoring of a dictator empowered by the masses. Here we touch one of the most disastrous consequences of the lack of Christian wisdom in modern political mass movements, movements which might well have profited by the church's knowledge of human nature. Christian experience in two thousand years could have taught the danger of deifying either masses or leaders. But how can Christians do this work when so many, perhaps the best of them, shun the company of political sinners? There is no record in the Gospels that Jesus Christ and his twelve secluded themselves from the world about them; they mixed with all sorts of people, even the most questionable characters.

SECURITY AND FREEDOM

As Christians we must be alarmed that in the struggle for social security millions of people are ready to let go their freedom. The slogan of the French Revolution was Equality, Liberty, Brotherhood. Modern revolutionists are inclined to push Liberty more and more to the background in the hope of gaining security by methods of dictatorship, forgetful that under such a system security is by no means general. In dictatorships security is available only to people who are ready for total submission to the ruling political caste. That admits the danger of spiritual corruption to an acute degree. Under such a system the man who keeps faith with his ideals must pay for it with economic insecurity, imprisonment, death, or exile. At such a price the many will choose submission or hypocrisy.

The problem of security and freedom is the most difficult problem under any political system because it is more deeply rooted than any other in our material institutions and routine. Man's inborn striving for freedom will always conflict with an economy which offers more to its loyal servants than to its opponents. No solution of the tension between security and freedom is possible if the individual is considered as a mere cog in a political and economic machine, with no higher responsibility than obedience to class or party or simply to a deified leader.

Oppression and persecution have been practised under many systems and in all nations. From the point of view of Christian democracy, it is necessary to stress this fact; it will save us from self-complacency. In the family of nations we can not pick the sheep from the goats. No nation is entirely good and none is entirely bad. Just as every individual is a composite of physical and mental traits, inherited and acquired, so every nation feels the interplay of positive and negative forces. As individuals we act differently under different conditions. Whether or not we have a hard struggle for existence, whether we are healthy or sick, whether we are in hope or despair, rich or poor, young or old, these factors influence our actions. Different circumstances may bring out very different sides of man's composite personality. Nobody can be sure how he would demean himself under certain conditions before he has experienced them.

Nations behave in a similar way. Those which are victorious, prosperous, satisfied, with ample territories, produce a different system of government and economy from those which are defeated, impoverished, dissatisfied, and confined within narrow boundaries. The sudden deep political change in France after a disastrous war of only a few weeks is the latest proof of this truth. Even a nation of old democratic traditions can not be sure that it would act differently if it had to go through the experience, let us say, of Germany after 1918 or France in 1940.

Therefore Christian democracy must reject self-righteousness and national self-complacency. But an attitude of comprehension must not lead us to under-estimate the immense danger which modern dicta-torships present for free personalities in the realm of ethics and religion. There are no good or bad na-tions. But there are bad systems of government. The unprecedented power of modern dictatorships lies in their efficiency in oppression, persecution, and cor-rupting propaganda. Religious people in free coun-tries must face this fact. All comparisons with dicta-torships in pretechnical times are misleading. There was never a total dictatorship before Lenin, Musso-lini, or Hitler. Only in our own age, which has con-quered space, is a highly centralized administration over large territory possible; only with our techni-cal instruments is a government able to control all aspects of public and private life. Former dicta-torships from Caesar to Napoleon were able to influence only certain aspects of human life, and even this control failed in the fringes of their em-pires. Now, for the first time in history, we have systems which can effectively regiment all human activities: politics, economy, art, entertainment, education from the kindergarten through the uni-versity. Love and marriage are regulated by laws for purifying the race. Religion must exalt the leader. Without exaggeration we may say that there is not one act between cradle and grave ex-cluded from control by the state. Totalitarian dicta-torship means what it says: total control of the total human personality. It is incorrect and unwise to talk as if there were only a difference of degree between modern democracy with its wide governmental ac-tivities and the totalitarian dictatorship with its omnipotent leader. The cleavage between them is deep and impassable. In the atmosphere of a democratic state we are apt to minimize the difference, but no one who has experienced both systems will deny the depths of the abyss which separates them. No critic of democracy would talk of "difference of degree" if he had once lived under a dictatorship and had there tried to lecture on Christian democracy, Christian pacifism, or Christian love for men of all races and classes.

CRITICISM OF DEMOCRACY

Christian criticism of democracy is as justifiable as is discontent with other human institutions. That does not alter the greatness of the democratic ideal to improve human society through the maintenance and development of liberty. A conviction of the profound importance of liberty is essential to only one political system, and that is democracy.

Democracy believes that human beings and their institutions may develop to a higher civilization only by a large degree of liberty for the individual. The democratic attitude demands respect for the dignity of every human being, equal rights for every citizen, laws expressing the free will of free citizens. Citizens! The democratic state is formed and governed by citizens. Even in its soldiers democracy sees only citizens temporarily under arms and in uniforms. Even in its army, democracy envisions only an instrument of the government of democratic civilians.

But modern totalitarian dictatorship rejects the idea of citizenship. In politics the dictator refuses to accept the point of view and methods of civilians. The soldier is his ideal; war is not an emergency but the highest manifestation of the moral strength of individual and nation. Under the modern dictator there are no longer citizens nor even civilians. Every man is a soldier. Employers and employees are soldiers of labor organized in a labor front, commanded by generals of labor whom they must obey without question; farmers wage the battle of agricultural production; teachers and their pupils form an educational front with boys and girls of the elementary schools marching in the ranks of a uniformed state youth; even mothers fight the battle by an increased birth rate to supply the greater armies of the future. Logically, then, state and society become completely masculine in character. The ideals of such a dictatorship may be summed up briefly: not citizens but soldiers; not liberty but obedience; not peace but conflict; not cooperation of free citizens and nations but the predominance of certain races, nations, and classes. This means the exclusion of all intellectual and spiritual challenge to the ruling philosophy, whether of class war, race war, or world revolution.

Where under such a system is there any place for Christianity? Let us look at the European continent: from Lisbon to Moscow, from the North Cape to Sicily, from the Black Sea to the Channel, not one political or pacifist or religious group is able to work for peaceful change in social and international relations on the basis of equality between nations, classes, and races. The only possible exceptions are in the two small democracies of Sweden and Switzerland. Let nobody mistakenly point to the agencies of the Quakers in Europe. The impressive relief work of the Society of Friends in Germany, Spain, France, Poland, Italy and certain other territories under dictatorship has been possible only because these agencies have for the time being wisely limited their activities to charity. A word against militarism, conscription, or conquest would result in long imprisonment, and the immediate suppression of the Society of Friends. Conscientious objection to military service means certain death. There are no exemptions or special courts for conscientious objectors; these are granted only by democracies. In the dictatorships a number of pacifists have already paid for their convictions with torture and death. Most of these were religious personalities.

The Christian may pray: "Father, forgive them; for they know not what they do." But he must not gloss over wrong-doing because he fears to stir up emotions. Where religion is prevented from judging the political system under which it lives by the moral standards of the Christian ethic, that system is contrary to religious freedom and truth.

Only in the democracies does religious freedom survive. Not by chance but by logical consistency, the highest degree of religious liberty and the widest variety of denominations exist in the United States of America. It is the oldest and deepest rooted democratic republic in modern history. Its constitution, its laws, and its statesmen have a long record of religious tolerance. This record has at times been marred by outbursts of fanaticism, but these have occurred only in small sections of a vast country and contrary to the policy of the federal government. On the whole, religious tolerance in this country is worthy of the spirit of democracy, and it could not have developed without political freedom.

To appreciate this fact is the first line of defense of spiritual freedom. A study of the religious situation throughout the world today should make Christians the staunchest defenders of democracy. I do not mean that this should make us complacent. Rather, it should stimulate us to improve democracy by making Christians more Christian and democrats more democratic in their way of life.

To complain of the shortcomings of democracy here in our country is useful only if we are ready to accept more duties and responsibilities as citizens. Neither defence nor improvement of democracy will be possible from the basis of a negative and unproductive criticism. Just as no church is better than its clergy and its members, so no democracy will be better or more mature than the citizens which compose it, both the governing and the governed. For a political system, like a religious institution, gains vigor only from the human beings who have put their whole physical, intellectual, and moral effort into making their ideals a reality. The democratic society of liberty, equality, and brotherhood will never be achieved by 'Blitzkrieg' methods. Such methods are capable of destroying obsolete institutions and of laying provisionary foundations for new ones. Nothing more. On the day of revolution the gradual evolution in state and society and in every human being must begin again. The belief that age-old problems of society and the human mind can be solved by quick decisions imposed by violence is typical of the dictator. It is undemocratic and unchristian. Democracy and Christianity have in common the conviction and the experience that real improvement requires slow growth. This is especially true in the effort to exclude force from the relations between individuals and the state. Baruch Spinoza's statement is as wise today as it was three centuries ago: "Peace is a virtue, growing from the strength of our soul." Democracy, too, is a virtue, flowering or withering in the human spirit.

This is true even if we accept the slogan that democracy is "liberty plus grocery". Incidentally, all dictatorships in our time prove that "groceries" are disappearing along with democratic freedom. "Guns instead of butter", Field Marshal Goering put it, and this is one promise which the Nazis have kept. Democracy may sometimes result in liberty on an empty stomach, but in a dictatorship liberty is always lacking and the cupboard is bare besides. Historically speaking, liberty and a full larder go hand in hand. In one thing Russia, Germany, Italy, Spain, Japan, and their vassals are united: if they want food stuffs they look toward the democratic republic of the United States. This being the case even pure materialism testifies against dictatorship.

MORAL GROWTH IS SLOW

But the justifiable struggle for better wages, better working conditions, and social security must not eclipse the fact that democracy has never been a material issue alone, nor will it ever be. Whether we study the records of the English revolution of 1689, or the American Declaration of Independence of 1776, or the French revolution of 1789, we shall always be struck by the moral aspect of democracy. One of the oldest democratic documents in modern history dates back to Cromwell's England; it is a report of a debate which took place at a meeting of the grand council of officers at Putney, the 25th of October, 1647. There a certain Colonel Rainboro sounded in one sentence the keynote of democracy: "I think the poorest he that is in England hath a life to live as the richest he." This officer of 300 years ago had no conception of a classless society, of Socialism, Communism, or Fascism. He thought of groups varying in social standing and earthly possessions as they do today. But he demanded for the humblest the right to live his own life however difficult and troublesome it might be. That right and responsibility belong to everyone. No system or leader has the right to deprive a human being of the deepest roots of personality. Nor will any class-consciousness, or national solidarity, or sense of community ever overcome man's consciousness of self and his eternal right to strive for its expression.

That is good democracy and good Christianity. It is impossible to see how Christianity could hold any other conception of the individual and the community. Neither a class society nor a classless one alters the human longing for redemption. The problem is: which helps more toward the attainment of this end? The question is as yet unanswered. Prominent socialist thinkers thought they had the answer some decades ago. But after twenty years of supposedly classless society in Russia and one decade of enforced people's community in Germany they are not so sure. And it is doubtful whether a classless society offers more opportunity for individual self-realization than does a society with a wide variety of social groups and class differences. The classless society may mean dictatorship of a small armed group over all others; it may bring material and spiritual poverty to everyone; it may impose physical and mental slavery upon a whole nation. The late German socialist, Dr. Emil Lederer, turning from Marxism, has made this important problem the subject of very enlightening research (*The State of the Masses, Threat of the Classless Society,* Norton & Co., New York). Lederer's book, written here in the United States shortly before his death, is an excellent antidote to the danger of oversimplifying and emotionalizing the class problem. Men like the farseeing Puritan, Colonel Rainboro, who have gone deep into the heart of democracy, may have known nothing of Capitalism, Marxism, Leninism, Trotskiism, Hitlerism, or any other ism, but they knew what is widely forgotten by many of us today — that democracy is not alone either a scientific or a common-sense doctrine, that it is more than constitution, parliament, or franchise. Democracy is a way of living with our fellow creatures. One may accept it or reject it, but one can not believe in the potential autonomy of all men and at the same time support political systems which proclaim super-classes, super-races, and the deification of one political philosophy and its leader.

Dissatisfaction with political democracy is deep and widespread because democratic governments have fallen so far short of the goal set before them by the early prophets of democracy. The contrast between that vision and the present reality is disillusioning indeed. Yet is the contrast any greater than that between the Christian ideal and Christian action? Suppose we turn on Christianity the same hard and pitiless judgment which innumerable Christians apply to democracy and its representatives. Would we not be justified in despairing of Christian institutions? The ultimate purpose of democracy is the brotherhood of men rising above social and national barriers; Christianity believes in the coming of the Kingdom of God on earth. These two ideals are very close together, and we are no nearer to one than to the other.

Because of its very nature democracy can not be developed rapidly. All really great things in life grow slowly; this seems to be an unavoidable law in nature and ethics. There is deep wisdom in the old practice of Quaker business meetings, the practice of not hurrying decisions:

> We exhort all who are concerned in the management of the discipline that they fervently seek to be clothed with a right mind therein that nothing may be done through rashness, strife or vain glory but all with a single eye to the honour of Truth and the good of individuals.*

Those who want to make sudden and radical changes in our social order would find it worthwhile to pause for a moment and think over this old-fashioned advice. Action is not everything. "Rashness, strife and vainglory" are noisy, but they lead to nothing except unsolvable conflict. There are no short-cuts to reason, understanding, justice, and love in the realm of human relations. The road to progress is long and winding, and each generation of mankind can make only microscopic contributions to its growth. That is the experience of the past, and there is no sign that the future will be different. To realize this and to accept it is by no means quietism or inactivity; it is the only sound basis from which to develop the spirit of political and religious democracy.

*Christian Advices by the Yearly Meeting of Friends held in Philadelphia, 1808.

History teaches us that premature actions are re-actionary rather than progressive in their effect, cre-ating national and international explosions no less evil than belated action. The counsel to "rashness and vain glory" is dangerous and it is typical of the short-lived dynamic of dictatorship. Such counsel has deceived some who should know better. How many sang the praises of Mussolini because the trains in Italy ran on time? Later they became dis-illusioned when the dictatorship which had imposed the new efficiency set out to conquer Ethiopia. How many others lauded the reforms of Hitler — until it became clear that his excellent program of physi-cal training was for military purposes only, that uni-versal employment had created the biggest war ma-chine in history, that the new-found German self-respect was racial fanaticism? And how many more hailed the dawn of the new order in Russia only to find one class tyranny substituted for another and a foreign policy which turned out to be the old imper-ialism in a new red dress? Then they cried out bit-terly against their former idol, but they had only themselves to blame. No Lenin or Stalin can alter the fact that real progress grows slowly and can not be imposed by the decrees of a few men, even if those men have the highest ideals.

The unnamed authors of the "Christian Advices" of 1808 may never have read a book on economy or government, but they had gathered a simple human wisdom from Jewish and Christian teachings based on the experience of three thousand years. They knew the essentials of Christian democracy: the striving for Truth and for the good of individuals. Scores of political scientists, economists, and states-

23

men in our time either know nothing of that wisdom or they dismiss it as irrelevant or reactionary. But the history of the European dictatorships has already shown their attitude to be superficial. Libraries of books written about Russia, Italy, and Germany before 1940 have since proved embarrassing to the hasty authors. All too many of them have praised as dynamic progress what was merely the return to a primitiveness which we had believed to have been overcome forever.

I remember meeting Jean Jaurès, perhaps the most universal mind that ever worked in the social democratic movement in Europe, certainly the greatest Frenchman in that field. (As a friend of European understanding and world peace he was murdered in Paris by a French nationalist at the outbreak of the first World War.) At our meeting Jaurès raised the question: "What does it mean to be a revolutionist?" And he answered with the words: "It means to become wiser." That is true. Lenin, one of the greatest and most daring of activists, may have had the same principle in mind when he spoke of "the children's disease of radicalism" and the necessity of "revolutionary patience." Growing wisdom, vigilant patience, and courageous action are the trinity of democratic needs. Without these three nothing worthwhile will be achieved in statecraft or in the spiritual growth of mankind.

DEMOCRACY IS YOUNG

Criticism of democracy is a symptom of increasing democratic consciousness. We should take courage from this fact. Democracy is young. Inequalities and injustices which our forefathers only some decades ago accepted or tolerated as unalterable are now violently opposed by millions of people. Visions of greater economic equality, of social justice, and of social security actuated the minds of some solitary thinkers and dreamers long ago, but mass movements organized for the purpose of embodying these ideals in the solid structure of government are not yet even a century old. In most countries they did not assume importance until the twentieth century. To the youthfulness of democracy we must assign its impatience with the lack of reason and justice in our society. A hundred years ago exploitation and brutality in economic life were much more general than now. This was especially true in regard to women and children. Evils were accepted with indifference by nearly everyone including most Christian churches. Why should we fear that democracy is doomed when we see how rapidly its conscience and vision are growing? It is not the fault of democracy that the complexity and the multitude of problems in our modern society obstruct men's plans for social progress. None of the dictatorships has been capable of solving these problems faster or more satisfactorily than the existing democracies. Switzerland, Denmark, Sweden, and the United States are still leading the world in material and spiritual standards, and the three small European democracies by no means belong to the so-called 'haves'.

Are we really disappointed in democracy? Or are we confused because in a democracy life is presented to us in all its confusing complexity? A dictatorship simplifies every issue. In dictatorships many disagreeable sides of politics, economy, and social life are hidden by censorship or varnished by propaganda, a fact which makes dictators of very moderate intellectual and moral stature appear to be great men. It is much more difficult to be great in a democracy, where the shortcomings of the most august leader must stand the harsh glare of public scrutiny. In a dictatorship only one voice is heard, that of the ruling caste praising the achievements of its system and judging all other systems and their leaders to be corrupt and backward.

No democracy can be one-sided in education or propaganda, for the variety of opinions aired by press and radio makes one-way influence impossible. In a democracy we must face life in all its contrasts of knowledge and ignorance, bravery and cowardice, tenderness and brutality, honesty and corruption. Because democracy permits human life to appear in all its conflicts it is the most open political system we know. Hypocrisy and complacency are under permanent attack. Nothing is less static than democracy. Democracy means eternal struggle between a multitude of interests, creeds, dreams. As each problem is solved, democracy moves on not only to face, but publicly to discuss, new problems. A democratic country never knows periods of rest, of settling down and enjoying the achievements of the past. Free criticism will always point to flaws and will always demand reforms. Probably democracy will never descend completely from the realm of ideas to the humdrum reality of daily life, for every new generation will have believers in and prophets of a still better society, citizens who will proclaim their vision in the clear bright atmosphere of intellectual freedom. Only in totalitarian systems is unvoiced surrender of the masses possible; the acceptance of poverty and hardship without eventual protest would be impossible in a democracy.

It is the lack of revealing criticism which has deceived so many well-meaning intellectuals into becoming supporters of Communism and Fascism. Even political scientists of note have made astonishingly superficial statements about conditions in totalitarian states, especially in Russia, statements which they could not have made if they had had at their disposal the multifold sources of information open, alike to friend and foe, in every democracy.

The present crisis of our civilization, often miscalled a crisis of democracy, is caused by many forces: tremendous capacity for production on one side, lack of purchasing power and narrowing foreign markets on the other, class interests and prejudices cleaving society from top to bottom, political sterility in the privileged classes, and political indifference in large sections of the underprivileged classes, lack of national and international cooperation, impoverishment of ethical and spiritual life, want of the audacity and imagination necessary to deal with the greatest world revolution in the history of human society. No one of these phenomena is caused or increased by democracy. They exist and carry on their disintegrating work in every type of government and economy. Democracy reveals, dictatorship conceals social disorders. Seeing and speaking the truth is a democratic virtue, not a reason for democratic defeatism. No cure is possible without finding the causes of the sickness and without the application of the best remedies made available by free research. There are conditions in the few remaining democracies which are not ideal. But these remaining democracies are certainly more highly developed than is any totalitarian system in all fields of human endeavor, with the single exception of military technique and preparation for total war unhampered by public criticism. A dictatorship is undoubtedly better able to prepare for total war than is a democracy. But whether a dictatorship is better fitted to hold out in a long war still remains open to question. The resistance of Great Britain has indicated that, after the first shock of surprise, a nation of free citizens is well able to match totalitarian soldiers in actual battle. At any rate, the efficiency of dictatorships in the building of unprecedented war machinery is of no permanent advantage; it only forces or seduces democracies to join the race for armaments. The only recognizable achievement in dictatorships turns out to be their hindrance of all constructive work in all countries whether dictatorships or democracies.

Mental Impoverishment

The forces which gave rise to dictatorships are complex and difficult to understand. All oversimplifications fail. For instance, we are told that nations like Germany and Italy turned to dictatorship because of unjust treatment in the family of nations, that they are 'have-nots' whose only weapon against the democratic 'haves' was totalitarian militarism. There is a certain amount of truth in this theory, but propaganda has exaggerated it tremendously. It takes into account only lifeless material, completely disregarding human talent. Germany has never really been a 'have-not' nation, nor will Germany ever be. Her people have that astonishing technical skill, scientific ability, discipline, order and thrift which made Germany one of the richest nations in the world before 1914, when in international trade she was second only to Great Britain. The spectacular rise of Germany between 1870 and 1914 was achieved by her own domestic strength, without colonies of any commercial value. For the German colonies, acquired in the 80's against the advice of Germany's one great and far-sighted statesman, Bismarck, were a liability rather than an asset. We must not yield to the imperialistic belief that a nation needs colonies in order to succeed. Germany's history before 1914 and after 1918 proves the contrary. After the Treaty of Versailles Germany, stripped of her colonial possessions, was supposed to be a hopeless 'have-not'. Yet she developed a higher industrial capacity and a more powerful military machine than any so-called 'have' in Europe. How else could she have overrun rich France in a few days? The theory of the 'haves' and 'have-nots' is more sentimental than realistic and completely leaves out of the picture small nations like Switzerland, Denmark, Norway, Sweden, the Baltic States, Poland, and Czechoslovakia, whose need was just as great as that of Germany, Italy, or Japan. Because these smaller nations lacked the money to spread propaganda abroad nobody became interested in whether they needed colonies or not.

Friends of Christian democracy and of peace should be cautious in using the purely materialistic division of nations into 'haves' and 'have-nots'. Such emphasis makes us dangerously susceptible to imperialistic arguments. To take from some in order

29

to give to others cannot be the aim of Christian democracy. This would be no better than an exchange between two imperialistic powers. And more important, it would exclude the self-determination of the inhabitants of colonies, a principle against which both dictatorships and democracies have sinned in the past. Christian democracy ought not to perpetuate the colonial system. We must envision a world-wide federation of free people with equal rights of access to markets and raw materials. Increased self-government in the colonies must follow. Such a process of evolution, which is under way in all existing empires, will only be hampered and slowed down by the exchange of colonies.

But if for the sake of argument we accept for a moment the theory of 'haves' and 'have-nots', we come to a conclusion which is not flattering to the dictators. They have turned their materially indigent nations into spiritual paupers as well. They have taken from their peoples the opportunity of utilizing all sources of intellectual and moral power. It may be doubted whether we can speak of education in dictatorships; their teaching is drill rather than education. Free research is abolished as well as free worship. The result is intellectual and spiritual indigence.

The mental impoverishment of dictatorships is certainly no cause for despair in democracy. Modern dictatorships are so unproductive of original ideas that often they have to use or abuse democratic methods. And this shows how strongly the democratic appeal persists even in dictatorships. The dictators organize plebiscites in order to create the impression that there still exists the right to vote; they maintain sham parliaments in order to perpetuate the belief that some democratic control of the government by the people still remains; they claim that they fight for social justice. That is a characteristically democratic idea. From the very beginning the dictatorships have complained about a lack of democracy in the international field, the same dictators who oppressed political, religious, and racial minorities at home demanded equal rights for their nations in international relations. What homage to the living power of democracy! Complaints against the Treaty of Versailles and the League of Nations were based on the fact that these instruments acted undemocratically because they refused equal rights to the defeated nations, and for years this appeal for international fair play had decisive influence with millions of people around the globe. Their response rose from a spirit of democracy. How then can that spirit be dead, or as impotent as many people want to make us believe? It is significant that Germany and Italy lost sympathy everywhere by their undemocratic invasion of foreign countries.

Totalitarianism does not pay; the undercurrent of democratic resistance is too strong. Neither in the domestic field nor in international relations have dictatorships produced a better way for men to live together. In spite of gigantic efforts they have only increased poverty within the nations and distrust and fear among the nations. That is incontestable from every point of view. Free cooperation is still unexcelled as a law of life. But cooperation is only possible between the free and equal; it is the principle and method of democracy. Enforcing one way of thought and action on people as is done by dictatorships is as irreconcilable with the principles of democracy as with the Christian faith that all men are children of God.

How strong must be the power of democracy when three decades of wars, civil wars, persecutions, and terrorism with all manner of modern physical and spiritual torture have been unable to crush it! The horrors of the dictatorships are not signs of their strength, but of their fear of a democracy undefeated and undefeatable in human souls. The democratic dream of work, food, knowledge, and beauty for all human beings was never before so strong and general as now. In accepting this vision the dictatorships pay reverence to the spirit of democracy. But they are not able to understand it; vainly they try to realize the dream of happiness for all by that most impossible method, force.

It is true that democracy is slow in producing justice and peace. But dictatorships will never achieve them. By their very terror dictatorships exclude or corrupt all moral forces that work for peaceful evolution to a higher type of human community. Only in democracy are men free to compete with the dark forces which they have inherited from the past.

INTERNATIONAL COOPERATION HAS WORKED

War is raging once more. A man is in danger of being considered a weak dreamer if he still believes that international cooperation is possible. Yet it is strange to see how many people despair of international cooperation in the future only because it broke down after the short-lived attempt to create through the League of Nations an international machinery for peace. The failure at Geneva is hailed as a failure of international democracy. But the truth is that the League of Nations failed because it was neither democratic nor universal. Based on the dominance of victorious over defeated nations, it clung too long to this undemocratic discrimination though it is not quite correct to assert that there was no change in favor of the defeated peoples. In addition, the reluctance of the United States to join the League deprived it of the cooperation of the most powerful and experienced of the democratic countries. The League itself may be considered a failure, but certainly not a failure in democratic method. And let us also remember that the League was sabotaged by the dictatorships. One by one they acted contrary to the will of the League and withdrew from it. There was political consistency in their action: international cooperation by means of mediation and arbitration is irreconcilable with that fundamental principle of dictatorship, domination by force. Nor is the belated and short-lived attachment of Soviet Russia to the League any evidence to the contrary, for it is clear enough now that this was only an opportunist move.

Yet there was a positive side to this first experiment in world-wide international cooperation. The League of Nations increased its membership from forty-two states to sixty at a time when there were only sixty-five sovereign states in existence on the globe. Unfortunately this increase in membership did not mean a similar growth in the spirit of world cooperation, but it proves that for a certain period after the World War the idea of the League had spread throughout the world. Two years after its inception the League created the World Court at the

Hague, to which more than seventy cases have been submitted. Although a new and inexperienced institution dealing with powerful sovereign states could not be expected to influence history decisively in the short period of its existence, this court stands as the first attempt to create world justice by law.

One success of the League which is now forgotten in the rapidly changing international scene was the administration of the Saar Territory between 1920 and 1935. The industrial Saar Valley was coveted both by France and by Germany, to whom it had belonged prior to 1918. The Versailles Treaty had assigned the responsibility of administering this territory to the League until a plebiscite in 1935 should determine whether it was to stay under the administration of the League, be given to France, or return to Germany. To govern this area was a difficult and highly explosive task. The administration of the League of Nations kept peace in the Saar for fifteen years and made possible a legal and peaceful plebiscite by which the overwhelmingly German population decided with a majority of 90% to rejoin the Fatherland. Thus the League was successful in liquidating one of the most dangerous conflicts between Germany and France. It is difficult to understand why friends of democracy and peace do not make use of this historic example as evidence that peaceful change, even the transfer of territory from one administration to another, is possible by democratic methods. Why do Christian pacifists join with enemies of international cooperation in blaming the League? They at least should not overlook its positive virtues. The failure of the League to settle the major conflicts in Manchuria, in the Chaco territory

in South America, in Ethiopia, Austria, and Czechoslovakia is standard material in all peace groups.
The peaceful solution of the Saar conflict by the
League in the midst of the nervous tensions in Europe is not so widely used. The temptation to yield
to negative criticism is strong even in Christian
pacifist circles.

Doing Justice to the League of Nations

The most frequent doubt of the possibility of international democratic cooperation is based on the fact
that the Disarmament Conference as an instrument
of the League failed in achieving its aim. But did
we not expect too much in too short a time? Is the
idea of international democracy wrong because in
ten years it could not eliminate the economic and
psychological tensions which have been present for
ten thousand years?

The idea of international institutions for preventing war is as young as modern democracy. Most of
the organizations working for international understanding and international law were founded at the
end of the 19th century or at the beginning of the
20th. Though political and religious appeals for
peaceful change are very old, an international peace
technique is completely new. It lacks experience with
the momentous question of how to reduce armament
without endangering national security and how to
give a feeling of security to disarmed nations. Nothing is easier than to depict the devastation of war and
to extol the blessings of peace. This is an old theme,
chanted in the holy scriptures of the most ancient
civilizations. But how can men achieve permanent
peace? Until very recent years there was no plan

which dealt with the complex problem of disarmament and security in technical terms. I myself was brought to realize this when, soon after the World War, the Inter-Parliamentarian Union in Geneva, preparing for the disarmament conference, appointed me as one of its experts. The literature on disarmament presented practically no technical answers to the technical questions. However much we may criticize the League it performed one immortal service: it brought disarmament out of the realm of moral speculation into the workshop of practical effort. The discussions, resolutions, and plans of Geneva are not lost. The first Disarmament Conference will find a successor which will lead us another step further along the road to world community.

The incomplete work of Geneva should not be scorned. Wars are not the fault of one generation; they are the inheritance of many. Neither is the building up of an effective democratic peace machinery the work of one generation. Hard and patient effort for many years to come will be needed before the world is blessed with permanent peace.

Meanwhile we believe: "First you must have faith, then you will have power." Our faith will grow in us and in others if we see that our democratic methods of peaceful change are able to work. Some people despair because they do not realize their own successes. They are so critical that they can not appreciate anything; they see only failure. It was this negative psychology which spread the legend that no concessions were made to disarmed Germany, and that therefore Hitler's war of revenge was bound to come. According to this theory Hitler's rearmament program and militant foreign policy were required to make Great Britain and France listen to German demands. Force and force alone makes history, we are told. But this is contradicted by historical truth in the case of Germany and the Treaty of Versailles. It is astonishing that so very few friends of international Christian democracy make use of the fact that years before Hitler rose to power disarmed democratic Germany nullified large parts of this militaristic treaty by passive resistance and patient diplomatic negotiations. In one decade the unarmed German Republic succeeded in reducing the payment of reparations from astronomical figures to zero. Germany also succeeded in manoeuvering the French army out of the Ruhr Territory and later all other foreign armies of occupation from German soil. She entered the League of Nations as a member with full rights only six years after Germany had been proclaimed unworthy of joining the family of nations; and obtained security for the western border-line of Germany by the Treaty of Locarno. Further, Germany was granted credits of some billions of dollars for the rebuilding of her economic capacity, and the League of Nations, supported by British opinion, was favorably considering Germany's complaints about one-sided disarmament. One may argue that these concessions to Germany were not made in time. But it is incorrect to claim that no concessions were made and that therefore peaceful change does not work.

To stress only the dark sides of the period between the two world wars is unwise. It will damage the cause of Christian democracy and of peace. One of the psychological reasons for the rise of dictatorships and the lapse into the second World War was that

the friends of democracy and peace did not appreciate and stress sufficiently their own successes.
Peace groups have no reason to be derogatory in regard to their achievement after Versailles. It was by
no means without lasting value. Though the enemies
of Christianity and humanism proved to be stronger
and are for the time being in control, theirs is a destructive victory. The peace treaty at Versailles was
unjust and unwise, but under this treaty Europe was
a paradise compared with its present state.

In the anarchy of Europe today Christian democracy has the right to raise the question: Would not
Germany have saved herself and the world from a
second World War if she had not lost her patience
and if she had continued to change the Versailles
Treaty by democratic criticism and diplomatic of-
fensives? Yes, Germany by abolishing the methods
of international democracy deprived herself and the
world of a unique opportunity. A disarmed democratic Germany in the midst of an armed world
would have been the strongest support to all friends
of peace, democracy, and Christianity. Such a Germany would also have been better off materially than
even a victorious Germany can be after this costly
war. When Germany renounced peaceful methods
she acted against her own interest as well as against
the interest of all nations. Democracy disappointed
many people because it fell so far short of its aims,
but dictatorships led us straight into the supreme
catastrophe of war.

NEED TO INFLUENCE THE MASSES

At present there is a growing inclination among
Christian democrats to start all over again, not in

large mass movements, but by education in small groups. The idea is to live the true spirit of community in such groups. These young people — for most of them are young — consider it impossible to permeate the existing large social units with a sense of brotherly solidarity. The hope is that from the example of such small groups and their ideal life there may start an economic, political, and moral reconstruction. Such experiments are interesting and of value to certain individuals. But one may doubt whether they will ever influence larger sections of society. For small groups can not reflect the variety, multitude, and complexity of our modern social life. Since the members of such groups usually practice the same type of thinking and acting, they are in danger of distorting the picture of our society because they are too far from its average members. Has Christianity a social and a democratic message only for small units of seekers or is the gospel capable of influencing large social units and nations? Do not Christians who work as Christians in private business or in other activities in the world with its interests and struggles do more for the growth of a Christian democracy? Jesus worked within the natural groups of his time. The power of his language and the truth of his parables would have been impossible without his knowledge of people. The same holds true for the one great religious activitist in our time, Mahatma Gandhi.

Christian democracy by its very nature has to deal with large numbers of peoples, their education for citizenship and their work toward the improvement of society as a whole. Democratic education may be prepared in small cells, but it must radiate into the minds of many millions of people if it is to lead to action. This truth is more valid than ever in this age of super-organization. Mass organization is everywhere, in factories, farms, banks, schools, even churches. Nor is there any evidence that we are headed towards a decline or dissolution of these gigantic social units. It is true that millions of small shops and farms survive and that art defies mass production. But the smallest economic units and even solitary individuals are drawn into mass organizations for the defense of their interests, the holding of their individual position, and even for their education.

A hundred and thirty million Americans cannot cooperate from individual to individual. They cannot make laws by talking personally with the President; they cannot have a plebiscite for every bill. The relations between the government and the citizens, between employers and employees, between conflicting interests and ideas can be reasonably adjusted and regulated only by well organized large units. Otherwise we would have a completely disintegrated society with perpetual clashes of individual interests and opinions. We may dream of free cooperation of free individuals without the machinery of organizations. This dream may even come true in some distant future. But today an atomized society is unworkable. We are too immature and morally we are too undisciplined. It would be a war of all against all. We need the principle and method of mass organization. Our choice is between the forced regimentation of totalitarian dictatorships and the cooperation of free organizations in a democracy.

In a totalitarian dictatorship the government controls and regiments all organizations. In a democracy the only way to influence mass organizations is to work in and through them. Christian democracy may sign its own death warrant if it neglects this truth. Are we really wise to leave leadership in modern organized democracy to religiously indifferent people, or even to enemies of religion and of democratic rights? How can we expect to influence the masses when we avoid them? How can Christian democracy be possible without a *demos*, in modern language, without mass organization? What right have we to criticize the unchristian acts of governments, political parties, employers, workers, if we do not make a patient and lasting attempt to spread the spirit of Christian democracy among them?

Neither Slave nor Master

A year before his presidency, Abraham Lincoln wrote this note about the democratic way of life: "As I would not be a slave, so I would not be a master. This expresses my idea of democracy. Whatever differs from this, to the extent of the difference is no democracy." This is a timely truth. The ideas of supermen and master races are alien to democracy and Christianity. The Christian conception of the human person as intrinsically sacred is incompatible with any type of totalitarian dictatorship. According to Fascism and National Socialism as well as Communism, all the interests of the individual are absorbed by and completely subjected to the state, and the individual exists for the sake of the nation or for the cause of the party, not the nation and party for the sake of the individual. But the relation between

Christianity and democracy is fundamental. They meet each other on the common ground of the worth and dignity of the individual.

According to democracy and Christianity all human beings are equal as persons whatever may be their social standing. All men have certain rights which come from their Creator. These they possess through life, regardless of race, country, class, creed, or sex. The American democracy, rooted in religious origins and still strongly influenced by religion, has recognized once more the essential of Christian democracy, the natural right of the individual to stick to his creed, by exempting the small religious minorities of conscientious objectors to military service. Such protection of minorities is possible only in a democracy.

In accepting and using the democratic right of free organization we cannot refuse it to any social group. The poor must have the same right as the rich, the workers the same right to unionize as the manufacturers to associate. In this age of mass production and mass distribution democracy is impossible without organized capital and organized labor. Everyone who wants cooperation in the spirit of Christian democracy must accept the principle and the right of free organization. This is just as important as the right of free worship, free assembly, and free speech. Equal opportunity for all is democratic and Christian. This equality must include the protection of weak individuals by strong organizations. The power of the strong organizations resides in the solidarity of their members.

Economic discontent occasions the most effective criticism of democracy at the present time. There is no use in trying to defend democracy by preaching its value in the lofty realm of ideas alone. Sound democracy has always been based on the economic independence of its citizens. As Aristotle said in his "Politics":

> Great then is the good fortune of a state in which the citizens have a moderate and sufficient property; for where some possess much, and others nothing, there may arise an extreme democracy, or a pure oligarchy; or a tyranny may grow out of either extreme — either out of the most rampant democracy — or out of an oligarchy; but it is not so likely to arise out of a middle and nearly equal condition.

The knowledge that freedom cannot exist without economic independence made it consistent for the ancient world to grant democratic rights to free citizens only, not to slaves. This practice continued for many centuries in spite of the power of medieval Christianity. Political privileges belonged to nobility, clergy, artisans, and farmers; they were not granted to journeymen, industrial workers, farm hands, serfs, or servants. All these were economically dependent on their employers or masters. In most countries until well into the present century two very large elements in the population were excluded from full political rights because they were considered dependent, namely, workers and women. In most democracies they were granted political equality only by 1919. In the late French democracy women in general never had the right to vote, and with comparatively few exceptions they did not even resent this restriction. In the United States of America the close connection between civil rights and economic status becomes clear when we consider the status of colored slaves before the War between the States. American democracy had never considered them as citizens. How could it? They were merely property. Without economic independence they were not entitled to enjoy political rights and influence.

In the American republic from its very beginning economic independence was assumed to be an essential of democratic freedom. At least the opportunity existed for all citizens of the republic to achieve that independence by acquiring property.

The poor people who formed the rank and file of the army of 1776 fought for both liberty and property. They were small farmers, discontended laborers, indentured servants who had served their time. To them the revolution against the king in England was not only a problem of political representation and of free worship; they also wanted free land, just wages, and the chance to own their workshops or stores. They disliked the gentry whether British or native.

The end of old privileged forms of land ownership, the confiscation of loyalist estates and of royal proprietary lands, and the opening of the west gave the revolution its necessary economic backbone. The founders of the republic based their constitution on individual liberty and on individual property, believing that these two together formed the basis of free citizenship. The American Constitution proves that the founding fathers were well aware of the dangers which might threaten both. They saw these social dangers from the top of society as well as from the bottom. They distrusted the collectivism of money power as much as the collectivism of propertyless masses. For this reason they placed checks and balances in the Federal Constitution. They wanted to protect material and spiritual freedom against majorities, whether of voters or of economic power.

The American Revolution was not an ideological movement born in the studios of intellectuals, but an upheaval rooted in the economic and social conditions of the young country. Out of this revolt came not only a new and still growing philosophy of democracy, but also a broader social equality by means of a broader distribution of property. The fusion of ideals with material advantages made the American dream a reality and attracted innumerable disowned men from Europe and from Asia.

CONTRASTING STATUS

In the sixties of the 19th century property or at least the chance or hope of acquiring property was still so common that Abraham Lincoln could demand from every American citizen the pledge of his life, his property, and his sacred honor for the support of the Constitution. That was the spirit and the language of the American dream. Now when about one-third of the nation has no property worth mentioning and very little chance of becoming proprietors, it is questionable whether Lincoln's demand would still be applicable.

Valid education for Christian democracy is impossible if we gloss over the fact that gigantic private economic powers are threatening freedom by economic despotism. The response of the propertyless masses may be violent. A conflict between massed property on one side and massed propertyless people on the other might well be fatal to our democracy.

45

And when democracy dies, with it will die religious freedom.

Massed property and massed proletariat work as destructive social forces against a balanced material and spiritual democracy. Privileged classes fearing to lose their power turn against democratic rights, while the unprivileged, resenting the fact that their civil rights do not prevent unemployment and poverty, become indolent and even hostile toward a system which they feel has done nothing for them.

Big business groups, on the one hand, are convinced that democracy grants too much power to the workers, especially to those who are organized in unions. Such business men may hold the honest opinion that certain labor activities are damaging the general economic status, but if they succeed in destroying a free labor movement, they will find that their own economic liberty has itself been lost under the heel of a totalitarian dictator.

On the other hand, many workers are inclined to underrate the value of democracy for themselves, and under the influence of communist slogans see only the incompleteness of the system. They talk of 'so-called' democracy, or of 'formal' democracy, not realizing that they could not even use these terms with safety if they were not blessed to a large extent with democratic rights. In many countries large groups of workers helped to destroy democracy by their propaganda of the dictatorship of the proletariat. This slogan had political consequences which its authors, Marx and Engels, could not foresee a century ago. They believed that everywhere the middle class and small farmers would be ruined and that they would join forces with labor against capital. But this was a huge miscalculation. The middle classes are not a diminishing, but a growing social stratum. They are growing faster than is labor. Even those who are financially ruined remain middle class in their psychology and do not want to be united with proletarians. Middle classes and farmers ally themselves to anyone who promises to protect them against the supposedly threatening dictatorship of the workers, and they dash into the anti-democratic camp in order to escape the dangers of communism. The end is that all social groups lose their political and economic freedom. For the totalitarian states there can be no rule by the masses, nor by a dominant aristocracy, nor by an influential middle class, but simply the dictatorship of a party militia and bureaucracy. This was the development in two leading Fascist countries, Italy and Germany. Class hatred was many times more responsible for the ruin of democracy in Europe than was the treaty of Versailles. Otherwise Fascism could not have become victorious in countries such as Spain which had no part in the war nor in the treaty. It is a dangerous over-simplification to blame the treaty of Versailles for nearly every adverse circumstance since 1918. Versailles itself has historical roots in at least one century of political and social evolution in central and western Europe. So also has Fascism, National Socialism, and Communism. They are all signs of the deep disintegration of Europe by unrestrained materialism in social and international relations. Marxists and Capitalists, protagonists of class war and imperialists alike refuse to bow to the universal moral law proclaimed by Christian democracy. The unbridled struggle between nations and classes led to the explosion of 1914, which in its turn accelerated the disintegration of Europe. The treaty of Versailles, monopolistic money power and the movements which developed in reaction against it, Communism, National Socialism, and Fascism, were all born out of the same inhumane and unchristian spirit. The Treaty of Versailles cannot be overcome by tearing up the paper on which it was written. We must overcome the social and spiritual disintegration out of which it grew. That will be difficult to accomplish because of the habit of Christians and pacifists to set off Versailles as if it were an isolated event. There is no isolation in history; all events are interwoven with one another. We cannot blame one treaty, or one country, one dictator, or one system alone. Our real trouble is that we have lost moral direction and are therefore unable to adjust our human relations to the current material conditions. That is the challenge. We must attack the total confusion with the total truth of Christian democracy. There lies our task.

It is obvious that the problems of democracy in this country are not basically different from those in Europe. Big employers and corporations in the United States distrust democratic development, especially in the field of taxation, social security, and economy in general. Whether they are right or wrong, the fact of their distrust remains. Farmers and the middle classes feel pinched and are afraid of losing their property by economic convulsions; professional and white collar people complain that their present jobs are inadequate to their education and that the future is uncertain; manual workers are restless and divided by unions of different types and by ideological and racial struggles. Incidentally the average manual worker in this country seems to be politically less educated than is the laborer in any industrialized country of Europe. There are plausible reasons for this. The rapid development of this continent required the influx of many millions of immigrants, many of them from countries which gave neither rights nor education to workers. The present political indifference of most American workers is a deplorable fact. It hampers the working of political democracy and hinders the growth of economic democracy. Increasing participation of the workers in the public administration and increasing cooperation between management and workers in private business require the best possible education for citizenship. That is not only the task of the public school system in this country, a system which is already second to none, it is also the task of the workers' organizations.

Union-consciousness is not enough. The worker no less than the employer must realize his responsibility as a citizen. Christian democracy demands that the employer treat the worker not as a machine, but as a human personality. The union, on the other hand, must not limit its aims to demanding higher wages and reduced working hours. Unionization and democratic rights entail upon every worker a degree of responsibility for the prosperity of the plant in which he earns his living. It is unwise and unfair to speak only of the employer's profit and to disregard his responsibility, his risks and losses. More rights will always mean more responsibilities; that is the moral law of democracy. To deny or to violate this means ruin to the newly gained privileges. This has been conclusively demonstrated by European history of the last twenty years.

INEVITABLE CHANGE

The personal attitude of most Americans is democratic. This is a revelation to anyone who has hitherto known democracy merely from constitutions and other documentary sources. Without any doubt the majority of people in this country believe in democracy, but we should get very different answers if we asked different individuals what they understand by democracy. This is not surprising. It is difficult, perhaps impossible, to propose a definition of democracy which would satisfy all those who believe in it. One of the inalienable rights of a democratic citizen is to define and to express his own pattern of democracy. Only dictatorial systems such as Fascism, National Socialism, and Communism can present in detail plans of their economic and social aims and enforce them on all citizens. And their practice is very different from their theory.

The very nature of democracy makes it impossible for any government or political party to successfully picture a democratic utopia, for in a democracy there would never be unity in regard to such a dream. Every group has the right to air its criticism and its counterplans. Thus democracy is seen to be a method of statecraft rather than a fixed goal. Every step forward has to be taken after consulting many interests; every reform has to be discussed in the light, or sometimes the darkness, of a variety of political and social philosophies. Democracy is eternal evolution, eternal change, eternal struggle. Government by democratic methods and ideas will always be a compromise between various interests and insights. Therefore government programs in democracies are bound to be more vague than the proclamations of dictators who need face no opposition. But democratic programs will be closer to reality. Their achievements will last longer and be of higher value.

Today we are in a rapidly changing world. The wars in Europe, Africa, and Asia with their already visible economic and social consequences manifest this current. Wars will themselves accelerate the tempo. Currencies break down. The British Commonwealth of Nations, the largest empire that has ever existed in history, is now unable to pay for its war purchases abroad. In nearly all countries the financial structure is upset. Foreign markets are lost through blockade and counter blockade. The highest capacity of production is directed towards vast destruction of national wealth. Old continents are impoverished. Boundless taxation and hazardous credit manipulations weaken the upper crust of the society and threaten to expropriate the middle classes. The workers, who are of decisive importance in the fantastic speed of war production, claim increasing rights and a higher share of income and property. The influence of war on youth and on the behavior of the young is unpredictable. Youth will certainly be more inclined to aggressive social action after this war. The war itself will have taught every child to trust in force and to crush his opponent. Our present society based on private ownership, competition, risk and profit, is under fire and Christians in a growing degree contribute to the challenge. After all, there must be something wrong with us if for decades we have seen all countries shaken by wars, civil wars, revolutions, counter-revolutions, and the results of wars, inflation, deflation, strikes, permanent economic and financial crisis, unemployment, general national and international unrest. Some countries are more affected and certain governments more responsible for this situation than others, but no country and no political system has escaped the cyclone. In the last fifty years there have been at least twenty-five major international conflagrations. No large country can claim to be free from responsibility for them. It is a world-wide phenomenon, not a German or an Italian or a French or a British problem, it is not even a European problem alone. All people are involved.

Powerful and Undefeated

Democracy could not survive if it had no remedy to offer. Its program is as simple as it is difficult to put into action. Democracy calls upon the different social elements in every country to solve their economic problems not by class rule but by cooperation of all social groups in the nation. Democracy calls upon nations to solve international conflicts by international cooperation. That means that within the nations free discussion and free decision must persist within the framework of democratically accepted constitutions. The same should apply to international relations. A democratic nation is a federation of free citizens; the world must become a federation of free states.

If we do not believe in the possibility of national and international cooperation, we deny democracy. We also deny Christianity. We deny our personal freedom. It is possible that the surging waves of

Fascist or National-Socialist or Communist dictatorships may overcome us, as they have overwhelmed other countries. That is no reason to succumb and to abandon our faith in the rights and in the brotherhood of man. As long as these ideals live in us Christian democracy is not dead. We must be careful not to deceive ourselves by believing an idea is dead or dying simply because our faith in it is weak. Not a single nation with any democratic experience has voluntarily given up democracy. Neither Germany, nor Italy, nor Japan, nor Russia, nor Spain can be said to have had a democratic tradition or education. The old democracies of France, Holland, Belgium, and Norway have temporarily broken down under the assault of invasion. Denmark, occupied by the army of a dictatorship, managed to retain some elements of democracy; the citizens of that small, unfortunate country have shown an admirable moral resistance through their democratic spirit. Switzerland and Sweden still hold to democracy in spite of their encirclement and the threat of the dictatorships. In Sweden the belief in democracy is today stronger than ever. For the first time in Swedish history the elections of 1940 gave a majority to the social democrats. The Communist votes declined to a hopeless minority of three seats in parliament, while the Fascists got no representation at all. This occurred at the very climax of the military victories of the dictatorships. In spite of its military glory and propaganda the totalitarian aim has no appeal for free people.

Great Britain and the United States have to some extent accepted restrictions upon democratic rights under the strain of warfare and of war production.

The restrictions were not made under the decrees of dictators but after free discussion and the regular procedure of parliaments democratically elected. It is important neither to forget nor to minimize this distinction, for out of this difference must grow the determination of the nations which are free to restore their temporarily restricted civil rights as soon as possible after the present emergency has passed. To assume that in Great Britain and in this country democracy is doomed under the impact of war is in ourselves to defeat democracy. We should tolerate restrictions of civil rights only as a measure of national need, not as a retreat from the principles of democracy. We may remember that soon after the first world war Great Britain as well as this country abolished all restrictions upon democracy and restored civil rights in full. They even extended the franchise to women and youth. Why should the development be different after this war? The answer depends on us. Without faith in democracy we can neither save nor improve it.

Strong Leaders of Free Citizens

Democracy is not incompatible with strong leadership. A president elected, as in this country, by the tremendous vote of twenty-five million free citizens must prove worthy of this confidence by the strength and boldness of his actions. No democracy can stand weak leadership for very long. This is especially true in critical times. The sound instinct of the nation turns to men of courage and daring. Even the party in opposition admires such characters and despises weaklings who, fearful of losing their mandate, follow every least murmur in their constituency. Democracy is lost without action, and action requires leadership. Democracy elects its leaders freely, and is able to depose them peaceably if they do not live up to the nation's expectation. But we misinterpret democracy if we demand that the duly elected President or representatives consult with every citizen before acting and that after election they follow every temporary change in public opinion. It is compatible with democracy, it may sometimes be the duty of the elected President and parliamentarians to act counter to the opinion of large sections of their electorate. In a democracy president and parliamentarians are servants of the nation, not slaves under pressure of groups and special interests. The integrity and the moral strength of a statesman will be revealed by his resistance to power groups of all kinds. Furthermore, it is technically impossible and it ruins democracy to turn over every momentous decision to the masses of the nation. In decisions where strong emotions are involved President and parliamentarians may show a more poised and balanced judgment than can millions of citizens swept away by propaganda and prejudice. Everyone who saw Europe at the outbreak of the war in the summer of 1914 will understand this point. Plebiscites may sometimes be useful. But it is a mistake to assume that they are bound to decide in a more democratic way than can a vote by parliament. In impoverished Germany after the war, the masses defeated a plebiscite which would have expropriated the wealth of former kings, granddukes, dukes, and princes in order to apply the property for public welfare. And what of that famous plebiscite by which Pontius Pilate asked the multitude whose blood they would spare: that of Barabbas or of Jesus of Nazareth? The mob voted for the murderer against the prince of peace. From democratic considerations we must be careful not to trust too much in plebiscites as such. A popular vote on war might turn out quite differently from the expectations of those who recommend it.

The Presidency of this country is an example of powerful leadership in a democratic republic. The executive powers of the President are unique: he is head of the strongest party in the country; he appoints cabinet ministers not as officials backed by a majority in parliament, as in other democracies, but dependent entirely on his good will; he is Commander-in-Chief of the army and navy; he is largely responsible for foreign policy; he controls the largest administration and the greatest economic power in the world. As the voice and symbol of national unity, he is leader of the greatest democratic federation.

Weak Presidents have been intimidated by so much power. They have not known how to use it; great Presidents have grown stronger under the burden. It is interesting and timely to remember that no weak President has ever recommended himself permanently to the affection of the American people, whereas strong men, who in the opinion of many contemporaries seemed to abuse their power, gained the lasting admiration and the love of the nation. This has been true since the days of Jefferson, who confessed to having acted unconstitutionally in purchasing Louisiana, but justified his action by pleading military necessity and the need of agricultural expansion. Yet Jefferson was the epitome of the great American dream. He is still its symbol. And though

Andrew Jackson was denounced by his opponents as 'King Andrew' because of his dictatorial methods, history now sees in him the first leader of modern American mass democracy. Abraham Lincoln, in the midst of a war for democracy, pushed his executive powers to the limit, and beyond. He started the war on his own responsibility, suspended the writ of *habeas corpus,* threw thousands of suspects into prison and detained them there; as Commander-in-Chief of the army he issued the Emancipation Proclamation. He defied Congress and the Chief Justice. In his own defense Lincoln stated: "I conceive that I may in an emergency do things on military grounds which can not constitutionally be done by Congress." That sounds dictatorial, but it is democratic wisdom and democratic action if done in the spirit of saving and not destroying the basis of democratic federation.

These historical incidents are cited to show that there is no reason for pessimism when, during a war or other national emergency, the forms of democracy must temporarily suffer. The result depends on the spirit which creates and controls such restriction.

The Spreading of Facts

When in this country authors, journalists, parliamentarians, teachers, and lecturers are deeply troubled by the trend toward dictatorship we should respect their arguments and ponder them. But intellectuals are prone to over-excitement. They do not reflect the true mental status of the nation. The confidence of the average American in the inborn democratic tradition may be as sound as it has ever been. Many Americans doubt the wisdom of their government in Washington; very few of them question the strength and future of American democracy. Perhaps they take too much for granted; re-education to democracy and its practical implications may be necessary. But education for democracy is never an intellectual problem alone. It can be achieved only by touching and moving the total human personality. One cannot have faith in democracy without knowing that it is rooted in the people. Democracy's fate will not be decided in editorial offices, class rooms, or studios. Though they make valuable contributions to the discussion of democracy, the life of democracy rests with the rank and file of the citizens. When it loses their support democracy is doomed. Intellectuals may be more stimulating than grocers, ranchers, and miners, but it is the latter who decide the survival or ruin of their country. These average people will also prevent us from falling into the error of believing that democracy can be separated from the problems of jobs, food, and housing. The democratic way of life recognizes that man lives not by bread alone, but that he needs bread first and above all to live on. Our modern capacity for production can meet this problem if we are ready diligently and reasonably to cooperate. Work is the first necessity; without work no consumption is possible.

But democracy must not only do its best along economic lines; it must also try to convince its citizens that everything possible is being done in their interest. It is not enough to accomplish something and to hope that the accomplishment speaks for itself. We must advertise the achievements of democracy. Fear of the term propaganda should not prevent us from spreading facts. Nor should we leave the field to agencies of propaganda. It is well to remember that ministries of propaganda are an invention of dictatorships, not of democracy. Adolf Hitler, in his book, *Mein Kampf,* claims that efficient propaganda can convince people that they enjoy paradise when they are actually living in hell. He should have added that such one-sided propaganda is possible only in a totalitarian state. Yet Hitler is right in pointing out certain weaknesses of democracies. Many of its citizens vie with one another in criticism of everything done or not done by the government. While democratic freedom grants the right to wide criticism it should also include the duty of doing justice to the existing administration. One-sided criticism is destructive and will result in the collapse of democracy.

THE CALL FOR ACTION

The program of modern Christian democracy is as easy to formulate as it is difficult to put into practice:

1. Work for all.

2. The highest development of useful production.

3. Just distribution of the wealth produced.

4. No economic monopolies by private corporations or governments.

5. Insurance for all needy citizens against private emergencies.

6. Mediation and arbitration between social groups in the nation.

7. Mediation and arbitration between nations.

8. A regional federation of free nations with the ultimate aim of a world federation of all nations.

9. Progressive limitation of armaments as gradual steps to disarmament. An international police force.

10. Education leading to voluntary national and international cooperation.

11. Emphasis on the supreme importance of liberty for the growth of the individual.

12. Fusion of individual liberty with a powerful leadership responsible to the people.

13. A new concept of the moral character of statecraft.

14. Strengthening of national and international solidarity.

15. Stress on the universal character of Christianity.

Out of such a program there is only one item which can be achieved in dictatorships and that is work for all. The second item, the highest development of useful production, is already irreconcilable with a totalitarian regime. In a dictatorship, production, like everything else, will be used and abused in the interest of the ruling group and its ideologies. Whether the aims are world revolution, class rule, or race rule, they always include waste of material and human activities and they exclude cooperation of people with different ideals. Therefore in a dictatorship neither in economy nor in the spiritual realm can there be full use of all productive forces.

In many Christian circles in the United States there is a fatalistic conviction that it is impossible to defeat political machines. Such machines are made by men and therefore can be destroyed by them. But most of the people who complain about party machines and their bosses have not expended nearly the same amount of time, effort, and enthusiasm in trying to wipe out these machines as politicians and racketeers have given to building them up. Why not learn from the politicians and apply a similar energy and daring to a good cause? In many religious groups of today the factor of aggressive energy is pitifully lacking, though it was this energy which gave power to leaders from Moses to Gandhi. The situation brings to mind an expression used by the religious fighter, Martin Luther, against one of his soft-speaking contemporaries: "He loves peace more than the cross."

In many cases when people loved justice more than peaceful acquiescence they have attacked corrupt politicians, and the machines have been defeated. It is significant in considering the possibilities of moral force in politics that many successful reform movements developed outside and against the political machine. Abolition, prohibition, unionization, women's rights, social security, low-cost housing, and cooperatives are among these causes.

Understanding of an education for democracy can be promoted in many groups which have no direct connection with politics such as families, schools, churches, and various types of clubs. Religious denominations have a task in educating for democracy which can not be tackled by other groups, for churches represent a cross-section of the population which is otherwise divided along lines of economic interests and social standing, in associations of employers and in unions of workers, in organizations of farmers, business men and professional people. The churches offer an opportunity for all of these to meet on neutral ground. As the Society of Friends has proved, it is possible to discuss successfully in groups of employers and employees the relation of Christianity to the social problems of today. Outside of parliaments with their purely political orientation no atmosphere offers so good an opportunity for the consideration of society and men on a broad basis as does the Church. Certainly nowhere else could the great moral issues of democracy be discussed better and more profoundly than in Christian denominations which claim to strive for the same goal as democracy: brotherhood of men in mutual understanding and by the free cooperation of many minds and hands.

Many Christians are convinced that democracy is possible only as religious democracy. We may endorse this conviction without overlooking the fact that there is a wide range of opinion as to what religion means. After all, Christianity is not the only answer to the relationship between God and man. Every religion could make a vital contribution by teaching that democracy like every other moral effort demands a hard, heroic, patient struggle, that we can expect little or nothing from political systems without the cooperative spirit and work of citizens, that no democracy is better than its citizens as no church is better than its members. Religion could spread the truth that with rights come duties, and that to win peace abroad and unity at home each must conquer the war lord in his own breast.

Democracy is the age-old belief in and struggle for the salvation of man from spiritual and material slavery. No democracy and no religion lives and acts in its true spirit if it does not work for more light in every human being and for more solidarity in the whole of human society.

Religion without democracy will be enchained. Democracy without religion, that means without developing and using its own deepest spiritual forces, will perish from dry rot. A Christian democracy may be the solution for the problems of the Western world. Are Christians ready not only to preach but to act, to teach, to write, to organize, to administer, to lead in politics? The answer is urgent. Upon it hangs the fate both of Christianity and democracy.

———